Modeling Maximum Trading Profits with C++

John Wiley & Sons

Founded in 1807, John Wiley & Sons is the oldest independent publishing company in the United States. With offices in North America, Europe, Australia, and Asia, Wiley is globally committed to developing and marketing print and electronic products and services for our customers' professional and personal knowledge and understanding.

The Wiley Trading series features books by traders who have survived the market's ever-changing temperament and have prospered—some by reinventing systems, others by getting back to basics. Whether a novice trader, professional, or somewhere in-between, these books will provide the advice and strategies needed to prosper today and well into the future.

For a list of available titles, please visit our Web site at www.WileyFinance.com.

Modeling Maximum Trading Profits with C++

New Trading and Money Management Concepts

VALERII SALOV

BICENTENNIAL 1807 WILEY 2007 BICENTENNIAL

John Wiley & Sons, Inc.

Published by John Wiley & Sons, Inc., Hoboken, New Jersey
Published simultaneously in Canada

For general information on our other products and services or for technical support, please contact our Customer Care Department within the United States at (800) 762-2974, outside the United States at (317) 572-3993 or fax (317) 572-4002.

Wiley also publishes its books in a variety of electronic formats. Some content that appears in print may not be available in electronic books. For more information about Wiley products, visit our Web site at www.wiley.com.

Library of Congress Cataloging-in-Publication Data:

Salov, Valerii, 1960–
Modeling maximum trading profits with C++ : new trading and money management concepts / Valerii Salov.
p. cm. — (Wiley trading series)
Includes bibliographical references and index.
ISBN: 978-0-470-08623-0 (paper/cd-rom)
1. Investment analysis—Computer programs. 2. Investments—Mathematical models. 3. C++ (Computer program language) 4. Financial engineering. I. Title.
HG4515.5.S34 2007
332.60285′5362–dc22

2006025197

Printed in the United States of America

10 9 8 7 6 5 4 3 2 1

Contents

Preface

From 1993 to 1995 I had been working on a project at Merrill Lynch of Japan in Tokyo. The project dealt with the development of trading systems that make automatic buy and sell decisions on futures, equity, and foreign exchange markets. The books of Perry Kaufman (1987), Robert Pardo (1992), and John Koza (1992) were driving forces of the project during this period. I was particularly interested in the book of Robert Pardo, which had become quite popular and quickly got the alternative name "The Black Bible." The adjective and the noun respectively reflected the color design of its front page and the short but relevant content.

The concept and description of *potential profit* attracted my attention because Robert Pardo believed that the idea of *what the market offered* was not a widely understood. He proposed a simple algorithm to compute this property. This algorithm buys every bottom and sells every top. I thought that under real conditions transaction costs could easily turn some of these trades into losses, even if they were successfully entered and exited at local bottoms and tops. I wanted to include this factor and began by manually trying different values to see how costs affected individual transactions and the final profit and loss. Surprisingly, I determined that the algorithm becomes substantially more complicated. Often, after the strategy was built and seemed to be generating the maximum profit, I was able to redistribute the transactions and get even more profits. This meant that the original result was inadequate. I also found that the distribution of transactions remained unchanged after small variations in costs, while at some higher cost levels it changed dramatically.

The task looked attractive to me from a pure algorithmic point of view. Soon I had created an algorithm that accepted arbitrary vectors of prices and transaction costs as input and generated a corresponding potential profit strategy as output. I discussed the result with the leader of the project, Dr. Ravi Chari, who found it very interesting. However, I did not program the algorithm, and it was not used as part of that project.

In 1996, while I was relocating with my family from Merrill Lynch of Japan to NumeriX LLC in the United States, I begin writing an article that described the basic properties of potential profit strategies and suggested using the new concepts of *s*-function, *s*-matrix, *s*-interval, and the *polarities* of *s*-intervals to create the *r*- and *l*-algorithms, which in turn would generate the accounting, including transaction costs, for potential profit strategies. However, at the same time, I read number of books, including those by Larry Williams (1979), Bruce Babcock (1989), and Ralph Vince (1992) and realized the tremendous profit potential of trading. It was clear to me that money management techniques that reinvested profits could improve any strategy that was already successful. I thought that writing about the potential profit strategy without the application of money management would be incomplete and premature, so I put my writings into the table drawer. Only my wife knew about this article.

Gradually, in the spare time available during parts of vacations and holidays, and without any time pressure, I have been able to improve the process and complete the missing parts, adding two new algorithms for manipulating margin requirements and applying trade offsetting rules that conform to the standards of the futures industry. I called them *the first* and *second P&L reserve strategies*. They both are based on fundamental properties of the potential profit and corresponding strategies.

I found that the material had grown from an article to a book. After adding fresh new price examples, this book is now offered for your interest. Needless to say, with my love of programming I have complemented each significant concept and each property requiring computation with a class, a compact framework, and/or a program. These are not fragments but form a complete program, ready to compile and run, and can be used for further market analysis and a better understanding of potential profit.

Over the years, I have come to the conclusion that the potential profit described by Robert Pardo as a "not yet widely understood idea" and the corresponding strategy is fundamental and the most goal-oriented trading property of the market. It will retain its meaning as long as trading exists and prices fluctuate.

Acknowledgments

Indeed, I have written this book in a "home laboratory" for my own enjoyment but always feeling that the subject goes beyond the interests of one individual. Nevertheless, a subject or a man cannot be taken out of his life context. If someone in July 1992 had told me that a Russian scientist doing research on inductively coupled plasma combined with mass spectrometry and chromatography under the guidance of Professor Masatoshi Morita of the National Institute for Environmental Studies would ever write a book on trading, I would have thought it ridiculous. Nothing in my background of analytical and computational chemistry, obtained from the Lomonosov's Moscow State University, or my scientific work at Vernadskii Institute of Geochemistry and Analytical Chemistry at the Russian Academy of Sciences, the scientific traditions and knowledge formed by close and fortunate cooperation with my teachers Professors Oleg Petrukhin and Boris Spivakov and the academician Yuri Zolotov, could predict such a turn. However, I had finished several successful software projects for personal computers in cooperation with Dr. Vladlen Taran, and my interest in software design in the late 1980s resulted in my creating a portfolio of programs, which I could then use as my calling card. Today, I am grateful to Dr. Richard Weisburd, my American colleague at the National Institute for Environmental Studies (Tsukuba, Japan), who noticed the programs and hinted that my computational background might be useful for a securities company such as Merrill Lynch. This idea seemed crazy enough to try.

I am grateful to Bob Samuels, Mark Young, Alec Clarke, Jiro Kawamura, and Carla Young, who worked from 1992 to 1993 in the Systems and Telecommunications Department, for opening the world of Merrill Lynch to me. I enjoyed working at Merrill Lynch of Japan from 1993 to 1996 and for a short time at Deutsche Morgan Greenfell Capital Limited in Tokyo with Dr. Ravi Chari, Dr. Richard Malone, Aaron Cooperwood, and Robert Stein. I am grateful to them for defining the unique project in which I participated, and which indirectly triggered the direction of this book. During the same time, the advice of Dr. Lubomir Gerginov formed my taste for C++, the encyclopedic knowledge of Japanese governmental bonds shared by Katherine Cash, and the lunch discussions about futures and markets with Russ Marcus were very useful for me.

The move to the United States and the work at NumeriX LLC began another new page. I am grateful to Dr. Alexander Sokol, Professor Nigel Goldenfeld, Professor Mitchell Feigenbaum, entrepreneur Michael Goodkin, Brian Cook, Craig Bouchard, Steve O'Hanlon, and Dr. Greg Whitten for the courage to create and successfully lead this excellent analytical company through its work in the area of pricing financial derivatives.

I am very grateful to Kevin Commins, senior editor at John Wiley & Sons, for his energy and valuable initiatives and advice, to his assistant Laura Walsh, and to Todd Tedesco, senior production editor, who brought this book to reality.

And, of course, I could not imagine in 1993, when I read the book of Perry Kaufman, that the swing in my career would ever result in my own book and that he would be the first reader. His experience in trading systems and the financial industry, friendly advice, fresh facts added for illustrations, critical review, and the work on each chapter and each paragraph make this book simply better. Benoit Mandelbrot wrote in one of his books: "No book is made alone." Considering the contribution of Perry Kaufman, I agree with this statement on 100 percent.

My full love is to my wife Natalia and the kids for making my life beautiful and for their moral support during the work on this book, and to my parents, who, unfortunately, will not see this unless there is some unknown side to the relationship between the two worlds. I also thank my son Victor, who, after a short description, proposed the title for the Chapter 6.

Valerii Salov
Savoy, Illinois
Winter 2006

CHAPTER 1

Potential Profit as a Measure of Market Performance

The goal of trading is to make money, and for many, profits are the best way to measure that success. It is one of the most important performance characteristics of trading. In this chapter, I would like to emphasize that in contrast with ordinary profit, potential or maximum profit—the central subject of this book—does not deal at all with the activity of an individual trader. Potential profit and the strategy producing it are market properties. Along with this, I will write a C++ program computing Pardo's potential profit.

PROFIT AND POTENTIAL PROFIT

What does a profit tell us? Is it a characteristic of the trader's skills? To some extent yes, but that is not all. The profit is a result of interaction of the human with the market. It characterizes the trader as well as the existing market conditions.

If we apply a mechanical trading system to several historical intervals of market data and get the average annualized return on investment, what does this value mean? Is it a system characteristic? In many respects yes, but not exactly. This value is a measure of both system and market performances.

If a developer says that his system produced a 60 percent return on investment, does it mean that the system is good? To make the hidden sense obvious, I will reformulate the question. Can we expect a 60 percent return on investment if we apply the same system to a flat market? One can argue that such markets luckily do not exist and that prices always fluctuate. This is not the point. We can find historical periods of very low price volatility and trend, where it is unreasonable to believe that 60 percent could be achieved. However, if one says that he made a 100 percent return on margin trading a *soybean futures contract* in the first quarter of 2005 (see Figure 1.1), should we conclude that the return is good?

FIGURE 1.1 Open, high, low, close prices for soybean contract SK05 expired in May 2005 and traded on the Chicago Board of Trade (CBOT) during January–March of 2005.
Source: Courtesy of XPRESSTRADE, www.xpresstrade.com.

One way to judge traders' performance is to compare it with results achieved by others. For our purposes the best example is Larry Williams, a well-known trader and writer of several best-selling books (Williams 1979, 1999, 2000, 2005), who has been documented as having demonstrated extraordinary performance participating in the Robbins Trading Company World Championship in 1987. Starting with $10,000, he increased the account value up to over $1 million in one year. This result remains the competition's record at the time of this writing, and it is certainly an extraordinary return for one year. Ten years later, in 1997, his daughter ended the year with more than $100,000, beginning with the same $10,000. It is interesting to compare the impressive results (see Table 1.1) shown in different years by other winners of this championship.

You would think that a return of 100 percent on margin in three months of trading soybeans would be considered a good return. But how much did the market offer during those three months? Although the returns in Table 1.1 show only the best of all participants, everyone should agree that potentially bigger or substantially bigger profits were possible in the markets during the time of the competition. Moreover, we understand that Larry Williams, in achieving his 1987 result, had his account equity exceed $2 millions before giving back part of

TABLE 1.1 Robbins World Cup Championships of Futures Trading—Top Overall Performances for All Divisions

Year	Winner	Return (%)
2004	Kurt Sakaeda	929
2003	Int'l. Capital Mngt.	88
2002	John Holsinger	608
2001	David Cash	53
2000	Kurt Sakaeda	595
1999	Chuck Hughes	315
1998	Jason Park	99
1997	Michelle Williams	1,000
1996	Reinhart Rentsch	95
1995	Dennis Minogue	219
1994	Frank Suler	85
1993	Richard Hedreen	173
1992	Mike Lundgren	212
1991	Thomas Kobara	200
1990	Mike Lundgren	244
1989	Mike Lundgren	176
1988	David Kline	148
1987	Larry Williams	11,376
1986	Henry Thayer	231
1985	Ralph Casazzone	1,283
1984	Ralph Casazzone	264

Source: Robbins Trading Company (http://robbinstrading.com/worldcup/standings.asp)

those profits to the market, of course, in the hope of getting even more. How can we know what the potential would have been? While I have no exact records of which futures contracts were traded by participants of the World Cup, we shall get an idea about potential profits by analyzing *daily prices* and *intraday tick prices* in later chapters. Meanwhile, these observations and formulated questions distinguish the actual profit obtained by a trader or a system from the potential profit that could be realized in the same market during the same time. The former deals with both trading activity and market behavior, and the last is a property of a market during any given time interval. This market property can be referred to as *potential profit, maximum profit, market profit,* or *market offer*. Therefore, we can conclude the following:

- If a market does not offer a profit, then there is no trader or system that can create profits in that market.
- If a market does offer a profit, then there is no trader or system that can create a bigger profit than one offered by the market. From this point of view, the market never can be beaten. In the best case, a trader can play a draw game with the market!

Robert Pardo (Pardo 1992) suggested dividing profit by potential profit and using the ratio as a new measure of *model performance*:

> *An excellent measure of model performance is the efficiency with which the trading model converts potential profits offered by the market into trading profits. This measure is simple to calculate: Divide the net trading profit by the potential market profit.... The model efficiency measure makes it easy to compare market-to-market performance and to evaluate model performance on a year-to-year basis.*

We shall see that it is easy to calculate potential profit under conditions where transaction costs are not involved. However, introducing even simple commissions makes things substantially more complicated. This and other transaction costs lead to algorithms and indicators described in the following chapters.

PRICE FLOW AND C++

Why C++?

The purpose of this book is not only to introduce solutions for the calculation of potential profit under different conditions but also to compute those values from real prices. To accomplish this, I need a programming language for writing corresponding programs, and a good candidate seems to be C++ (Stroustrup 2000). It has excellent capabilities to express concepts in terms of *classes* and supports several programming paradigms, including *procedural programming*, *programming with abstract data types*, *generic programming*, and *object-oriented programming* (Stroustrup 2000, Booch 1994). Conveniently, there are several different C++ compilers commercially and publicly available. The modern C++ Standard Library (International Standard ISO/IEC 14882 2003) and Standard Template Library (STL), which is a part of it (Musser 1996) contain rich data collections and algorithms that can serve our purpose very well and simplify design and coding. Over the next few chapters, I shall gradually introduce the necessary notions and related C++ representations. In this chapter, we need to work with a sequence of prices that we will call *price flow*.

Why Skip Date and Time Classes?

Market prices come sequentially in time and are referred to as a *time series*. The most detailed information is called *tick data*. Every new transaction on an exchange is a discovery process that identifies the traded price and makes it known to the public. The time of each transaction is registered. Each time-price pair becomes a single point on an intraday price chart. In active or liquid markets, the time interval between two transactions can be just a fraction of a second. This is why in order to keep accurate records of this information and write corresponding software, one needs a class representing and measuring time with a precision of at least one second.

If we work with intraday prices and combine them across consecutive days into a single stream, a developer would need a date class. Alternatively, one could develop a class that combined both time and date computations. Such an aggregate would serve the use of intraday as well as daily price flows. A most common example of *daily price information* is a set of open, high, low, closing, and/or settlement prices. For trading either futures or equities, a daily record may also contain trading volume. For futures contracts, most analysts also include open interest. The calculation of annualized profit or return, the times and dates of the investment activity, and a sequence of realized profits and losses are crucial. In order to satisfy the complex requirements and conventions of the variety of fixed income and other investment instruments, and to compute the present values of cash flows and discount factors, a software library must have date, calendar, day fraction, and time classes. By contrast, for only profit computations, based wholly on prices, the knowledge of time and date intervals is not critical. Then, for our purposes, we can simplify the program by skipping date and time classes in this book.

Vector for Price Flow

Although date and time classes will be omitted, we still need to pay attention to the fact that a price flow is a sequence of prices. Ignoring time difference between elements of the sequence does not eliminate the need to reference and access each of them. This sequence can be expressed and implemented as a *sequence container*. In STL such sequence containers are *deque*, *list*, *queue*, *stack*, and *vector* (International Standard ISO/IEC 14882 2003). The last, *vector*, is very useful for our application. Because it is a template, the class `vector` may contain elements of different built-in types or classes. It automatically and efficiently handles memory management when objects are added to the collection or removed from it. The class `vector` gives multiple advantages compared to the C++ built-in arrays. It helps the writing of programs without *memory leaks* caused by a failure explicitly to release a dynamically allocated memory consumed by objects and makes development pleasant.

Classes for Prices

One way to program prices is to use the C++ built-in type `double`. If this low-order level type is used to express the notion of price, then it is up to us to make sure that wrong values do not find their way into our program. Such wrong values can be zero and/or negative numbers and those that are not whole multiples of minimal price increments—*ticks*. It is easier to organize these two verification tasks in a class or a *framework* (a collection of classes providing a set of services for a particular domain [Booch 1994]) encapsulating the built-in type `double`. In describing the evolution of prices by differential stochastic equations, one of the goals of modern theoretical approaches is to move from discrete cases to continuous functions or processes as soon as possible (Hunt 2000). In contrast with this tendency, I will emphasize the discrete properties of prices and transactions.

Prices either do not change or change by increments of minimum ticks. Each market has its conventions. For instance, the minimal nonzero price fluctuation of a soybean futures contract, traded on the Chicago Board of Trade (CBOT), is one quarter of a cent per bushel. When one sees soybean prices in Figure 1.1 or in an issue of the *Wall Street Journal* as 661.75, it is read as 6 dollars 61 cents and three quarters of a cent per bushel. For accounting matters one does not need to know that a soybean contract assumes that a trading unit is 5,000 bushels. The only important information is that when the price changes by one tick up or down, the value of a bushel changes by +0.25 or –0.25 cents, the futures contract value changes by $12.50, higher or lower, respectively, and the value of the account gains or loses, depending on whether a single contract was bought or sold. If you bought and the price increased or sold short and the price decreased, then you've gained; otherwise, you've lost. Clearly, all these numbers relate each to other: the value 12.5 [dollars] is equal to 0.25 [cents per bushel] × 5000 [bushels]/100 [cents per dollar]. There are days when a soybean contract, which is traded on the CBOT from 9:30 A.M. to 1:15 P.M., can range from up 20 points to down 20 points (each point is 1 cent per bushel). A net rise or fall of 20 cents per bushel results in a profit or loss of $1,000 per contract without commissions and other fees.

C++ provides convenient and helpful tools to encapsulate details of price checking while hiding the internal state of an object of a price class. In the *object model* (a collective name of elements of a sound engineering foundation), which serves as a basis for modern programming, the main *object characteristics* are *identity*, *state*, and *behavior* (Booch 1994). In C++, the *state of an object* as a concept denotes collectively all values of the class members and other objects referred to by class members. It is a software design goal that an object is maintained in a well-defined state. The property making the state of an object well defined is known as *invariant* (Stroustrup 2000). A useful invariant for our price object means maintaining positive price values represented by a whole number of minimal price ticks. In particular, a *constructor* of a price class can create and initialize an object, where invariant holds. This can be achieved by checking that the input price is positive and consistent with market conventions. Once an invalid price is detected, a constructor may *throw* (`throw`) a C++ *exception*. All other *class operations* should maintain this invariant.

Sometimes certain operations have to violate an invariant. In such situations, it is assumed that several operations must be called in sequence, with the final effect recovering the invariant. If such operations are called outside of the sequence, then this can violate the invariant and bring an object into an inconsistent state. The best practice is to prohibit the use of everything that may violate an invariant. In C++ operations, violating an invariant, can be encapsulated as `private` or `protected`. Preferably, a `public` interface of a class should consist of operations maintaining the invariant of the objects of the class.

The design of a price class that solves the two price-checking tasks can be more complicated than the simple wrapper of the C++ built-in type `double`. While the constructor of such a wrapping class would be able to check that the input price is positive for any market data, the second task, checking that the price is in the correct increment of minimal ticks, depends on a concrete market convention. Literally, part of the code that validates soybean and gold prices cannot be the same. This is because a one-tick move for the *gold futures contract*, traded on the Commodity Exchange (COMEX), is 0.1 dollars per ounce and one contract is 100 troy ounces. This makes the *dollar value of one tick* equal to $10 per contract. This convention differentiates gold futures contract specifications from those of soybeans. Object-oriented or generic programming techniques are valuable for solving both of these verification tasks.

Object-orientation implies developing a hierarchy of price classes based on *inheritance* (Rumbaugh et al. 1999). The Unified Modeling Language (UML) (Rumbaugh et al. 1999) defines this term as:

The mechanism by which more specific elements incorporate structure and behavior defined by more general elements.

With my choice of the programming language, the inheritance relationship between classes is expressed using the syntax and mechanism of C++ inheritance, which distinguishes base and derived classes. The *interface inheritance* can be useful in order to access objects of different price classes in run time conveniently by means of a single *interface* (a named set of operations that characterize the behavior of an element) (Rumbaugh et al. 1999). It is defined as:

The inheritance of the interface of a parent element but not its implementation or data structure.

In C++, this can be achieved by defining a base price class without any data members and with `public`, `virtual`, *pure operations* (Stroustrup 2000) and deriving from it the classes supplying definitions of the pure operations. I will use object-orientation but not for the class `Price`.

For the development of the major class `Price` I have chosen generic programming—programming with types efficiently supported in C++ by the *class* and *function templates*. In our case, this means a parameterization of the class template Price by classes, checking prices in accordance with a particular contract specification.

Procedural Programming

Let me begin with the classes to be used for *default* (an *abstract contract* with the minimum tick 0.0001 and the tick dollar value 0.0001), gold and soybean futures contracts specifications. They are defined in the header file `Spec.h`.

```
#ifndef __Spec_h__
#define __Spec_h__

namespace PPBOOK {

    class SpecDefault {
    public:
        static  const char* name(){return "default";}
        static  double      tick(){return 0.0001;}
        static  double      tickValue(){return 0.0001;}
    };

    // Gold
    class SpecGC {
    public:
        static  const char* name(){return "GC";}
        static  double      tick(){return 0.1;}
```

```
        static  double      tickValue(){return 10.0;}
    };

    // Soybean
    class SpecS {
    public:
        static  const char* name(){return "S";}
        static  double      tick(){return 0.25;}
        static  double      tickValue(){return 12.5;}
    };
    //...

} // PPBOOK

#endif /* __Spec_h__ */
```

The notation ... means that more lines in the file are possible. In the code above, this notation is shown as a C++ comment so that one can copy and paste this text as it is and use it in a real program. I have verified that all code extracted in this manner will compile without errors. In order to avoid collision of a class name with the same name used in other libraries, I place the definition of the class inside the `namespace PPBOOK`, which means "potential profit book." Similar `namespace` syntax will be used for other identifiers.

The gold contract with the ticker symbol GC is traded on the COMEX division of the New York Mercantile Exchange (NYMEX). The soybean contract with the ticker symbol S is traded on the CBOT. The symbol, minimum tick value, and dollar value of the tick (the tick value times the contract size) are only a part of what can constitute the contract specifications. I have selected only those specifications that are needed for profit computation and can improve diagnostics.

The three classes contain only `static` functions. No objects are required in order to call them. Calling these functions is applying C++ for procedural programming: the interfaces use only functions and no objects of classes. However, compared to other procedural programming languages, such as C, C++ still gives technical advantages by using namespace, class scope, and stronger type checking (Stroustrup 2000).

While the three classes that we have defined, `SpecDefault`, `SpecGC`, and `SpecS`, are different they have the same number and type of `static` functions—the same interfaces. Combining these functions into a class scope creates a new quality. This quality already distinguishes the obtained result from pure procedural programming, where nine stand-alone functions would need to be introduced to handle the three contracts. It is quite common that several programming paradigms can be mixed together in a software project.

Once the number of selected futures contracts or stocks increases, more specification classes can be defined and added in different header files in the same manner. Next, I am going to introduce the class `Price` parameterized by a specification class.

Object-Based and Generic Programming

The definition of the class `Price` is in the header file `Price.h`:

```
#ifndef __Price_h__
#define __Price_h__

#include <cmath>
#include <sstream>
#include <stdexcept>
using namespace std;

namespace PPBOOK {

    template<class S>
    class Price {
    public:
        Price(double p) : p_(p){check(p);}
        Price(const Price<S>& p) : p_(p.p_){}
        double          price() const {return p_;}
        Price<S>&       operator=(double p)
                        {check(p); p_ = p; return *this;}
        Price<S>&       operator=(const Price<S>& p)
                        {p_ = p.p_; return *this;}
    private:
        double          p_;
        static  void    check(double p)
        {
            if(p <= 0.0) {
                ostringstream   s;
                s   << S::name() << " price " << p
                    << " must be positive.";
                throw   invalid_argument(s.str());
            }
            double  nt = p / S::tick();
            if(fabs(floor(nt) * S::tick() - p) > 1.0e-8 &&
                fabs(ceil(nt) * S::tick() - p) > 1.0e-8) {
                ostringstream   s;
                s   << S::name() << " price " << p
                    << " must be a whole number of ticks " << S::tick();
                throw   invalid_argument(s.str());
            }
        }
    };

    // Only for illustration
    //template<class S>
    //double
    //operator-(const Price<S>& lhs, const Price<S>& rhs)
    //{
```

```
//    return  lhs.price() - rhs.price();
//}

} // PPBOOK

#endif /* __Price_h__ */
```

Programming with objects, which are instances of classes not related through an inheritance relationship (see previous sections), is known as object-based programming or programming with abstract data types (Booch 1994). However, in this design a specification class parameterizes the class template `Price`. The last can be successfully instantiated, if the public interface of a specification class contains the `static` functions `name()` and `tick()`. All three classes—`SpecDefault`, `SpecGC`, and `SpecS`–satisfy this requirement. Using them as parametric types to change the behavior of an object of the class `Price` is known as *generic programming*—programming with types. This small example shows a hybrid of object-based and generic programming paradigms.

The `private static` function `check()` throws an exception if a price is not positive or not equal to whole multiples of ticks. For making error messages more descriptive I use the C++ Standard class `ostringstream`. The normal work of the function `check()` is based on the two assumptions that `S::name()` may not return a zero pointer and `S::tick()` may not return a zero value. Of course, I could make the function longer and check both conditions; however, returning zeros in both cases is out of the problem's domain. Even if this is done by mistake, it must be corrected in the trivial implementation of the specification classes. Hence, instead of writing additional checking code, which should never be used under the normal conditions existing at compile time, I am omitting it.

The function `check()` is called explicitly by the constructor creating a price object from raw `double` data and by the overloaded `operator=()` assigning the new `double` value price to the existing object. This design closes all gates and prevents the input of inconsistent prices into an object of the class `Price`. For better invariant protection, I excluded the *default constructor*. There is no reasonable value for a price created by a constructor without arguments. This is because zero prices have been excluded from our domain. Sometimes the lack of a default constructor may cause a technical inconvenience because a built-in array cannot be created from a class without it (Koenig 1996). However, I am going to reuse the Standard C++ class `vector` not requiring a constructor without arguments for a class of an element.

One may say that it would be convenient to have an operator that converts a price object to a `double`. Then class does not need the operation `price()` and can behave in many situations in the same way as the built-in type `double`. However, it has been pointed out (Stroustrup 2000) that the presence of both a nonexplicit constructor from a type and a conversion operator to the type can lead to ambiguity or surprises when conversion is unexpected. For instance, the C++ Standard class `string` has a constructor from `const char*`; however, it supplies the explicit operation `c_str()` in order to convert it to `const char*` and does not allow automatic user-defined conversion by an `operator const char*()`.

You may notice that if I do not supply an automatic conversion operator, then at least I may need to overload global arithmetic and input/output operators so that they could accept objects of the class `Price` as well as values of the type `double`. The way this is done is shown right after the definition of the class `Price` in a comment. However, I will not use this approach because, in my opinion, it compromises the safety that has already been achieved in the introduced classes.

Example Test1.cpp

From time to time I shall apply the C++ `typedef` specifier. It helps to create a new identifier for naming already existing types. This does not introduce new classes but alias names making the code shorter and more readable. The program `test1.cpp` containing a few `typedef` and C++ `main()` function is:

```
#include <vector>
#include <iostream>
using namespace std;

#include "Spec.h"
#include "Price.h"
using namespace PPBOOK;

typedef Price<SpecGC>               GoldPrice;
typedef vector<GoldPrice>           GoldPrices;
typedef Price<SpecS>                SoybeanPrice;
typedef vector<SoybeanPrice>        SoybeanPrices;

int main(int, char*[])
{
    try {
        GoldPrices      gp;
        gp.push_back(449.10);

        SoybeanPrices  sp;
        sp.push_back(661.74);
    }
    catch(const exception& e) {
        cerr    << e.what() << endl;
    }
    catch(...) {
        cerr    << "Unknown exception" << endl;
    }
    return  0;
}
```

If we are going to use new identifiers such as `GoldPrices` and `SoybeanPrices` in multiple source and header files, then the `typedef` statements should be placed in a separate C++ header file. Notice how prices can be appended to the collections using `push_back()`. In this case, an implicit user-defined conversion of `double` to object of the class `Price` works because I added the constructor from `double` and did not declare it using the C++ keyword `explicit`. The number of currently available prices in the collection is returned by the operation `vector::size()`. A price can be extracted given an index by `operator[]`. An object of the class `GoldPrices` accepts only positive numbers, which are whole multiples of 0.1 (the minimum price move). An object of the class `SoybeanPrices` accepts only positive numbers, which are whole multiples of 0.25. This program generates the following output:

```
S price 661.74 must be a whole number of ticks 0.25
```

The wrong soybean price has been rejected!

This simple framework consisting of the specification classes, price class, and sequence vector collection illustrates another important principle of software design known as the *Open-Closed Principle* (Meyer 1988, Martin 1996). It is opened for extensions assuming adding new specification classes and closed for modifications. "Closed for modifications" means that in extending this framework one does not need to change existing code, which might introduce bugs into a program that is already working. Of course, "closed for modifications" assumes that we do not extend our problem domain by changing the number of requirements. For instance, if a common default price value is known for each price specification, then specification classes might get the additional `static` function `S::defaultPrice()`. It would then be reused for defining the default constructor in the class `Price`. Adding those operations would be a modification of existing classes and a violation of the principle. The need to make these changes would indicate that our original design was not adequate to the solving task.

Object-Oriented Programming

Working with a class template `Price` and corresponding `vector` means that template parameters must be known in compile time. Consequently, I would need to write a template version of each algorithm calling the *vector of prices*. However, in order to apply such template algorithms, the price specification template parameters again must be known in compile time. This can easily fulfill our application working with prices of different specifications by `if-else` or `switch` statements. The introduction of new specification classes would require the changing of these places in the code, which is very likely prone to errors. I would like to simplify the writing of these applications so that they select the correct algorithms in run time based on the contract price specifications. To accomplish this, we will need a class in run time that manages either the algorithms or the vectors of prices. I have chosen the last option.

In order to reach the goal, I apply object-oriented programming. This means that the fundamental, logical building blocks should be objects. The objects must be instances of some classes. The classes are related via inheritance relationships (Booch 1994). I build a hierarchy of the classes available through a common interface, where each concrete class implements a sequential collection of prices with given contract price specifications. This hierarchy is encapsulated within a concrete class managing collections of different price types. This managing class aggregates an object of an appropriate concrete class from the hierarchy and delegates to this object a subset of its own collection responsibilities. The *aggregation* and *delegation* techniques and also multiple *design patterns* based on object-oriented programming are described in Gamma et al. (1994). The following code shows the interface class `IPrices` from the header file `IPrice.h` (the leading character "I" stands for "interface"):

```
#ifndef __IPrices_h__
#define __IPrices_h__

namespace PPBOOK {

    class IPrices {
    public:
        virtual ~IPrices(){}
        virtual IPrices*    clone() const = 0;
        virtual const char* name() const = 0;
        virtual double      tick() const = 0;
        virtual double      tickValue() const = 0;
        virtual size_t      size() const = 0;
        virtual double      operator[](size_t n) const = 0;
        virtual void        assign(size_t n, double price) = 0;
        virtual void        append(double price) = 0;
        virtual void        clear() = 0;
    };

} // PPBOOK

#endif /* __IPrices_h__ */
```

It is always necessary to decide if a `virtual` operation (method) should be declared constant. This issue is discussed in Lippman (1996). In this case, distinguishing between operations accessing and modifying an object's state seems straightforward. The operation `clone()` plays a role of so-called "virtual copy constructor" (Stroustrup 2000). The template class `CPrices` from the header file `CPrices.h` implements the interface (the leading character "C" means "concrete"):

```
#include <vector>
using namespace std;

#include "Price.h"
#include "IPrices.h"
using namespace PPBOOK;

class Prices;

namespace PPBOOK {
```

```
    template<class S>
    class CPrices : public IPrices {
        friend  class Prices;
    public:
        virtual CPrices*    clone() const {return new CPrices(*this);}
        virtual const char* name() const {return S::name();}
        virtual double      tick() const {return S::tick();}
        virtual double      tickValue() const {return S::tickValue();}
        virtual size_t      size() const {return p_.size();}
        virtual double      operator[](size_t n) const
                            {return p_.at(n).price();}
        virtual void        append(double price){p_.push_back(price);}
        virtual void        assign(size_t n, double price)
                            {p_.at(n) = price;}
        virtual void        clear(){p_.clear();}
    private:
        vector<Price<S> >   p_;
        CPrices(){}
    };

} // PPBOOK

#endif /* __CPrices_h__ */
```

In defining this class template, I introduce the entire hierarchy of concrete classes implementing the interface `IPrices`. The creator of C++ Bjarne Stroustrup (2000) discussed this very powerful technique, where a template class is derived from a nontemplate *abstract class*. The default constructor is made `private` and the class `Prices` is declared as `friend`. Default copy and assignment semantics are suitable in this case. Let me introduce the last item of this triad: the managing class defined in the header file `Prices.h`:

```
#ifndef __Prices_h__
#define __Prices_h__

#include <string>
using namespace std;

#include "IPrices.h"
using namespace PPBOOK;

namespace PPBOOK {

    class Prices {
    public:
        Prices(const string& s) : p_(create(s)){}
```

```
        Prices(const Prices& src) : p_(src.p_->clone()){}
        ~Prices(){delete p_;}

        const char* name() const {return p_->name();}
        double      tick() const {return p_->tick();}
        double      tickValue() const {return p_->tickValue();}
        size_t      size() const {return p_->size();}
        double      operator[](size_t n) const {return (*p_)[n];}
        void        assign(size_t n, double price){p_->assign(n, price);}
        void        append(double price){p_->append(price);}
        void        clear(){p_->clear();}
        Prices&     operator=(const Prices& rhs)
        {
            if(this != &rhs) {
                IPrices*    tmp = rhs.p_->clone();
                delete  p_;
                p_  = tmp;
            }
            return  *this;
        }
    private:
        IPrices*    p_;
        static IPrices* create(const string& s);
    };

} // PPBOOK

#endif /* __Prices_h__ */
```

An object of the class `Prices` is a sequential collection of prices similar to a vector. It does not provide for a reference to an element in the collection because such a reference would depend on a price specification class. Nor does it have `operator[]` returning a reference to the built-in type `double` allowing left-hand side assignment. This class is concrete and has no `virtual` operations. The default constructor is not available. The copy constructor as well as assignment operator is defined. An object of this class can be an element of a value-based data container such as the class `vector`. The `private static` function `create()` is a factory producing objects of different types from our hierarchy. If either this function or the operations `clone()` return a valid nonzero pointer or throw an exception, then constructors either create an object with invariant hold or an object will not be created at all. Hence, it is an implementation task to ensure that `create()` and `clone()` possess this property. This simplifies implementation of other operations, because it is no longer necessary to check that pointer `p_` is zero. In this situation using a zero pointer without checking would be a software disaster. This will not happen if the `operator new` on failure throws `bad_alloc` exception instead of returning 0. If this is not the case, then it is clear that modification of `create()` and `clone()` would be straightforward. Basically, it is easy to write implementations where the `create()` and `clone()`

operations act independently on the behavior of the operator new and never return 0 but throw an exception if something is wrong.

Exception Safety

It is important to note the *exception safety* properties of the class Prices. To do this, it is useful to follow the classification of levels of exception safety discussed in Stroustrup (2000). The level *no guarantee* means that if an exception is thrown by an operation working on an object, then the object is left corrupted. The invariant is not hold. The level *basic guarantee* means that after an exception is thrown, basic invariants are hold and no memory or other resources leak. The level *strong guarantee* means that after an exception is thrown the object remains in the same state as it was before, calling the operation throwing the exception. The level *no throw guarantee* means that an operation never throws an exception. Careful examination shows that operations in the class Prices belong to the strong guarantee level and the *destructor* belongs to the no throw guarantee level. The definition of the assignment operator shows how this is reached. If clone() possess the properties required in the previous section, then it either throws an exception and nothing changes in the object, or it returns a valid pointer. After the last is returned, the operator delete does not throw exception (no throw guarantee for destructor). Assignment of one pointer to another pointer may not throw an exception either. Here the order of lines is important. For instance, if one deleted p_ and after that called clone(), then an exception thrown by clone() would leave the object in a corrupted state because the pointer would contain an address of a destroyed object. A suitable order of lines here is a very cheap way to reach the strong guarantee.

Production of Concrete Objects

The static function create() plays the role of a *factory* producing price objects of a given type dependent on a specification passed as a string. In order to maximally restrict access to this function, it is declared private and defined in the source file Prices.cpp:

```
#include <stdexcept>
using namespace std;

#include "Spec.h"
#include "Prices.h"
#include "CPrices.h"
using namespace PPBOOK;

namespace PPBOOK {

    IPrices* Prices::create(const string& s)
    {
        if(s == SpecDefault::name())
            return  new CPrices<SpecDefault>;
        if(s == SpecGC::name())
```

```
        return  new CPrices<SpecGC>;
    if(s == SpecS::name())
        return  new CPrices<SpecS>;
    throw   invalid_argument(
                "Cannot create object of class Prices for " + s);
  }

} // PPBOOK
```

This function parses the string parameter and decides the object of which concrete type should be created. If the specification is not in the list, then an exception is thrown. The parsing is character case sensitive. If one needs a new type of specification in the system, then a new class is written similar to `SpecDefault`, `SpecGC`, and `SpecS`. This is added in new header files. Until this point, the Open-Closed Principle discussed earlier is obeyed: there are to be no existing code changes while a new price specification is introduced. However, the function `create()` violates this principle. For a class `Prices` based on a new contract specification, an additional `#include` statement, `if`, and `new` operators must be added in the source file `Prices.cpp`. True, these are only three lines, but the file and function `create()` must be changed within this design every time a new contract specification is added.

You may recognize in the design based on the functions `clone()` a variation of the design pattern *Factory Method* also known as the design pattern *Virtual Constructor* (Gamma et al. 1994). The factory method `clone()` was used in order to implement the copy constructor and assignment operator in the class `Prices`. In the context of factories, it makes sense to mention interesting alternative variations of the prototype-based *abstract factory* (Gamma et al. 1994), (Vlissides 1998, 1999).

We are now fully equipped to write a program computing Pardo's potential profit.

PARDO'S POTENTIAL PROFIT

Simple Algorithm for a True Reverse System

Robert Pardo (Pardo 1992) formulated a definition of *potential profit* and an algorithm of its computation in this statement:

> *Potential profit is the profit that could be realized by buying every bottom and selling every top. More precisely, it is the sum of every price change where each change is taken as a positive number.*

Are the first and second sentences in agreement? Yes, they are if we assume that selling every top means short selling so that the result of this transaction is a net short position in the market. In other words, if we were long one *unit* (a contract or share) before the transaction, then the transaction liquidates the long position and enters a new short position at the same price. The same process occurs when buying every bottom. We are always in the market and our trading strategy is a true reversal system, switching our position from long to short and back again. Only under these conditions will the sum of every price change, where each change is taken as a positive number, give us the right result. This number is substantially greater than a long-only strategy where we buy a bottom, then sell the next top in order to exit the market, then wait until the price drops to the next bottom before buying again. The C++ implementation of this algorithm is placed in the header file `PardoPotentialProfitAlg.h`:

```
#include "Prices.h"
using namespace PPBOOK;

namespace PPBOOK {

    inline  double
    pardo_potential_profit(const Prices& prices)
    {
        double  ppp = 0.0;
        for(size_t j = 1; j < prices.size(); j++)
            ppp += fabs(prices[j] - prices[j - 1]);
        return  ppp * prices.tickValue() / prices.tick();
    }

} // PPBOOK

#endif /* __PardoPotentialProfitAlg_h__ */
```

This algorithm returns zero if the collection of prices is empty. The code of the function `pardo_potential_profit` is my interpretation of Robert Pardo's algorithm description. It does not mean that the same or similar code or formulas are used by Robert Pardo. In order to emphasize his contribution, I am applying the prefit "pardo" in function name `pardo_potential_profit` and file names `pardo.cpp` and `PardoPotentialProfitAlg.h`.

The Program Computing Pardo's Potential Profit

It is convenient to have a program that works as a filter with the following interface on Microsoft Windows: type prices.txt | pardo or on UNIX it might look like cat prices.txt | pardo (in both cases the same effect is reached using the syntax pardo < prices.txt). Both programs, "type" on Windows and "cat" on UNIX, send the contents of text files to the standard output. A *filter program* takes information from *standard input*, processes it, and sends the result to the *standard output*. The *pipe syntax* (|) is a mechanism that passes the output of one program to the input of another, and is supported by the operating system (Stevens 1999). This program may determine the type of a price by reading a conventional descriptor from input. The final program from the file `pardo.cpp` is:

```
#include <iostream>
```

```
#include <string>
using namespace std;

#include "PardoPotentialProfitAlg.h"
using namespace PPBOOK;

int main(int, char*[])
{
    try {
        string  market;
        cin >> market;
        Prices  p(market);
        double  price;
        while(cin >> price)
            p.append(price);
        cout    << market << " " << pardo_potential_profit(p) << endl;
    }
    catch(const exception& e) {
        cerr    << e.what() << endl;
    }
    catch(...) {
        cerr    << "Unknown exception" << endl;
    }
    return  0;
}
```

This program assumes that the input file has a descriptor of the market (default, GC, S) as the first token. Because this is a filter program it can operate in all possible ways, where the input is obtained from standard input object `cin`. The "echo" command can be applied as follows:

```
echo S 661.50 662.75 659.25 | pardo
S 237.5

echo S 661.50 662.75 659.21 | pardo
S price 659.21 must be a whole number of ticks 0.25

echo HG 661.50 662.75 659.25 | pardo
Cannot create object of class Prices for HG
```

The program rejects the soybean price 659.21 because it is not a multiple of 0.25, the minimum move. It also knows nothing about HG. The last entry could be a copper contract but has no identification. Adding a *copper futures contract* specification class should extend the program. However, even if this is not yet done, you still can get Pardo's potential profit for such a contract. To accomplish this, you can apply the extended capabilities based on the *descriptor default* and the class `SpecDefault`. This class has the minimum tick 0.0001 and the dollar tick value 0.0001. This makes the dollar value of one point (*tick value/tick*) equal to one dollar. If you know the dollar value of one point for the contract, which is not yet programmed, then you can multiply the "default" Pardo's profit by this value and get the correct final result.

For instance, the soybean contract S is already in the list. However, if it would not be yet included, then the task could be solved as:

```
echo default 661.50 662.75 659.25 | pardo
default 4.75
```

The command line contains the descriptor *default* and the same set of soybean prices. These prices are certainly whole multiples of 0.0001 and will be accepted. The *default* Pardo's profit value is equal to 4.75. The value of one point in the soybean contract is $50. Multiplying 4.75 by 50 we get 237.5. This is the right profit observed earlier. Of course, using *default* means that you need now to take care about correct input prices. The program will accept everything that is a multiple of 0.0001. However, once a specification for a new contract is added permanently, the input prices will be verified automatically.

In practice, most prices will be available as a long list of records in a text file. Such a text file must begin with the character descriptor of the market or stock, which is followed by prices. The descriptor and individual prices must be separated by a delimiter, which can be space, tab, or new line characters. The program allows arbitrary combinations of these delimiters, collectively known as *white spaces*. The program reuses the magic C++ Standard `operator>>` to read the input token by token.

This program performs many operations: reading and checking prices, creating appropriate objects in run time, filling them with prices and managing memory, and applying a simple mathematical algorithm. It consists of exception safe building blocks. At the same time, it is compact. Implementation of many operations can be done in just one line of code. A combination of generic and object-oriented programming, reusing variations of sound design patterns and the C++ Standard Library classes, makes the system stable and open for extensions. A minor drawback—that the existing code is not completely closed to modifications—is well compensated because new changes inside `create()` can be done in a simple and safe manner, localizing the place of changes. Another benefit of this design is that modifications that extend the specifications will not require recompilation of other modules but only the file `Prices.cpp`.

CONCLUSIONS

- Potential or maximum profit is a market property.
- Pardo's algorithm computes potential profit with all transaction costs taken as zero.
- Pardo's algorithm implies a true reversal trading strategy.
- A simple program illustrating major C++ design principles and programming paradigms is written to calculate Pardo's potential profit.

CHAPTER 2

Potential Profit and Transaction Costs

Pardo's algorithm for evaluating potential profit includes even the tiniest price changes and uses them to his advantage. These small price changes can be profitable because it assumes that transaction costs are zero. In real life, transaction costs can turn winning trades into losing ones. A price change should be large enough to compensate for all costs and still net a profit. Transaction costs are an important factor that influence trading decisions and change the number of profitable trades, their distribution in time, and the size of the profit. An algorithm for evaluating potential profit when costs are taken into account becomes more complicated. In this chapter, I analyze the properties of the potential profit strategy we began in Chapter 1 and introduce some notions necessary for building an algorithm to generate that strategy. The algorithm itself will be constructed in the next chapter.

WHAT IS A TRADING STRATEGY?

There are several definitions of *trading strategy*. At the time of this writing, Wikipedia (the free encyclopedia available on the Internet) contains an article with the definition: "a Trading Strategy is a predefined set of rules to apply." This can be extended to be *a set of rules that are followed in a precise order when deciding whether to enter or exit a trade*. At any moment, for a given market the application of the strategy must clearly result in whether we should be holding a long or short position as well as the size of that position. These transactions, or trades, are to be done sequentially. A strategy may also be defined by a set of trades, but this does not give you a way to make trading decisions in the future.

Other definitions (Hunt and Kennedy 2000; Harrison and Pliska 1981) formalize a trading strategy as a *portfolio process* developing through time. At any given time a *portfolio* is specified, listing all the holdings of assets that could be a combination of negative *short market positions*, zero (*out of the market*), and positive *long market positions*. Typically, it is required that at any time this process would not depend on knowledge of a future state (*nonanticipative process*). For accounting purposes we do not need to know why the portfolio changes. That deals with decisions and actions. However, we do need to access the changes or know the actions.

A trading strategy must be represented in a way that is sufficient for writing computer programs. I shall follow the definition of a portfolio process. Our portfolio will consist of a single asset such as a futures contract or a share of stock. There are two ways of supplying information about changes in the portfolio. The first is to record the holdings as a time sequence (1, –1, –1, 0). These numbers mean that the first position (at time 1) was long one contract, the second and third positions (at time 2 and 3) were both short one contract, and at the fourth time we are out of the market. These are not our buy or sell actions but simply a record of our long or short positions in terms of the number of contracts and without any idea of their dollar values. Does it mean that at the first time we bought one contract? We do not know that unless more information is given. Maybe this vector is a part of a longer record: (–1, [1, –1, –1, 0]). In this scenario the position was short one contract before the "first time." In order for the position at time 1 (the "first time") to be 1, we had to start by buying two contracts. If we had had the position 0 at the beginning, we would have had to buy only one contract as the "first" transaction. This illustrates that, given a *vector of positions*, we can reconstruct the "buy," "sell," or "do nothing" actions except for the uncertainty of the first action (*, –2, 0, 1). If our position was zero before the "first" transaction, then we would have enough information to complete the *vector of actions* as (1, –2, 0, 1).

The second way of supplying information about changes in the portfolio is to specify actions and show how many trading units (contracts or shares) are bought or sold at one time. The class `Strategy` from the header file `Strategy.h` is suitable for representation of both simple positions and actions. A way to use it becomes a subject of negotiation:

```
#ifndef __Strategy_h__
#define __Strategy_h__

#include <vector>
using namespace std;

namespace PPBOOK {
    typedef vector<int>     Strategy;
} // PPBOOK

#endif /* __Strategy_h__ */
```

As you can see, I have used it for recording actions. The positive or negative sign of an element means "buy" or "sell," respectively. The absolute value of an element is the number of trading units. Zero denotes the "do nothing" action. For instance, the strategy (1, –2, 0, 1) means that the first action is "buy one unit." The second action is "sell two units," and the third is just waiting. The fourth and final action is "buy one unit."

Another reason why I have not used the class `Strategy` for recording positions is that it is not suitable for *complex positions* consisting of several units traded at different prices. Consideration of such positions is essential for the strategies that reinvest profits. This is done later in the course of the book. The class `Position`, developed in further chapters, handles complex positions as well as simple ones. This class keeps track of associations between all actions and prices leading to a given complex position.

Can we reconstruct positions from the actions (1, –2, 0, 1)? Yes, if we must know the initial position, the one existing prior the application of the strategy. If we were out of the market, then the positions would be (1, –1, –1, 0). The final position can also be viewed as the initial position plus the sum of all elements (actions) of a strategy. Using the Standard Template Library's (STL's) algorithm, `accumulate` is the straightforward way to get this sum, which can be called the *net strategy action:*

```
...
#include <algorithm>
using namespace std;
#include "Strategy.h"
using namespace PPBOOK;
...
Strategy s;
s.push_back(1);
s.push_back(-2);
s.push_back(0);
s.push_back(1);
cout << accumulate(s.begin(), s.end()) << endl;
...
```

The ellipsis (. . .) without a comment prevents extracting and compiling this code fragment. However, the code can be used as a part of a program. If the sum from `accumulate` is zero, then the application of the strategy does not change a position established before its application. In our example, we can see that it bought two units (one for each of two trades) and sold two units (in a single transaction). The net strategy action is zero. If we were long one contract before application of the strategy, then we remained long one contract after its application. If the initial position is zero but the net strategy action is not, then there is an open position and an unrealized profit or loss at the end of the sequence. Any open positions must be accounted for when calculating the final strategy profit and loss (P&L).

I use the term *transaction* to denote an individual buy or sell action. I use the term *trade* to denote a completed set of transactions entering (from being out of the market status) and exiting (to being out of the market status) a position of one type (long or short). If we have a sequence of reversal transactions then, for the purposes of accounting, they can be combined into a sequence of completed trades plus maybe the initial and/or the final open position. If a sequence of transactions gradually increases or decreases the size of a position (the number of contracts or shares of a stock), then, as we can see in later chapters, the transactions still can be combined into a sequence of trades using the notion of the complex position mentioned earlier.

PROPERTIES OF POTENTIAL PROFIT STRATEGY

In this book, I shall introduce three types of strategies called *potential profit strategy*, *first P&L reserve strategy*, and *second P&L reserve strategy*, respectively. A potential profit strategy maximizes profits taking long and/or short positions of the same size in a single market. It does not reinvest profits. By contrast, the first and second P&L strategies do reinvest profits and consequently are more complicated. Nevertheless, the potential profit strategy has a fundamental meaning and serves as the basis for building the other two P&L "reserve" strategies. We shall also see that it is the second P&L reserve strategy that answers the question "What is a maximum profit that can be achieved in a time interval under given market conditions and trading rules?" One of these conditions is the account value specified at the beginning of the time interval.

A potential profit strategy is one that creates the maximum profit in a time interval under given market and trading conditions, which include price movement, transaction costs, and the assumption of fixed-size trades for long and/or short positions. In other words, this is a vector of the type `Strategy` of "buy," "sell," and "do nothing" actions that maximize profit for any given pair of vectors of prices and costs. It will be clear that sometimes the same maximum profit is created by more than one `Strategy` vector.

Some useful properties of a potential profit strategy, taking into account transaction costs, are derived from understanding that such strategy (1) cannot lose money and (2) results in the maximum profit.

"Do Nothing" Strategy

If a strategy is empty or contains only "do nothing" actions, then it will be called a "do nothing" strategy. It can be applied under any market condition. The P&L value of it is equal to zero. A "do nothing" action is not considered a transaction.

Property 1

A potential profit strategy generates P&L ≥ 0. This is because for any market the "do nothing strategy" can be applied if any other strategy loses. If there is no strategy with P&L > 0, then the potential profit strategy is "do nothing."

Property 2

If a potential profit strategy is not a "do nothing" strategy, then it has at least two transactions. It always closes a position if it entered one, because it must take some profit from the market. It is not possible to have a potential profit strategy with only one transaction.

In the case where there is an open position at the end of a time interval, that position should be resolved by adding an offsetting transaction at the end of the list of transactions.

By the same reasoning, each time interval should have at least two points. A single-point time interval is losing if a transaction cost is not zero. This is because entering and offsetting a position only in one time point and, as a result, at one price gains no profit but still pays the cost. If transaction cost is zero, then a net profit and loss on a single-point time interval is zero.

Property 3

If a potential profit strategy is not a "do nothing" strategy and contains transactions, then any pair of transactions that enter and exit a market (a "round trip" trade) has a P&L > 0. If the trade is not profitable, then one can eliminate this losing (P&L < 0) or breakeven (P&L = 0) trade and create a new strategy with profits that are at least as large (but without breakeven trades). Then this new strategy can be named a potential profit strategy.

Property 4

If a potential profit strategy takes long and short positions of the same size and has more than two transactions, then it is a true reversal system. At each transaction point, except the initial entry and final exit points, such a system reverses its position from long to short or from short to long. This switching has a very symmetrical sense in the futures market, where there is not any additional cost for going long or short and no rules that favor longs over short (such as the uptick rule). A true reversal strategy is always long or short except on the initial and final positions.

A reversal point is usually a single point in time. One simply buys or sells a sufficient number of units in order to close out the previous position and enter the opposite one. The entire transaction occurs at the same price. However, if the price remains unchanged for several time points, one could close a position at one point and enter the opposite position at another point with the same resulting profit. This can still qualify as a reversal system. I will not differentiate between these cases. This also explains why several maximum profit strategies may exist. All of them generate the same profit but different transactions are done at different times, making them unique. However, from a purely financial viewpoint, these strategies are not equivalent. For instance, a profit obtained from one strategy is realized sooner than the other. This profit can be reinvested and result in a larger annualized return. This is especially true when trading or investing in more than one market. The presence of several markets will further complicate an algorithm for evaluating maximum potential profit when total capital is limited and when transaction costs are taken into account.

While the properties 1 through 3 may be obvious, property 4 requires a proof. In order to prove it, I shall apply the rule of contraries (by discovering the contrary hypothesis) by assuming that a potential profit strategy that consists of more than two transactions is not a true reversal system. This means that before the first and after the last transaction, when the strategy is out of the market, there is at least one more interval where the strategy is also out of the market. The goal is to show that there is a finite number of cases that describe how the strategy can exit an existing position and enter a new one in order to create this added interval in which it is out of the market. In each of these cases the strategy leaves a part of the potential profit in the market and cannot be called a potential profit strategy.

We recognize that, before exiting the market in the special interval, a position must be either long or short. These two possibilities are denoted as $L1$ and $S1$, respectively. After reentering the market after this special interval, the newly established position is again either long or short. These two possibilities will be named $L2$ and $S2$, respectively. The indicators 1 and 2 simply denote the points where the strategy exits and reenters the market. Similarly, the prices $P1$ and $P2$ are introduced to correspond to the exit and reentry points. Clearly, there are only three possible combinations of these two prices: $P1 < P2$, $P1 = P2$, $P1 > P2$. Additionally, at exit point 1 there are two combinations of position types, L1 or S1. The product $2 \times 3 = 6$ corresponds to the number of combinations of exit positions and exit and reentry prices. Two combinations corresponding to the final reentry position $L2$ or $S2$ must multiply this number to get the total number of cases equal to $6 \times 2 = 12$.

Using this notation it is easy to mark each of the 12 cases. For instance, $L1$, $P1 < P2$, $L2$ should be read as follows: Before exiting the market the position is long. The price of exiting is $P1$. After reentry the position is again long $L2$. The price of reentry is $P2$. Additionally, $P1$ is less than $P2$. Clearly, if one exits a long position and then reenters a long position again at a higher price, then some potential profit corresponding to the price difference $P2 - P1$ is left unrealized. Moreover, additional commissions are paid for these "extra" exit and reentry transactions. Continuing to hold the long position between points 1 and 2 would be a more profitable strategy.

All 12 cases are listed below with comments explaining why some profit is either left unrealized or the net profit is less than the case where reversing the position could gain additional profit. In these cases the fixed transaction costs at the points 1 and 2 are assumed to be equal one to another.

1. ***L*1, *P*1 < *P*2, *L*2.** There are additional transactions costs, plus the difference $P2 - P1$ is not a profit; therefore, staying in the original long position is a better choice.
2. ***L*1, *P*1 = P2, *L*2.** There are additional transaction costs; staying in the long position is a better choice.
3. ***L*1, *P*1 > *P*2, *L*2.** The strategy is out of the market before the price drops; if the difference $P1 - P2$ offsets the transaction costs, then reversing instead of exiting the long position at point 1 would gain added profit; if the price drop does not offset the transaction costs, then staying in the original long position would have avoided additional transaction costs.
4. ***L*1, *P*1 < *P*2, *S*2.** The strategy exits the market too early before finally reversing the long position; the difference $P2 - P1$ is an unrealized profit.
5. ***L*1, *P*1 = *P*2, *S*2.** This is an example of the type of reversal system discussed in the previous paragraphs.
6. ***L*1, *P*1 > *P*2, *S*2.** The strategy reverses the long position too late; the price difference $P1 - P2$ is an unrealized profit.
7. ***S*1, *P*1 < *P*2, *L*2.** The strategy exits the market at point 1, while reversing the short position to long would gain additional profit associated with the price difference $P2 - P1$.
8. ***S*1, *P*1 = *P*2, *L*2.** This is another example of the type of reversal system discussed in the previous paragraphs.
9. ***S*1, *P*1 > *P*2, *L*2.** Price drops and the short position exit occurs too early;

10. ***S*1, *P*1 < *P*2, *S*2.** If the price difference offsets the transaction costs, then reversing the position instead of exiting at point 1 is preferable; if it does not offset costs, then staying in the short position would avoid additional commissions.
11. ***S*1, *P*1 = *P*2, *S*2.** There are additional transaction costs; staying in the short position is a better choice.
12. ***S*1, *P*1 > *P*2, *S*2.** There are additional transaction costs, plus the difference $P1 - P2$ is not a profit; staying in the short position would be a better choice.

As we see, there are additional losses in all cases except 5 and 8. The last two cases are variations of a true reversal system. Hence, our strategy does not realize some potential profit and cannot be considered as a maximum profit strategy. This means that our original assumption that the potential profit strategy is not a reversal system is wrong.

If transaction costs at points 1 and 2 are not equal, then we need to compare prices adjusted by costs. These adjustments must be done in a manner that reduces potential profit. The price of exiting a short or entering a long position must be shifted up $k \times P1 + C1 = P1^u$ or $k \times P2 + C2 = P2^u$ (this can be considered the same as always buying at a higher price). At the same time, the price of exiting a long or entering a short position must be shifted down $k \times P1 - C1 = P1^d$ or $k \times P2 - C2 = P2^d$ (this can be considered the same as always selling at a lower price), where k denotes the dollar value of a one-point move. $C1$ and $C2$ denote transaction costs as absolute dollar amounts at points 1 and 2, respectively. This may influence whether the position should be reversed at point 1 or 2; however, the potential profit strategy still remains a true reversal system.

It is worth noting that if costs are zero, then Pardo's potential profit, which is equal to a sum of absolute price changes, can be considered the result of applying a true reversal strategy. This means that an algorithm that correctly accounts for transaction costs should lead to Pardo's potential profit value, provided these costs are zero. If the costs are not zero, then the net profit should be less than Pardo's potential profit.

Proving that for a single market the potential profit strategy is a true reversal system substantially simplifies building and understanding corresponding computational algorithms.

Property 5

If the absolute cost is constant for each transaction, then the potential profit strategy has transactions at time points that correspond to local price extremes (maximums and minimums). This is because the differences between opposite local extreme price values are greater than between other points. Of course, in order to be counted, the net difference must be greater than all transaction costs.

However, if the absolute cost for each transaction is not constant, then optimal trades may not necessarily occur at extreme price points. This complicates the algorithm for constructing the maximum potential profit strategy and can be illustrated by a simple example. Let us consider just three sequential prices, 150, 170, 166, and corresponding costs, 5, 6, 1. Buying at the local price minimum 150 and selling at the local price maximum 170 generates the profit 170 – 150 – 6 – 5 = 9. This is less than the profit generated by selling at 166 with lower costs, 166 – 150 – 1 – 5 = 10. Of course, if the cost per transaction is the same, then the local extreme prices 170 and 150 are the best for this trade.

Property 6

If costs increase to infinity, the potential profit strategy becomes a "do nothing" strategy with zero P&L and zero transactions. If the costs are equal to zero, then the potential profit strategy consists of as many trades as there are local price extremes during the time interval. Intuitively, this property is useful because by varying transaction costs as a parameter we can find the most optimal price swings. These selected movements can be associated later with trading patterns and/or other events and initiate interesting investigations.

TRANSACTION COSTS

The most obvious transaction cost is the commission, but other market effects may influence the ability to create a profit from every price change.

Commissions

A broker executes orders on your behalf. The *commission* is a payment for that work. In the futures markets, commissions per contract are fixed for each market, although they are negotiable. Normally, they are collected after a trade is completed and include both the entry and exit costs. Some brokers charge half of the commission when a position is entered and a half when it is closed, but that is less common. Commissions per trade may vary greatly from one brokerage to the next, even when they are not negotiated. Full-service companies may charge up to $150 per contract per trade, while discounts companies that provide no added value may charge from $15 to $40 per contract per trade. Even within the same company, commissions may vary for different commodities. A company may also provide a commission discount per contract, on a monthly basis, if the number of contracts traded increases above a preset volume level. There may also be additional fees that are typically less than a dollar per contract per trade. In order to attract clients, brokerage companies do their best to charge lower commissions than other firms for comparable services. The actual transaction costs for executing an order are less than $4.

Stock commissions have traditionally been charged as a percentage of price. Typically, these commissions are separately charged when a position is entered and later exited due to the longer holding period for these transactions. It is simpler and often cheaper (Babcock 1989) to deal with fixed commissions available on the commodities markets than with stock commissions. It is also possible that professionals, such as hedge funds, pay a fraction of a cent (as low as 1/20) for each share transacted. More recently, discount houses have adopted the policy of charging a fixed fee for up to a certain number of shares bought or sold (usually limited to 500 or 1,000).

Slippage

Every practical guide for trading discusses the effect of *slippage* on trading results. The definition taken from Babcock (1989) is:

> *Slippage refers to the difference between the price at which you want to execute your trade and the price at which it is actually executed. Depending on the type of orders you use and your trading tactics, slippage can reduce profits or increase losses significantly.*

Slippage reflects the current dynamic properties of both the market and the way in which orders are executed. The volume of transactions on the market at the time of your order greatly affects slippage. On highly liquid days, in markets such as U.S. 10-year Treasury note futures, orders are executed within seconds and slippage should be no more than one tick, or 1/64 of a point. The cost of this is about $16 per contract, but the contract value is $100,000.

Market Orders A *market order* requires that the broker buy or sell a certain number of contracts for your account immediately at the current market price, accepting either the bid or offer regardless of price. This is the fastest way to enter, change, or exit a position. With modern computerized trading programs, Internet Web sites, and fully electronic markets, such as NASDAQ (originally an acronym for the National Association of Securities Dealers Automated Quotations) or the e-mini Standard and Poor's (S&P—a stock market index futures contract traded on the Chicago Mercantile Exchange's Globex electronic trading platform), the entire process after you enter your order is electronic, and execution may take just a fraction of a second. Some "electronic order entry systems" have manual intervention, which can add significant delay to the execution. Even if a market order is given by phone, for a liquid market, you can expect the order to be filled before the conversation is over. However if the price is quickly changing or if the market is not liquid, then even this fastest order may result in a very undesirable fill price, where several ticks or even whole points are lost. In a "fast" market, which occurs frequently at the time of government economic releases, the amount of slippage can be shocking.

Stop Orders A *stop order* is most often used to limit a loss on a position when the price moves the wrong way, but it can also be used to enter a new position. For traders concerned with unlimited risk, a long position in soybeans entered 661.75, could be limited to a $500 loss per contract by setting a sell stop 10 cents below the entry level. This can be done as a day order (assumed unless otherwise indicated) or "good 'til canceled" order (GTC). While a day order is active only until the close of the current session, a GTC order is active until it is executed, canceled, or replaced. In futures markets, which are subject to expiration dates, a brokerage company may obligate a trader to close a speculative position a certain number of days before the contract expiration. Because margins increase substantially just prior to delivery, traders are reminded, by a request for additional money, that they need to exit their trades.

The price at which a stop order is placed depends on money management considerations, technical analysis, market volatility, and other factors. Let us say that one does not want to lose more than $500 per contract on the soybean position. If this loss amount also includes commissions of $30 per contract, then the stop price is calculated as 661.75 – ($500 – $30)/$50 (per one cent per bushel) = 661.75 – 9.40 = 652.35. We need to round this price to a higher tick level, 652.50. Clearly, the program `pardo.cpp` described in Chapter 1 would report 652.35 as invalid price for soybeans. The loss corresponding to the price 652.50 is $492.50. The discontinuous nature of prices means that the next higher loss obtained from the price 652.25 would be $505. This exceeds the loss that the trader is willing to take.

The stop order becomes a market order when the price touches the stop order price. It is very possible that the stop order will be filled a few ticks lower than the order price (if a sell stop) due to the intraday price movement. One can lose as much as 2 cents in soybeans, where each cent per bushel translates into $50 per contract. A horrible scenario may occur when a position is held on the day prior to an important monthly production report released by the U.S. Department of Agriculture. As often happens in April or May, this report may show that farmers substantially changed their planting intentions and used more land originally devoted to corn for soybean crops. The implication is that there will be more soybeans and less corn this year. The market reacts by opening 20 cents below yesterday's close and your stop order is filled on the open, much lower than the price given in the order. This loss will partly go to those people, who had previously taken a short position, and partly to the floor traders, who can act quickly to enter new shorts before your order is triggered. Your only consolation is that the loss may be taken into account when you file your taxes.

The Commodity Futures Trading Commission (CFTC), the futures market regulatory agency, correctly states that trading futures (or any trading) is risky and not suitable for everybody.

If we want to enter a new long position only if prices rise from their current level of 661.75 to 665.25, but only if it happens today, then we place the order "buy at 665.25 stop." This is always treated as a day order. We know that the fill may come at a less attractive, higher price because of slippage. If the stop order is not filled today, then it is automatically canceled at the end of the trading session.

Limit Orders A *limit order* is another way of limiting risk and is used for entering or liquidating a position at a specific price. The order is entered as "buy at 661.75," where 661.75 is lower than where the market is now trading. It is common to hear this order entered as "buy 661.75 limit" or "buy 661.75 or better." In all cases the broker will understand, but the words *limit* and *or better* are not necessary. A buy limit is always placed below the market and a sell limit above the market. Should you do otherwise, the order will be filled immediately at the market. To be reasonably sure of a fill for a limit order, prices must go through your price, not just touch the price. In a less liquid market, even a penetration of your order price cannot guarantee that you will fill part or all of your order. There must be enough shares or contracts traded below your buy limit, and you may need to beat out the competition. While a limit order succeeds at controlling risk, it does so with a chance that you will not get filled.

The two types of frequently used orders, market and stop, can each result in the added cost of slippage. Limit orders cannot show slippage but risk being unfilled, which is just another form of market risk. Unfortunately, slippage can be comparable to or even greater than commissions. In some cases, it can be very large.

The Bid/Asked Spread

The *bid/asked spread* is a basic market function, but many retail customers do not recognize it because it is a hidden cost. It is well described in Babcock (1989) as:

When a price is being quoted in the trading pit, there are actually two prices, the bid and the asked. They are usually, but not always, one tick apart with the bid being the lower of the two. . . . The public trader always buys at the asked price and sells at the bid price, while the floor trader (who takes the other side of the transactions) will be buying at the bid and selling at the asked.

The bid/asked spread partly explains why, in almost all situations where a price touches the level specified in a limit order several times but never penetrates that price, the limit order remains unfilled. It also comes into play with market orders, where the fill is never at the price seen on the screen (assuming there is no viewing delay). For our purposes it is important only that we can measure this cost as a specific number of ticks.

The Total Transaction Cost

The total transaction cost can be estimated as the sum of the components:

- Commissions and fees on futures markets can be in the interval \$15 to \$150 per contract per trade.
- Commissions on stocks may range from \$10 for a fixed-size order to 1 percent of price
- Slippage in a futures contract is normally assumed to be one to four ticks but in a fast market may be much, much larger.
- Bid/asked spread may add one to four ticks, depending on market liquidity.

Let us look once more at the soybean contract. A trader can pay a \$25 commission to a discount broker. To this cost add sixteen ticks (4 cents per bushel) for intraday slippage—eight ticks for entering and eight ticks for exiting. Another two ticks are added for bid/asked spread if a market order is used. The dollar value of these 18 ticks means 18 × \$12.5 = \$225. The total cost per contract per trade is \$25 + \$225 = \$250. Under these conditions the price fluctuation must be at least 5 cents per bushel before the trade reaches a breakeven point. An algorithm that takes into account the costs when computing potential profit should filter out all price swings less than 5 cents.

A constant cost per contract or a cost expressed as a percentage of price can be captured equally well by the same algorithm that evaluates potential profit for a single market. It is clear, however, that the frequency and magnitude of price fluctuations may affect transaction costs when we are including slippage.

The price fluctuations in equity markets over a short time interval are often considered to be following a *lognormal stochastic process* (Hull 1997; Bachelier 1900). This means that a price increment can be expressed as $dP = m \times P \times dt + s \times P \times dz$, where dP is a price change, m is a coefficient, P is a current price, dt is a short time interval, s is a price volatility, and dz is a change in the basic *Wiener process* during the time interval dt. The change in price is represented as a sum of the nonrandom drift contribution $m \times P \times dt$ and the random volatility component $s \times P \times dz$. Both of them are proportional to price. This leads to a property that the *asset return* dP/P is normally distributed with mean $m \times \mathrm{dt}$ and variance $s^2 \times dt$. This mathematics also ensures that prices never become negative if the initial price is positive. In more sophisticated models, volatility itself is considered a stochastic process. If these or similar stochastic processes do indeed take place, then the cost due to slippage may also be subject to random shocks and could be neither constant nor a constant percentage of price. For instance, we could use a *random numbers generator* and *Monte Carlo simulation* in order to fill a *vector of costs*. While this consideration leads in general to complicated cost models and simulations, we should note that constant and percentage costs are good first approximations of the real situations and that the algorithm described in the next chapter can be applied to any vector of costs without analyzing how these costs were obtained.

TRANSACTION COSTS AND C++

To program transaction costs, we could apply something as simple as

```
...
namespace PPBOOK {
    typedef vector<double> Costs;
} // PPBOOK
...
```

This should remind you of the previously introduced type `Strategy`. The template type parameter in `Strategy` is the C++ built-in type `int` while here it is `double`. However, in the type `Strategy` the intention was to use numbers of units with positive and negative signs to mean buy or sell transactions. For costs, all numbers must be of one sign (positive) or zero. The current collection is not able to protect an object from negative numbers. Additionally, if a transaction cost is represented as a percentage, then we would want that value to be nonnegative numbers less than 1.

Classes are needed to represent costs and for checking their values. The classes are similar to the class `Price` and related specification classes. This similarity is expressed on the design level by the concept "design pattern" (Gamma et al. 1994). The C++ implementation of the class `Cost` may look like the one in the header file `Cost.h`:

```
#ifndef __Cost_h__
#define __Cost_h__

namespace PPBOOK {

    template<class S>
    class Cost {
    public:
        Cost(double c) : c_(c){S::checkCost(c);}
        Cost(const Cost<S>& sp) : c_(sp.c_){}
        double      cost() const {return c_;}
        Cost<S>&    operator=(double c)
                    {S::checkCost(c); c_ = c; return *this;}
```

```
        Cost<S>&    operator=(const Cost<S>& sp)
                    {c_ = sp.c_; return *this;}
    private:
        double      c_;
    };

} // PPBOOK

#endif /* __Cost_h__ */
```

Two cost specification classes are sufficient for our purposes. They are in the header file `SpecCost.h`:

```
#ifndef __SpecCost_h__
#define __SpecCost_h__

#include <sstream>
#include <stdexcept>
using namespace std;

namespace PPBOOK {

    class SpecAbsoluteCost {
    public:
        static  void    checkCost(double c)
        {
            if(c < 0.0) {
                ostringstream   s;
                s   << "Absolute cost " << c
                    << " must be non negative.";
                throw   invalid_argument(s.str());
            }
        }
    };

    class SpecFractionCost {
    public:
        static  void    checkCost(double c)
        {
            if(c < 0.0 || c > 1.0) {
                ostringstream   s;
                s   << "Fraction cost " << c
                    << " must be from interval [0, 1].";
                throw   invalid_argument(s.str());
            }
```

```
        }
    };

} // PPBOOK

#endif /* __SpecCost_h__ */
```

Now we can create objects of the classes `Prices`, `Strategy`, and vectors of costs, the major building blocks of our applications.

PROFIT-AND-LOSS FUNCTION

The Main Equations

Let us assume that three vectors of prices, costs, and bought and sold units (in contracts or shares) are given and have the same number of elements n: $\boldsymbol{P} = \boldsymbol{P}(P_1, \ldots, P_i, \ldots, P_n)$, $\boldsymbol{C} = \boldsymbol{C}(C_1, \ldots, C_i, \ldots, C_n)$, $\boldsymbol{U} = \boldsymbol{U}(U_1, \ldots, U_i, \ldots, U_n)$. The bold font is used to denote vectors. Scalars are shown using the regular font. The elements of the vector $\boldsymbol{P}$ are all positive numbers. The elements of the vector $\boldsymbol{C}$ are all non-negative numbers. The elements of the vector $\boldsymbol{U}$ are all integer numbers. If $U_i < 0$, then $|U_i|$ units are sold at time i. The vertical lines denote the absolute value of a number. If $U_i > 0$, then U_i units are bought at time i. If the $U_i = 0$, then no transaction is done at time i. The profit or loss (PL) is calculated:

$$PL = -k(\boldsymbol{P}, \boldsymbol{U}) - (\boldsymbol{C}, abs(\boldsymbol{U})) + kP_n\, sum(\boldsymbol{U}) - C_n|sum(\boldsymbol{U})| \tag{2.1}$$

where k is conversion factor, the dollar value of a one-point move. This coefficient can also be thought of as equal to the dollar value of one tick divided by minimal tick. For instance, for the gold (GC) futures contract $k = \$10 / 0.1 = \$100$ per point. For the soybean (S) futures contract $k = \$12.5/0.25 = \$50$ per point. The parentheses with two vectors inside separated by the comma denote scalar product of two vectors. The scalar value is computed as:

$$(\boldsymbol{P}, \boldsymbol{U}) = \Sigma P_i U_i \tag{2.2}$$

where Σ denotes summation and the index i takes all values from 1 to n. In C++ the first element of a `vector` or built-in array has the index value 0. This explains why the index often takes all values from 0 to $n - 1$ in the programs. The $abs(\boldsymbol{U})$ means that the absolute value function is applied to the vector $\boldsymbol{U}$. As a result we get a new vector $\boldsymbol{U}^*$ with the same number of elements n, where each element is an absolute value of the corresponding element in the original vector:

$$abs(\boldsymbol{U}) = abs(\boldsymbol{U}(U_1, \ldots, U_i, \ldots, U_n)) = \boldsymbol{U}^*(|U_1|, \ldots, |U_i|, \ldots, |U_n|) \tag{2.3}$$

The $sum(\boldsymbol{U})$ function adds all elements of a vector (in this case vector $\boldsymbol{U}$) and returns a result—a scalar number. If $sum(\boldsymbol{U}) \neq 0$, then the last position has not been closed and there is an unrealized profit or loss. The last open equity is also called the marked-to-market value as of the final time increment. It can be computed using the assumption that the position is liquidated at the current or last price. This current price is the last value in the vector $\boldsymbol{P}$.

While price fluctuations can result in profits or losses, all transaction costs by definition represent a loss and are subtracted in Equation (2.1). Finally, this equation can be rewritten as

$$PL = k\,(P_n\, \Sigma\, U_i - \Sigma\, P_i U_i) - \Sigma\, C_i\, |U_i| - C_n\, |\Sigma\, U_i| \tag{2.4}$$

Equations (2.1) and (2.4) imply the cost given as absolute amount of money. Two special cases are interesting: (1) transaction cost is a constant fraction of price $\boldsymbol{C} = a\boldsymbol{P}$ meaning $a\boldsymbol{P}(P_1, \ldots, P_i, \ldots, P_n) = \boldsymbol{C}(aP_1, \ldots, aP_i, \ldots, aP_n)$, where the fraction a is from the interval $0 \leq a < 1$ and $k = 1$ and 2) transaction cost is a constant $C_i = C$ per transaction. They reflect conditions existing in trading equities and futures contracts, respectively. Consequently, Equation (2.4) is translated into the following two equations:

$$PL = P_n\, \Sigma\, U_i - \Sigma\, P_i U_i - a\, \Sigma\, P_i\, |U_i| - aP_n\, |\Sigma\, U_i|\ (equities) \tag{2.5}$$

$$PL = k\,(P_n\, \Sigma\, U_i - \Sigma\, P_i\, U_i) - C\,(\Sigma\, |U_i| + |\Sigma\, U_i|)\ (futures) \tag{2.6}$$

In Equation (2.6) C is a constant cost per transaction. For instance, if a cost is just commissions C paid at the end of trade after closing a position, then commissions per transaction are equal to $C/2$. It is worth noting that if the number of trading units m times greater than $\boldsymbol{U}$ meaning $m\boldsymbol{U}$, then the common multiplier m can be taken out of the expressions on the right side of Equations (2.1), (2.4), (2.5), and (2.6) and in all cases the new P&L value will be equal to mPL.

C++ Implementation

The function for Equations (2.1) and (2.4) is in the header file `ProfitAndLossAlg.h`:

```
#ifndef __ProfitAndLossAlg_h__
#define __ProfitAndLossAlg_h__

#include <cmath>
#include <vector>
#include <sstream>
#include <stdexcept>
using namespace std;

#include "Prices.h"
#include "Strategy.h"
#include "Cost.h"
#include "SpecCost.h"
using namespace PPBOOK;

namespace PPBOOK {
```

```
    inline double
    profit_and_loss(const Prices& prices, const Strategy&
        units, const vector<Cost<SpecAbsoluteCost> >& costs)
    {
        size_t  n = prices.size();
        if(n != units.size() || n != costs.size()) {
            ostringstream   s;
            s    << "profit_and_loss: prices[" << (unsigned int)n
                 << "], units[" << (unsigned int)units.size()
                 << "], costs[" << (unsigned int)costs.size()
                 << "] must have the same size.";
            throw   invalid_argument(s.str());
        }
        if(!n) return 0.0;
        int     su = 0;
        double  spu = 0.0;
        double  scau = 0.0;
        for(unsigned int i = 0; i < prices.size(); i++) {
            su += units[i];
            spu += prices[i] * units[i];
            scau += costs[i].cost() * abs(units[i]);
        }
        return  prices.tickValue() * (prices[n - 1] * su - spu)
            / prices.tick() - scau - costs[n - 1].cost() * abs(su);
    }

} // PPBOOK

#endif /* __ProfitAndLossAlg_h__ */
```

This function checks that all three collections have the same size. If all are empty, it returns zero. If not, then it proceeds to the Equation (2.4) and accumulates three terms: sum of units, sum of products price by unit, and sum of products cost by absolute value of unit. Combining those three terms in the final statement is straightforward. In order to understand how the formulas and the function work, consider a simple example.

Example Test2.cpp

Let the vector of gold prices for the GC contract have four elements: $\boldsymbol{P}(427.3, 423.5, 439.1, 433.3)$. The trading strategy is $\boldsymbol{U}(-1, 2, -2, 0)$. Since the sum of elements is equal to –1, the final short position is left open. Then the last price 433.3 should be used for computing the unrealized profit (in this case). The commissions and other fees per round-turn trade are equal to \$25. This means that for each transaction (a buy or sell) it is \$12.50. Our vector of costs is $\boldsymbol{C}(12.5, 12.5, 12.5, 12.5)$. By following the strategy, we go short one contract at the price 427.3, then reverse the position from short to long at 423.5. Because the minimum tick for this contract is 0.1 and tick value is \$10, our first trade results in a profit after commissions equal to (427.3 – 423.5) × 100 – 25 = 380 – 25 = \$355. The second trade brings an additional gain of (439.1 – 423.5) × 100 – 25 = 1,560 – 25 = \$1,535 plus a new position reversed from long to short at price 439.1. We are holding the short position until the price drops to 433.3. The marked-to-market value of this position after commissions is also profitable (439.1 – 433.3) × 100 – 25 = 580 – 25 = \$555. Hence, the total P&L value under these conditions is equal to 355 + 1,535 + 555 = \$2,445. The same example is programmed in the source file test2.cpp:

```
#include <iostream>
#include <string>
#include <cmath>
using namespace std;

#include "Prices.h"
#include "Strategy.h"
#include "Cost.h"
#include "SpecCost.h"
#include "ProfitAndLossAlg.h"
using namespace PPBOOK;

int main(int, char*[])
{
    try {
        Prices  p("GC");
        p.append(427.3);
        p.append(423.5);
        p.append(439.1);
        p.append(433.3);

        Strategy                        u;
        u.push_back(-1);
        u.push_back(2);
        u.push_back(-2);
        u.push_back(0);

        vector<Cost<SpecAbsoluteCost> > c(p.size(), 12.5);

        cout    << profit_and_loss(p, u, c) << endl;
    }
    catch(const exception& e) {
        cerr    << e.what() << endl;
    }
    catch(...) {
        cerr    << "Unknown exception" << endl;
    }
    return 0;
}
```

When this program is compiled, linked, and run, the output is a single number, 2,445, confirming our calculations.

In this example, it is clear that the selected strategy is the best, provided only one unit is held for any position. However, some profit is lost due to commissions, which is inevitable. It is easy to see that, if commissions are zero, then the value is Pardo's potential profit, equal to $(|427.3 - 423.5| + |423.5 - 439.1| + |439.1 - 433.3|) \times 100 = \$2,520$. It is \$75 greater than our real profit, the result of paying commissions of \$25 for each (a total of three) round-turn trade.

At first glance, it looks as though commissions do not add much complication in getting the potential profit value. Just separate each deal in a true reversal system into independent trades, sum the price differences as absolute values, and subtract commissions from each trade. However, this simplicity is an illusion. The main problem is to build the potential profit strategy selecting only price differences that offset transaction costs. In our example, I intentionally selected large price fluctuations while using small commissions. Instead, let's say that the cost is \$600 (too big for gold commissions but possible if we add slippage when gold is trading at \$700/oz) and/or price fluctuations are smaller due to low volatility. Then the first and the last trades must not be taken since they both would generate a loss. An algorithm must filter out those transactions. A maximum profit strategy for a \$600 per trade cost is **U**(0, 1, −1, 0). The profit is equal to $(439.1 - 423.5) \times 100 - 600 = 1,560 - 600 = \$960$. However, if the costs are equal to \$400, then only the first trade must be skipped and the best strategy would be ***U***(0, 1, −2, 0) or the same ***U***(0, 1, −2, 1). The profit is equal to $1,560 - 400 + 580 - 400 = \$1,340$.

CONCLUSIONS

- Some important properties of the potential profit strategy working under conditions of transaction costs are deduced and proved.
- The size of transaction costs is estimated for futures and equities markets.
- The classes `Cost` and `Strategy` complementing previously created `Price` framework are developed.
- Equations and the function are written for profit-and-loss computation from objects of the class `Prices`, and `Strategy`, and vector of objects of the class `Cost` using absolute cost specification.
- Transaction costs reduce not only profits of individual trades but also influence on the number of potentially profitable trades and their distribution in time.

CHAPTER 3

R- and *L*-Algorithms for Maximum Profit Strategy

The profit-and-loss function that has the arguments prices, strategy, and transaction costs and returns the profit or loss value helps in understanding the concepts of *s-function*, *s-matrix*, and *s-interval*. Having developed these three concepts, they will be useful for construction of the algorithm that evaluates potential or maximum profit and for building the corresponding strategy.

S-FUNCTION AND *S*-MATRIX

Let me define the following scalar function, $S = S(\boldsymbol{P}, \boldsymbol{C}, i, j, k)$, where $\boldsymbol{P}$ and $\boldsymbol{C}$, both containing n elements, are the vectors of prices and transaction costs, respectively; i and j are indices taking arbitrary integer values from the closed interval $[1, n]$; and k is a coefficient converting contract prices into absolute dollar amounts. The vector of transaction costs contains elements expressed as absolute dollar amounts paid per contract per transaction. The coefficient k can be computed as the *tick value/tick*, which is equivalent to the value of a full-point move.

Definition 3.1: *S*-Function

The following equation defines the s-function:

$$S = S(\boldsymbol{P}, \boldsymbol{C}, i, j, k) = k\,|P_i - P_j| - C_i - C_j \tag{3.1}$$

If $\boldsymbol{P}$, $\boldsymbol{C}$, and k are constant, meaning that a historical interval of prices and costs is selected for a contract with given specifications, then S is a function of the indices i and j only. The symbol S_{ij} in this case denotes a return value of the function.

Definition 3.2: S-Matrix

All values of the *s*-function S_{ij} on the interval [1, *n*] form an *s*-matrix with *n* rows and *n* columns, where *i* is the row index and *j* is the column index.

It is easy to see from Equation (3.1) that the *s*-matrix is a square symmetric matrix with $S_{ij} = S_{ji}$. If $i = j$, then the diagonal elements are equal to $-2C_i$; therefore, it is enough to consider elements for which $i \leq j$.

The *s*-function and *s*-matrix are easy to understand. If $S_{ij} > 0$, then the dollar value of price difference is greater than corresponding transaction costs. Hence, entering and exiting the market at times *i* and *j* can be profitable. If $S_{ij} \leq 0$, then the price difference cannot offset the costs and the corresponding trade would be either a loss or at best a breakeven (zero profit).

S-INTERVAL AND ITS BOUNDARIES

Definition 3.3: S-Interval

Any subinterval [*l*, *r*] of the main interval [1, *n*] is referred to as an *s*-interval if, for any pair (*i*, *j*) from [*l*, *r*], the value of the *s*-function is nonpositive $S_{ij} \leq 0$. It is denoted as s-[*l*, *r*].

An *s*-interval is a range of price stability, or relatively low volatility sideways movement, where price fluctuations are not big enough to generate profits. This is why the letter *s* (stability) is used to name this concept. Clearly the one point $l = r$ is always an *s*-interval. Any subinterval of an *s*-interval is also an *s*-interval. The following three definitions will help to understand what happens to an *s*-interval when the left *l* and the right *r* boundaries are gradually expanded.

Definition 3.4: S-Interval with the Right-most Boundary

s-[*l*, *r*] has the *right-most boundary* r^* if $r = n$ or if there is a point *e* on the interval *s*-[*l*, *r*] such that $S_{e,r+1} > 0$. Then it is denoted as *s*-[*l*, *r**].

It follows from Equation (3.1) and the Definition 3.4 that, if $r^* < n$, then there is no point *e* on an interval *s*-[*l*, *r**] such that $P_e = P_{r^*+1}$. Indeed, in this case, the value $S_{e,r^*+1} = -C_e - C_{r^*+1} \leq 0$.

Definition 3.5: S-Interval with the Left-most Boundary

The interval *s*-[*l*, *r*] has the *left-most boundary* l^* if $l = 1$ or there is a point *e* on *s*-[*l*, *r*] such that $S_{l-1,e} > 0$. Then it is denoted as *s*-[*l**, *r*].

It follows from Equation (3.1) and Definition 3.5 that, if $l^* > 1$, then there is no point *e* on *s*-[*l**, *r*] such that $P_e = P_{l^*-1}$. In this case, the value $S_{l^*-1,e} = -C_{l^*-1} - C_e \leq 0$.

Definition 3.6: S-Interval with the Left-most and the Right-most Boundaries

The interval *s*-[*l*, *r*] has the left-most and the right-most boundaries l^* and r^*, if it is simultaneously *s*-[*l**, *r*] and *s*-[*l*, *r**]. It is denoted as *s*-[*l**, *r**].

Let us select an interval s-$[l, r]$. This can always be done, if an interval contains at least one point, because any point is an s-interval. If we begin to expand the interval adding points from the left and the right sides, then we arrive at the l^* and r^* boundaries of s-$[l^*, r]$ and s-$[l, r^*]$, which must include the original s-$[l, r]$. The new s-$[l^*, r^*]$ contains the original s-$[l, r]$.

THE BEST BUYING AND SELLING POINTS ON THE S-INTERVAL

The best point to buy on s-$[l, r]$ corresponds to the minimum of $kP_i + C_i$. It is possible that several values of i from the interval $[l, r]$ lead to the same minimum value given by this expression. Then from a pure profit point of view, all of these moments are equivalent.

The best point to sell on s-$[l, r]$ corresponds to the maximum of $kP_i - C_i$. It is also possible that several values of i from the interval $[l, r]$ yield the same maximum value of this expression. Then from a pure profit point of view, all of these moments are equivalent.

It will become clear that it makes sense to buy or sell only on s-$[l^*, r^*]$. Whether the best strategy should be to buy, sell, or do nothing depends on the price history prior to the boundary l^* and after the boundary r^*. We now need the additional concept of *polarity* of s-intervals in order to move forward.

POLARITY OF S-INTERVALS

Definition 3.7: Right Polarity

s-$[l, r^*]$ possesses a *right polarity* property. The right polarity is neutral (0), if $r^* = n$, it is positive (+1) if there is a point e on s-$[l, r^*]$ such that $kP_e + C_e < kP_{r^*+1} - C_{r^*+1}$, or it is negative (−1) if there is a point e on the interval s-$[l, r^*]$ such that $kP_e - C_e > kP_{r^*+1} + C_{r^*+1}$.

The positive right polarity implies that $P_e < P_{r^*+1}$. From the definition it follows that $kP_{r^*+1} - C_{r^*+1} - kP_e - C_e > 0$. Because $C_{r^*+1} \geq 0$, $C_e \geq 0$, $k > 0$, $P_e > 0$, $P_{r^*+1} > 0$, it must follow that $P_e < P_{r^*+1}$. The positive right polarity means that the price substantially increases after the right boundary of the s-interval as we move from left to right.

The negative right polarity implies that $P_e > P_{r^*+1}$ and from the definition it follows that $kP_e - C_e - kP_{r^*+1} - C_{r^*+1} > 0$. Because $C_e \geq 0$, $C_{r^*+1} \geq 0$, $k > 0$, $P_e > 0$, $P_{r^*+1} > 0$, then $P_e > P_{r^*+1}$. The negative right polarity means that the price substantially decreases after the right boundary of the s-interval as we move from left to right.

Theorem 3.1

The right polarity cannot be simultaneously negative and positive for the same s-$[l, r^*]$. This can be proved as follows:

Let us assume that this is not true and the right polarity is both negative and positive simultaneously. In accordance with Definition 3.7, this means that there are two points ep and en on the s-$[l, r^*]$ such that $P_{ep} < P_{r^*+1} < P_{en}$. Because $P_i > 0$, $k|P_{ep} - P_{r^*+1}| + k|P_{en} - P_{r^*+1}| = k|P_{ep} - P_{en}|$ it follows from Equation (3.1) and Definition 3.4 that $S_{ep,r^*+1} = k|P_{ep} - P_{r^*+1}| - C_{ep} - C_{r^*+1} > 0$ and $S_{en,r^*+1} = k|P_{en} - P_{r^*+1}| - C_{en} - C_{r^*+1} > 0$. Hence, $S_{ep,r^*+1} + S_{en,r^*+1} = k|P_{ep} - P_{en}|$

$- C_{ep} - C_{en} - 2\,C_{r^*+1} = S_{ep,en} - 2C_{r^*+1} > 0$ and $S_{ep,en} > 2C_{r^*+1}$. Because $C_{r^*+1} \geq 0$, we get $S_{ep,en} > 0$. However, in accordance with Definition 3.3, the points *ep* and *en* cannot both belong to one *s*-interval. Hence, our assumption about the existence of simultaneous positive and negative polarity of *s*-$[l, r^*]$ is wrong.

Definition 3.8: Left Polarity

Let *s*-$[l^*, r]$ possesses a *left polarity* property. The left polarity is neutral (0), if $l^* = 1$, it is positive (+1), if there is a point *e* on the *s*-$[l^*, r]$ such that $kP_e - C_e > kP_{l^*-1} + C_{l^*-1}$, or it is negative (–1), if there is a point *e* on the interval *s*-$[l^*, r]$ such that $kP_e + C_e < kP_{l^*-1} - C_{l^*-1}$.

The positive left polarity implies that $P_e > P_{l^*-1}$. From the definition it follows that $kP_e - C_e - kP_{l^*-1} - C_{l^*-1} > 0$. Because $C_e \geq 0$, $C_{l^*-1} \geq 0$, $k > 0$, $P_e > 0$, $P_{l^*-1} > 0$, then $P_e > P_{l^*-1}$. The positive left polarity means that the price substantially increases after passing the left boundary of the *s*-interval moving from left to right.

The negative left polarity implies that $P_e < P_{l^*-1}$. From the definition it follows that $kP_{l^*-1} - C_{l^*-1} - kP_e - C_e - > 0$. Because $C_{l^*-1} \geq 0$, $C_e \geq 0$, $k > 0$, $P_{l^*-1} > 0$, $P_e > 0$, then $P_e < P_{l^*-1}$. The negative left polarity means that the price substantially decreases after passing the left boundary of the *s*-interval moving from left to right.

Theorem 3.2

The left polarity cannot be simultaneously negative and positive for the same *s*-$[l^*, r]$.

The proof is similar to one given for the Theorem 3.1.

It follows from Definitions 3.6, 3.7, and 3.8 that an interval *s*-$[l^*,r^*]$ possesses the left and the right polarity properties. There is only one interval such that *s*-$[1, r^*]$. This interval has both the left-most and the right-most boundaries. The left polarity of this interval is zero. There is only one interval such that *s*-$[l^*, n]$. This interval also has both the left-most and the right-most boundaries. The right polarity of this interval is zero.

R-ALGORITHM

Let us assume that the vectors of prices ***P*** and absolute transaction costs **C** are given and have the same number of elements *n*. This number is greater than zero. The goal is to find a vector of trading units (a strategy) ***U*** maximizing the trading profit on the price and cost interval $[1, n]$. More precisely, we would like to find the most profitable points on the interval $[1, n]$ to enter buy, sell, and exit orders. We discussed in Chapter 2 that the best trading strategy is a true reversal system. The questions of money management will be left for later chapters, and we will assume here that any open position (long or short) consists of the same number of contracts or shares denoted *U* (do not confuse this single constant value with the vector ***U*** marked in bold). The letter *r* in the name of the algorithm means that the interval is scanned from the left to the right, which is the normal time sequence.

The value given by the variable *begin* used below is equal either to 1 or to any value between 1 and *n*, if only a part of the original interval is to be scanned, with the unscanned portion being on the left. The value *end* is equal to either n or to any value between 1 and n, if only a part of the original interval is to be scanned, with the unscanned portion being on the right. We require that: $begin \leq end$. At the beginning of processing, all elements of the vector $\boldsymbol{U}$ are initialized to zeros. The following steps should be done sequentially unless within the step there is a specific command to stop or go to another step.

1. Set the indices i = min = max = begin; set the variable polarity = 0.
2. Increment i by one unit. If i > end, then STOP.
3. Calculate $S_{\min,i}$ and $S_{\max,i}$.
4. If $S_{\min,i} \leq 0$ and $S_{\max,i} \leq 0$, then test for conditions (a) through (c).
   a. (If $kP_{\min} + C_{\min} > kP_i + C_i$, then set min = i.
   b. If $kP_{\max} - C_{\max} < kP_i - C_i$, set max = i.
   c. If i = end, then (set $U_{\min}$ = polarity * U * (polarity – 1) / 2;
   set $U_{\max}$ = –polarity × U × (polarity + 1) / 2;) go to STEP 2).
5. If $kP_{\min} + C_{\min} < kP_i - C_i$, then (set $U_{\min}$ = (1 – polarity) × U; set polarity = 1; set min = max = i).
6. If $kP_{\max} - C_{\max} > kP_i + C_i$, then (set $U_{\max}$ = (–1 – polarity) × U; set polarity = –1; set min = max = i).
7. If i = end, then (set U_i = –polarity × U;) go to STEP 2.

The *r-algorithm* is a one-path algorithm. It starts from a single point at the left side of the interval [*begin, end*]. This point is an *s*-interval. Incrementing the index i by one unit expands the right side of the interval while checking that it is still an *s*-interval. During this expansion the algorithm searches for a local minimum $kP_i + C_i$ and maximum $kP_i - C_i$. These quantities represent the contract value plus or minus transaction cost. These local extremes would be the best buying or selling points, depending on the polarity of the next interval, which can be found on the right side. If the absolute transaction cost is the same for each point, as it was illustrated in a comment to property 5 in Chapter 2, it would be enough to search for local minimum or maximum of the price only.

If the *s*-property remains intact at the end of the scanned interval, then the number of units remains equal to zero because the initial zero value of the variable *polarity* does not change. This corresponds to the "do nothing" strategy. However, once the first r^* boundary is determined, the initial value of units is set either to U or $-U$. This is again because the initial polarity is set to zero (see the expressions in step 4). At this point, the strategy enters the market going either long or short. The algorithm resets the *polarity* value to the current one.

Once the strategy is in the market, it switches from long to short by buying or selling $2U$. It is never out of the market during the remainder of the interval once it has set an initial position. This corresponds to property 4 proved in Chapter 2. Once the r-algorithm comes to the end of the interval, it resets the last transaction from $2U$ or $-2U$ to U or $-U$ exiting the market, or sets the last point to U or $-U$ units. This corresponds to property 2 discussed in Chapter 2.

As a result, the vector $\boldsymbol{U}$ is filled.

L-ALGORITHM

The *l-algorithm* is named to mean that the interval is scanned from the right side to the left side. The *l*-algorithm is a transformation of the *r*-algorithm by replacing the words *begin* with *end*, *end* with *begin*, increment by decrement, and > by < in the expression $i > end$ found in step 2.

1. Set the indices i = min = max = end; set the variable polarity = 0.
2. Decrement i by the unit. If i < begin, then STOP.
3. Calculate $S_{\min,i}$ and $S_{\max,i}$.
4. If $S_{\min,i} \leq 0$ and $S_{\max,i} \leq 0$, then test for conditions (a) through (c).
   a. (If $kP_{\min} + C_{\min} > kP_i + C_i$, then set min = i.
   b. If $kP_{\max} - C_{\max} < kP_i - C_i$, set max = i;
   c. If i = begin, then (set $U_{\min}$ = polarity × U × (polarity – 1) / 2; set $U_{\max}$ = –polarity × U × (polarity + 1) / 2;) go to STEP 2.)
5. If $kP_{\min} + C_{\min} < kP_i - C_i$, then (set $U_{\min}$ = (1 – polarity) × U; set polarity = 1; set min = max = i).
6. If $kP_{\max} - C_{\max} > kP_i + C_i$, then (set $U_{\max}$ = (–1 – polarity) × U; set polarity = –1; set min = max = i).
7. If i = begin, then (set U_i = –polarity × U;) go to STEP 2.

The right and left algorithms may result in two different strategies but will have the same maximum profit (see explanation to property 4 in Chapter 2). Once we have all three vectors ***P***, ***C***, ***U***, the maximum profit value can be computed using the profit-and-loss function from Chapter 2.

C++ IMPLEMENTATION

Coding the *R*- and *L*-Algorithms

For the purpose of coding the *r*- and *l*-algorithms, we can reuse classes for prices, absolute transaction costs, and strategy developed in previous chapters. The header file `PotentialProfitAlg.h` contains the definitions of `s_function` and the two algorithms `potential_profit_ralg` and `potential_profit_lalg`:

```
#ifndef __PotentialProfitAlg_h__
#define __PotentialProfitAlg_h__

#include <cmath>
#include <vector>
```

```
using namespace std;

#include "Prices.h"
#include "Cost.h"
#include "SpecCost.h"
#include "Strategy.h"
using namespace PPBOOK;

namespace PPBOOK {

     inline  double
    s_function(const Prices& prices,
        const vector<Cost<SpecAbsoluteCost> >& costs,
        size_t i, size_t j, double k)
    {
        const double    SMALL_NUMBER = 1.0e-10;
        double  s = k * fabs(prices[i] - prices[j]) - costs[i].cost()
                    - costs[j].cost();
        return  fabs(s) < SMALL_NUMBER ? 0.0 : s;
    }

    inline  Strategy
    potential_profit_ralg(const Prices& prices,
        const vector<Cost<SpecAbsoluteCost> >& costs,
        unsigned int nContracts)
    {
        if(prices.size() != costs.size()) {
            ostringstream   s;
            s    << "potential_profit_ralg: vectors prices["
                 << (unsigned int)prices.size() << "] and costs["
                 << (unsigned int)costs.size()
                 << "] must be of one size.";
            throw   invalid_argument(s.str());
        }
        Strategy    units(prices.size(), 0);
        double      k = prices.tickValue() / prices.tick();
        int         polarity = 0;
        size_t      minI = 0;
        size_t      maxI = minI;
        for(size_t i = 1; i < prices.size(); i++) {
            double s_min_i = s_function(prices, costs, minI, i, k);
            double s_max_i = s_function(prices, costs, maxI, i, k);
            if(s_min_i <= 0.0 && s_max_i <= 0.0) {
                if(k * prices[minI] + costs[minI].cost() >
```

```
                k * prices[i] + costs[i].cost()) {
                minI = i;
            }
            if(k * prices[maxI] - costs[maxI].cost() <
                k * prices[i] - costs[i].cost()) {
                maxI = i;
            }
            if(i == prices.size() - 1) {
                units[minI] = polarity * (int)nContracts *
                                (polarity - 1)/2;
                units[maxI] = -polarity * (int)nContracts *
                                (polarity + 1)/2;
            }
            continue;
        }
        if(k * prices[minI] + costs[minI].cost() <
            k * prices[i] - costs[i].cost()) {
            units[minI] = (1 - polarity) * nContracts;
            polarity = 1;
            maxI = minI = i;
        }
        if(k * prices[maxI] - costs[maxI].cost() >
            k * prices[i] + costs[i].cost()) {
            units[maxI] = (-1 - polarity) * nContracts;
            polarity = -1;
            maxI = minI = i;
        }
        if(i == prices.size() - 1)
            units[i] = -polarity * (int)nContracts;
    }
    return  units;
}

inline  Strategy
potential_profit_1alg(const Prices& prices,
    const vector<Cost<SpecAbsoluteCost> >& costs,
    unsigned int nContracts)
{
    if(prices.size() != costs.size()) {
        ostringstream   s;
        s   << "potential_profit_1alg: vectors prices["
            << (unsigned int)prices.size() << "] and costs["
            << (unsigned int)costs.size()
            << "] must be of one size.";
```

```
        throw   invalid_argument(s.str());
    }
    Strategy    units(prices.size(), 0);
    double      k = prices.tickValue() / prices.tick();
    int         polarity = 0;
    int         minI = (int)prices.size() - 1;
    int         maxI = minI;
    for(int i = (int)prices.size() - 2; i >= 0; i-) {
        double s_min_i = s_function(prices, costs, minI, i, k);
        double s_max_i = s_function(prices, costs, maxI, i, k);
        if(s_min_i <= 0.0 && s_max_i <= 0.0) {
            if(k * prices[minI] + costs[minI].cost() >
                k * prices[i] + costs[i].cost()) {
                minI = i;
            }
            if(k * prices[maxI] - costs[maxI].cost() <
                k * prices[i] - costs[i].cost()) {
                maxI = i;
            }
            if(i == 0) {
                units[minI] = polarity * (int)nContracts *
                                (polarity - 1)/2;
                units[maxI] = -polarity * (int)nContracts *
                                (polarity + 1)/2;
            }
            continue;
        }
        if(k * prices[minI] + costs[minI].cost() <
            k * prices[i] - costs[i].cost()) {
            units[minI] = (1 - polarity) * nContracts;
            polarity = 1;
            maxI = minI = i;
        }
        if(k * prices[maxI] - costs[maxI].cost() >
            k * prices[i] + costs[i].cost()) {
            units[maxI] = (-1 - polarity) * nContracts;
            polarity = -1;
            maxI = minI = i;
        }
        if(i == 0)
            units[i] = -polarity * (int)nContracts;
    }
    return  units;
}
```

```
} // PPBOOK

#endif /* __PotentialProfitAlg_h__ */
```

The sequence of steps in the algorithm is represented by `for` loops. Each `for` loop contains four sequential `if` statements. The first three of them check mutually exclusive conditions. However, because of rounding and truncation errors, the expressions may give different results and the exclusiveness of the three conditions can be violated. There are situations where straightforward computation of the *s*-function is supposed to return the exact value zero, but returns a small positive value of the magnitude 10^{-12}. This is a problem with many systems due to the representation of real numbers. Instead of recognizing that the *s*-interval is not yet finished, the program begins to check the polarity of the next interval. To fix this computational instability we must force the `s_function` to return exactly zero if the absolute value of the result is less that some minimum absolute value, which will be called `SMALL_NUMBER`.

The flow of the code directly corresponds to the steps described in the previous two sections. The following example will give you a better understanding of the process.

Example Test3.cpp

The program `test3.cpp` applies both algorithms and the profit-and-loss function from Chapter 2. Once it is compiled and linked, this program uses a set of hard-coded gold contract prices and a transaction cost specified in the command line of the program. If no number is supplied in the command line, then the transaction cost is set to zero.

```
#include <iostream>
#include <iomanip>
#include <string>
#include <cmath>
using namespace std;

#include "Prices.h"
#include "PotentialProfitAlg.h"
#include "ProfitAndLossAlg.h"
using namespace PPBOOK;

int main(int argc, char* argv[])
{
    try {
        double  transactionCost = argc > 1 ? atof(argv[1]) : 0.0;
        Prices  p("GC");
        p.append(427.3);
        p.append(426.5);
        p.append(426.7);
        p.append(426.6);
```

```
        p.append(430.6);
        p.append(432.1);
        p.append(432.1);
        p.append(430.7);

        vector<Cost<SpecAbsoluteCost> > c(p.size(), transactionCost);
        unsigned int    nContracts = 1;

        Strategy    ru(potential_profit_ralg(p, c, nContracts));
        Strategy    lu(potential_profit_lalg(p, c, nContracts));
        cout    << setw(8) << "Price" << " "
                << setw(8) << "Cost" << " "
                << setw(3) << "R" << " "
                << setw(3) << "L" << " "
                << endl;
        for(size_t i = 0; i < p.size(); i++) {
            cout    << setw(8) << p[i] << " "
                    << setw(8) << c[i].cost() << " "
                    << setw(3) << ru[i] << " "
                    << setw(3) << lu[i] << " "
                    << endl;
        }
        cout    << "R-P&L = " << profit_and_loss(p, ru, c) << " "
                << "L-P&L = " << profit_and_loss(p, lu, c) << endl;
    }
    catch(const exception& e) {
        cerr    << e.what() << endl;
    }
    catch(...) {
        cerr    << "Unknown exception" << endl;
    }
    return 0;
}
```

The program outputs prices, the corresponding transaction costs input from the command line, and transactions (the number of units bought and sold) calculated by *r*- and *l*-algorithms. The program was run with the transaction costs of 0 ($0 per trade), 13 ($26 per trade), 40 ($80 per trade), 70 ($140 per trade), and 280 ($460 per trade). As discussed in Chapter 2, the costs can be interpreted as a combination of commissions ($140 per trade is a realistic number for a full-service broker and $26 is quite reasonable for a discount broker) and slippage. The following are the outputs from five runs:

```
test3
   Price     Cost   R   L
   427.3        0  -1  -1
```

```
   426.5        0   2   2
   426.7        0  -2  -2
   426.6        0   2   2
   430.6        0   0   0
   432.1        0  -2   0
   432.1        0   0  -2
   430.7        0   1   1
R-P&L = 800 L-P&L = 800
```

With zero transaction cost, the program returns a strategy giving Pardo's profit. This corresponds to property 6 from Chapter 2. Profit-and-loss values are identical for r- and l-algorithms. However, the strategies are different because two identical prices, 432.1, can be chosen at different times.

```
test3 13
   Price      Cost   R   L
   427.3        13  -1  -1
   426.5        13   2   2
   426.7        13   0   0
   426.6        13   0   0
   430.6        13   0   0
   432.1        13  -2   0
   432.1        13   0  -2
   430.7        13   1   1
R-P&L = 702 L-P&L = 702
```

Using the cost of $26 dollars per trade (round trip) eliminates a few transactions from the list. However, the first and second points are still profitable.

```
test3 40
   Price      Cost   R   L
   427.3        40   0   0
   426.5        40   1   1
   426.7        40   0   0
   426.6        40   0   0
   430.6        40   0   0
   432.1        40  -2   0
   432.1        40   0  -2
   430.7        40   1   1
R-P&L = 540 L-P&L = 540
```

Further cost increase to $80 dollars per trade eliminated even more transactions. Still, the position is reversed one time at the price 432.1.

```
test3 70
   Price      Cost   R   L
   427.3        70   0   0
   426.5        70   1   1
   426.7        70   0   0
   426.6        70   0   0
   430.6        70   0   0
   432.1        70  -1   0
   432.1        70   0  -1
   430.7        70   0   0
R-P&L = 420 L-P&L = 420
```

Paying $140 per trade leaves us with only the initial entry and final exit points. The number of transactions can never be equal to one for the best strategy (property 2 from Chapter 2).

```
test3 280
   Price      Cost   R   L
   427.3       280   0   0
   426.5       280   0   0
   426.7       280   0   0
   426.6       280   0   0
   430.6       280   0   0
   432.1       280   0   0
   432.1       280   0   0
   430.7       280   0   0
R-P&L = 0 L-P&L = 0
```

The cost of $460 per trade makes all transactions senseless. The result is the "do nothing" strategy predicted by property 6 from Chapter 2.

C++ PROGRAM EVALUATING POTENTIAL PROFIT

The program from the previous section is hard-coded for a few gold prices and is useful only for illustration and testing. It would be more practical to a have a program similar to the filter program created in Chapter 1 for computing Pardo's profit but taking into account transaction costs. The classes and algorithms already developed are sufficient for writing such a program. This new program can also evaluate Pardo's profit after setting all costs to zero.

It would also be very good if the program "understands" two input formats using space, tab, and new line characters as delimiters between tokens. The first is specified as: `descriptor cost price1 price2`, etc. The second is specified as: `descriptor price1 cost1` `price2 cost2`, etc. The first format simplifies writing data files for futures markets, where transaction cost can be selected as a constant. This avoids the inconvenience of replicating the same number again and again. The program from the file `maxprof.cpp` does exactly that. If there are no command line arguments given to the program, then it "assumes" the first format. If there are command line arguments (it does not matter which), then the program "assumes" the second format. The input is taken from the standard program input.

```
#include <iostream>
#include <iomanip>
#include <string>
using namespace std;

#include "Prices.h"
#include "SpecCost.h"
#include "Cost.h"
#include "ProfitAndLossAlg.h"
#include "PotentialProfitAlg.h"
using namespace PPBOOK;

int main(int argc, char*[])
{
    try {
        string  market;
        cin >> market;
        Prices                          prices(market);
        vector<Cost<SpecAbsoluteCost> > costs;
        double  cost, price;
        // Fills prices and costs depending on the requested format
        if(argc > 1) {
            while(cin >> price && cin >> cost) {
                prices.append(price);
                costs.push_back(cost);
            }
        }
        else {
            cin >> cost;
            while(cin >> price) {
                prices.append(price);
                costs.push_back(cost);
            }
        }

        // Builds strategies
```

```
        Strategy    rs(potential_profit_ralg(prices, costs, 1));
        Strategy    ls(potential_profit_lalg(prices, costs, 1));

        // Reports results
        cout    << setw(4) << "#" << " "
                << setw(9) << prices.name() << " "
                << setw(8) << "Cost" << " "
                << setw(5) << "R" << " "
                << setw(5) << "L"
                << endl;
        for(unsigned int i = 0; i < prices.size(); i++) {
            cout    << setw(4) << i << " "
                    << setw(9) << setprecision(9) << prices[i] << " "
                    << setw(8) << costs[i].cost() << " "
                    << setw(5) << rs[i] << " "
                    << setw(5) << ls[i]
                    << endl;
        }
        cout    << "R-P&L = " << profit_and_loss(prices, rs, costs)
                << " L-P&L = " << profit_and_loss(prices, ls, costs)
                << endl;
    }
    catch(const exception& e) {
        cerr    << e.what() << endl;
    }
    catch(...) {
        cerr    << "Unknown exception" << endl;
    }
    return  0;
}
```

A test of the program and output is:

```
echo S 70 599.5 601.75 594.25 597.25 597.25 | maxprof
   #         S     Cost     R     L
   0     599.5       70     0     0
   1    601.75       70    -1    -1
   2    594.25       70     2     2
   3    597.25       70    -1     0
   4    597.25       70     0    -1
R-P&L = 245 L-P&L = 245
```

As we see, not all price changes in this fragment would be profitable.

CONCLUSIONS

- The concepts of *s*-function, *s*-matrix, and *s*-intervals help to determine price and cost ranges, where a pair of opposite transactions cannot produce a profit.
- The left-most and the right-most boundaries of *s*-intervals help to divide the main interval into a set of adjacent *s*-intervals of maximum length.
- The concept of polarity of *s*-interval is useful for determining the type of transaction.
- *R*- and *l*-algorithms are offered as a way of building the potential profit strategy under a condition of transaction costs.
- A C++ program filter and a test program implementing *r*- and *l*-algorithms are constructed and confirm, with simple examples, the main properties of the potential strategy discussed in Chapter 2.

CHAPTER 4

Money Management and Discrete Nature of Trading

Realizing what to trade and when to trade is the key to successful trading. Because nobody can know a potential profit strategy in advance, losing money is an inevitable part of trading. It then becomes very important to decide how much money to allocate to each trade. This question addresses the issue of money and risk management and is found in many of the familiar writings of Ralph Vince (1992, 1995), Ryan Jones (1999), and Larry Williams (1979, 1999, 2000). While money and risk management are important for trading any financial instrument, we will continue to focus on trading futures contracts. My particular interest in this chapter is to identify the optimal allocation of money for each trade and to recognize the discrete nature of the allocated amounts.

DENOMINATIONS

Let me introduce the notation that will be used throughout this chapter and discuss the underlying concepts.

N, *W*, and *L*: *N* is the total number of trades in a specific sequence. Some of them win (profit and loss [P&L] > 0), others lose (P&L < 0), and some will break even (P&L = 0). *W* is the number of winning trades. *L* is the number of losing and breakeven (P&L = 0) trades. By including breakeven trades in the count of losing trades, we avoid thinking that we have a successful system simply by having no losses. Then $N = W + L$. As *N* grows because more and more trades are completed, the ratios *W*/*N*, *L*/*N*, and *W*/*L* will become more stable and fluctuate around some values representing the long-term profile of this strategy. For instance, if a coin has regular properties, then one can expect that the ratio of the number of heads (*H*) to the number of tails (T) will get closer to unity (1.0) as the number of flips (F) increases. Mathematically, this can be written as:

$$\lim_{F\to\infty} H/T = 1,\ \lim_{F\to\infty} H/F = 0.5,\ \lim_{F\to\infty} T/F = 0.5 \tag{4.01}$$

In this case, we all know that the probability of a head or tail occurring is 0.5 for any single trial. An interesting question is: "Do the limits $\lim_{N\to\infty} W/L$, $\lim_{N\to\infty} W/N$, $\lim_{N\to\infty} L/N$ exist?" If they do exist, then they could be associated with the probabilities p_w and p_l that any single trade will win and lose respectively (breakeven trades are included as losing trades), and we could write:

$$\lim_{N\to\infty} W/N = p_w,\ \lim_{N\to\infty} L/N = p_l,\ \lim_{N\to\infty} W/L = p_w/p_l \tag{4.02}$$

A key point in Chapter 1 was that trading performance depends not only on a trader or a system but also on the potential profit offered by the market. Under these conditions, it is unreasonable to expect that the ratio W/L is only a characteristic of a trader or a system and does not depend on market conditions.

The ratios W/N, L/N, and W/L should depend on a trader and/or a system as well as on the potential profit and the nature of the price movement that occurs in a market. Under these conditions, it is difficult to expect that corresponding limits of the ratios, where $N \to \infty$, exist. An assumption of their existence means that the market will offer the same potential profit and corresponding strategy and the trader or the system will continue extracting a part of it in the same manner as in the past.

A_w, A_l. A_w is a constant amount of money won per contract for each winning trade. We will assume here that this return is a net profit after subtracting all commissions and fees, and $A_w > 0$. A_l is a constant amount of money lost per contract during for losing trade (or zero) and that it already includes all commissions and fees, then $A_l \le 0$. In real trading these amounts are not constant. One can estimate the average profit or loss per contract per trade by applying a trading strategy to historical prices. Alternatively, real trading records can be analyzed in order to evaluate this information. Typically, information about average profits, average losses, breakeven trades, the maximum *drawdown*, and the biggest winning run are among the measurements common when describing trading performance (Babcock 1989; Pardo 1992; Williams 1999). These important characteristics that show average and extreme profits and/or losses are still not as informative as a complete distribution of individual trade amounts.

A profit or loss per contract per trade depends not only on systematic application of a strategy and its properties but also on the potential profit offered by a market.

An interesting representation of trading performance is the complete distribution of profits and losses per contract per trade showing how many trades correspond to consecutive intervals of certain length on the scale of loss-to-profit.

A_0, A_N, A_0 is the initial account value to be used for trading futures contracts. A_N is the account value after N trades have been completed. Similarly $A_1, A_2, \ldots$ denote account values after 1, 2, ... trades. The generic denomination A_i means account value after i trades. Every trade requires a specific allocation of funds per contract (less than or equal to the total account value). The total amount depends on the type and number of contracts and is determined by both the exchange and the brokerage firm. A part of this invested amount, the entire amount, or even more (in futures trading the allocated amount is a "good faith deposit," while the actual loss is determined by the market price) can be lost by the time the trade is exited. Alternatively, the trade can be profitable.

M denotes a constant *margin* per contract. Because of the many regulations that apply to futures trading, a trading account must have a minimum amount that includes both an *initial margin* plus enough reserves to satisfy your brokerage firm in the event of an adverse price move. Babcock (1989) describes this as:

> *Unlike the stock market, where the broker uses money in your account to buy shares, the money in your commodity account is not used to buy anything. It is the guarantee that when you are wrong about the price change, the broker will have the money to pay off the person on the other side of the transaction. For each commodity, the exchanges and your brokerage firm set an amount that you must have available in your account for this guarantee before initiating a trade in that market. This is called margin.*

This amount is not necessarily constant. Although margins can remain unchanged for months or years, they are subject to change based on factors such as daily price volatility and speculative interest. Once a position is open, a brokerage firm requires that the value of each account remain above a level known as *maintenance margin*. Typically, maintenance margin is 75 percent of initial margin. If an account falls below this maintenance margin threshold, the broker will issue a *margin call*. This call means that more money must be added to the account, normally within 24 hours, bringing the account back to the full margin level. If the margin call is not satisfied, then the broker will liquidate the positions at-the-market. For intraday trading, where positions are opened and closed during the same day, formal margin requirements do not normally apply. In that case, each brokerage firm has its own rules that determine the minimum account value based on the trading activity and market risk.

The parameter b is a fixed or constant money allocation fraction. This means that the product bA_i is the total amount of money allocated in order to enter a new trade, where i number of trades have been completed. The fraction b must be positive $b > 0$. If it is zero, then no money is allocated. The zero case is not interesting because b is a constant for all trades and $b = 0$ would mean no trading. The value of $b > 1.0$ would mean that the allocated amount comes not only from the existing account but also from another source. For this evaluation, we will consider only *self-financing accounts*, where $b \leq 1$. This means that the original account value A_0 evolves during trading and that only gains and losses from trading are used to finance further trades. This is quite similar to the concept of *self-financing strategies* (Hunt and Kennedy 2000) actively applied in pricing derivatives. A self-financing strategy replicating all cash flows from an instrument is one of the bases of modern no-arbitrage pricing approaches (Harrison and Pliska 1981).

Clearly, the expression bA_i/M corresponds to the maximum number of contracts that can be traded using the amount of money allocated to the trade that follows the ith trade. In practice, it would be unusual if the values of this expression were integers. Hence, because at any time i we can trade only a whole number of futures contracts, we must round the result of this expression to the nearest (less or equal to) whole number using the following equation:

$$n_i = \text{int}(bA_i/M) = \text{static\_cast<int>}(bA_i/M) \tag{4.03}$$

The intermediate expression above uses the so-called *cast operator* `int()`, which is well known to C and C++ programmers. If the value in brackets is a positive fractional number, then the operator reduces the fraction and returns only the smaller integer part. The `int()` is a C-style cast operator, which is a deprecated feature in C++. The `static_cast<int>()` is a more explicit and more visible alternative syntax of C++ (Stroustrup 2000). Rounding to a lower integer number of contracts is analyzed in Vince (1995). Ralph Vince writes the equation as *number of units to trade = int(account equity/f$)*. The number of units to trade relates to the risk. Changing the formal denominator *f$* allows you to choose the number of trading units as a function of the individual comfortable level of the market risk. For a futures market, Equation (4.03) seems very natural because all risk considerations can be absorbed in b, the allocation fraction. At the same time the value of M simply reflects trading rules assigned by the futures industry for a specific market. Under these conditions:

$$n_i = \mathrm{int}(bA_i/M) \le bA_i/M \qquad (4.04)$$

This implies that the amount of money allocated for each new trade is always equal to or less than the one determined by the fraction b:

$$M \times \mathrm{int}(bA_i/M) \le bA_i \qquad (4.05)$$

Regardless of that, we will begin with a case representing the noninteger number of contracts. Why? That will be shown in the next sections.

INDUCTION AND TRADING ACCOUNT SIZE

If the first trade is a profit, then the account value increases to $A_{1w} = A_0 + A_w bA_0/M = A_0(1 + bA_w/M)$. If the first trade is a loss, the account shrinks to $A_{1l} = A_0 - A_l bA_0/M = A_0(1 - bA_l/M)$. Both equations imply that the number of contracts traded can be noninteger including the situation where it is between zero and 1 unit. Considering the losing case, we would postulate that:

$$0 < 1 - bA_l/M \text{ meaning that } b < M/A_l \qquad (4.06)$$

If this is not so, then after the first loss it would be impossible to continue trading because the account value is either zero or even negative. Hence, the fraction b must obey the condition:

$$0 < b < M/A_l \qquad (4.07)$$

At the same time b must be < 1 for a self-financing account. Which condition prevails, $b < 1$ or $b < M/A_l$, depends on the ratio M/A_l. If it is > 1 ($M > A_l$), then b must be < 1. If the ratio is less than 1 ($M < A_l$), then b must be less than the ratio. This is the intersection $\cap$ of the two open intervals:

$$0 < b < M/A_l \cap 0 < b < 1 \tag{4.08}$$

After two consecutive gains the account grows to $A_{1w1w} = A_{1w} + A_w bA_{1w}/M = A_{1w}$ $(1 + bA_w /M) = A_0$ $(1 + bA_w/M)(1 + bA_w/M) = A_0$ $(1 + bA_w/M)^2$. To get the final relationship, A_{1w} was replaced by the expression in the first paragraph, A_0 $(1 + bA_w/M)$. After two consecutive losses the account drops in value to $A_{1l1l} = A_{1l} - A_l bA_{1l}/M = A_{1l}$ $(1 - bA_l/M) = A_0$ $(1 - bA_l/M)(1 - bA_l/M) = A_0$ $(1 - bA_l/M)^2$. Here again, A_{1l} was replaced by the expression A_0 $(1 - bA_l/M)$, explained in the first paragraph. The two other possible combinations, win-lose and lose-win, lead to the equations $A_{1w1l} = A_{1w} - A_l bA_{1w}/M = A_{1w}$ $(1 - bA_l/M) = A_0$ $(1 + bA_w/M)(1 - bA_l/M)$ and $A_{1l1w} = A_{1l} + A_w bA_{1l}/M = A_{1l}$ $(1 + bw_l/M) = A_0$ $(1 - bA_l/M)$ $(1 + bA_w/M)$ respectively. In each case, we can express the final account value, using the initial account value and constant per each trade parameters. Further application of induction to the case of W winning trades and L losing or breakeven trades gives the equation

$$A_N = A_0 (1 + bA_w/M)^W (1 - bA_l/M)^L \tag{4.09}$$

for the account value after N trades, where $N = W + L$. Equation (4.09) is the same independent of the order of wins and losses. Because of the conditions in Equation (4.07) and/or in (4.08) and the hypothetical ability to trade a noninteger number of contracts, even the case where the number of contracts is < 1, the right side of the equation is always positive. This implies that trading may not stop even if the number of consecutive losses is endless.

- If fractional number of contracts can be traded and the account value is assessed in fractions of a penny, and $0 < b < M/A_l \cap 0 < b < 1$, then such trading account is never wiped out, if the amount lost, A_l, is a constant per contract per trade.

GROWTH FUNCTION AND OPTIMAL *B*

The ratio of the account value after N trades to the initial account value is given by:

$$A_N/A_0 = (1 + bA_w/M)^W (1 - bA_l/M)^L \tag{4.10}$$

Taking a natural logarithm of the left and right sides of the Equation (4.10) and dividing the result by N gives:

$$\ln(A_N/A_0)/N = (W/N) \ln(1 + bA_w/M) + (L/N) \ln(1 - bA_l/M) \tag{4.11}$$

Of course, there are already two unrealistic assumptions that ignore the discrete nature of money: (1) trading a fractional number of contracts and (2) accounting for fractional values less than a penny. Having already accepted those conditions temporarily, you might excuse a third assumption about the existence of the limits p_w and p_l for the ratios W/N and L/N, where $N \to \infty$. This helps to introduce the *growth function G:*

$$G = \lim_{N\to\infty} (\ln(A_N/A_0)/N) = p_w \ln(1 + bA_w/M) + p_l \ln(1 - bA_l/M) \qquad (4.12)$$

The G function expresses an average logarithmic increment or decrement of the account associated with one trade, as the number of trades goes to infinity. Whether this will be an increment or a decrement depends on the parameters from the right side of Equation (4.12). Now consider the function G as a continuous function of a single independent variable b and write $G = G(b)$. All other parameters, such as p_w, p_l, A_w, A_l, M, are fixed. The higher the value of G the faster the account grows. This function may have a maximum in the interval of b satisfying the conditions (4.07) and/or (4.08). If it does have a maximum G^* at some point b^*, then the first derivative dG/db must be equal to zero at point b^*. This can be written as $dG/db(b^*) = 0$. A calculus exercise gives the expression for the derivative:

$$\begin{aligned} dG/db &= p_w (A_w/M)(M/(M + bA_w)) - p_l (A_l/M)(M/(M - bA_l)) \\ &= p_w A_w/(M + bA_w) - p_l A_l/(M - bA_l) \end{aligned} \qquad (4.13)$$

The second denominator is strictly positive because $b < M/A_l$. The right side of Equation (4.13) is equal to zero, if $p_w A_w (M - bA_l) - p_l A_l (M + bA_w) = 0$. This results in the optimal equation for b:

$$\begin{aligned} b^* &= ((p_w A_w - p_l A_l)/(p_w A_w + p_l A_w)) M/A_l \\ &= ((p_w A_w - p_l A_l)/A_w) M/A_l \\ &= (p_w - (1 - p_w)A_l/A_w) M/A_l \end{aligned} \qquad (4.14)$$

The right side of Equation (4.14) contains three equivalent expressions. To derive them it is necessary to use the property $p_w + p_l = 1$. In the first and second expressions, the term $p_w A_w - p_l A_l$ represents the mathematical expectation of the dollar amount gained during a single trade. The presence of the minus sign in this expression should not obscure that fact that this is a formula for mathematical expectation used in a finite discrete case. From the beginning, A_l has been treated as a positive number and systematically complements the lost amount by the minus sign. Another interesting observation is that, if $M = A_l$, then the last expression becomes:

$$b^* = p_w - (1 - p_w)A_l/A_w \qquad (4.15)$$

Equation (4.15) is widely cited as the famous *Kelly formula* (Kelly 1956). John Kelly used the growth function $G = q \log(1 + l) + p \log(1 - l)$, where $q + p = 1$, q and p are probabilities of correct symbol transmission and error respectively, and log is logarithm with base 2. The maximum value of G is reached if $(1 + l) = 2q$ or $(1 - l) = 2p$ (this can be verified by solving the equation $dG/dl = 0$). Equation (4.14) contains Equation (4.15) as a special case.

Substituting the right side of Equation (4.14) into Equation (4.12) gives the maximum value G^* of the growth function for the case of futures contracts. This is an algebra exercise:

$$G^* = p_w \ln(p_w) + p_l \ln(p_l) + p_w \ln(1 + A_w/A_l) + p_l \ln(1 + A_l/A_w) \tag{4.16}$$

Two interesting observations can be made by examining Equation (4.16). The first is that it does not contain the parameter M. This means that while the optimal allocation fraction b^* does depend on margin, the maximum account growth rate does not depend on margin. The second is that, if the binary logarithm (logarithm with base 2) was used instead of the natural logarithm and the gains and losses are equal, $A_w = A_l$, then Equation (4.16) transforms into:

$$\begin{aligned} G^*_{bin} &= p_w \log(p_w) + p_l \log(p_l) + p_w \log(1 + 1) + p_l \log(1 + 1) \\ &= p_w \log(p_w) + p_l \log(p_l) + 1 \end{aligned} \tag{4.17}$$

This is because $\log(2) = 1$ and $p_w + p_l = 1$. The right-most side of Equation (4.17) is the famous *equation for the rate of transmission* defined by Claude Shannon (1948). A similar relationship between Kelly's and Shannon's equations is shown in Kelly (1956).

The condition given in Inequality (4.08) can now be combined with Equation (4.14):

$$0 < b^* = (p_w - (1 - p_w)A_l/A_w)\, M/A_l < M/A_l \cap 0 < b^* < 1 \tag{4.18}$$

The left inequality means that $0 < (p_w - (1 - p_w)A_l/A_w)\, M/A_l$. This is true if the mathematical expectation of the money gained $p_w A_w - p_l A_l$ in a single trade is positive. The right inequality means that $(p_w - (1 - p_w)A_l/A_w)\, M/A_l < M/A_l$. Clearly, this is equivalent to the condition $p_w - (1 - p_w)A_l/A_w < 1$ or $p_w A_w - p_l A_l < A_w$. The last is always true except where $p_l = 0$. Indeed, if $p_l = 0$, then $p_w = 1$ and it cannot be so that A_w is less than itself. When is p_l equal to zero? Well, this is the case of the potential profit strategy—the main subject of this book. The best strategy however does not guarantee that A_w is constant. The positive impact of proper money management on the best trading strategy will be discussed separately. Meanwhile, it is necessary to check the second part of the intersection $(p_w - (1 - p_w)A_l/A_w)\, M/A_l < 1$. This last condition is equivalent to

$$p_w A_w - p_l A_l < A_w A_l/M \tag{4.19}$$

which means that the mathematical expectation of the money gained in a single trade is less than product of individual profits and losses divided by the margin. It is only under this condition that the optimal allocation fraction b^* is < 1 and can be used for a self-financing account. If this is not the case, then in order to reach the optimal allocation fraction b^* the account must get financing from outside sources. If outside sources were not available, then the best strategy would be to allocate everything $b = 1$. However, this would still lead to a smaller growth rate than G^*.

If a fractional number of contracts is allowed, then substituting b with b^* from Equation (4.14) into the equation $n_i = bA_i/M$ gives the optimal number of contracts n_i^* for a next trade after i number of trades have been completed. If the inequality (4.19) is satisfied and b^* can be obtained with a self-financing account, then $n_i^* = (p_w - (1 - p_w)A_l/A_w)\, A_i/A_l$. The optimal number of contracts is similar to the optimal growth rate in that neither of them depends on margin. If $b^* > 1$ is not attainable and $b = 1$ is set for a self-financing account, then the number of contracts cannot be optimal and is determined by $n_i = A_i/M$. It then depends on the amount of margin required.

The main equations and conditions of this section can be summarized as:

- The *best allocation fraction* $b^* = (p_w - (1 - p_w)A_l/A_w)\, M/A_l$
- The *maximum growth rate* $G^* = p_w \ln(p_w) + p_l \ln(p_l) + p_w \ln(1 + A_w/A_l) + p_l \ln(1 + A_l/A_w)$
- The condition making b^* attainable $0 < p_w A_w - p_l A_l < A_w A_l/M$

DISCRETE NATURE OF TRADING

In order to simplify the approach in the previous sections, derive new formulas for futures account management, and find their relationships with the known Kelly and Shannon formulas, it was helpful to use a fractional number of contracts and accounts containing fractions of penny. For real trading, these simplifications are too unrealistic. This means that neither these new formulas nor the Kelly formula can be directly applied to trading. Nevertheless, they can improve our feeling about some extreme cases. Different limitations of the Kelly formula are discussed in Vince (1992). Now let me return to condition (4.04) $n_i = \text{int}(bA_i/M) \le bA_i/M$. What is changed by the presence of the operator int()?

First, induction no longer leads to a single formula for the evolution of the account size as in the previous sections. For instance, the right side of the equation $A_{1w} = A_0 + A_w\, \text{int}(bA_0/M)$ cannot be decomposed so that the common multiplier A_0 is taken out of the sum. Second, the account size after i number of trades is now written as $A_{i+1} = A_i + A_w\, \text{int}(bA_i/M)$ for a next winning trade and as $A_{i+1} = A_i - A_l\, \text{int}(bA_i/M)$ for a next losing trade. Both expressions mean that, if bA_i/M is < 1, then trading is terminated since the next number of contracts after i trades is equal to zero. Third, the order of winning and losing trades becomes important. Depending on the parameters, several consecutive losses can now wipe out the account. What is important here is that it now looks like real trading! What is bad is that it is hardly possible to get closed formulas as we did it in the previous sections. However, some assistance can come from a computer simulation.

Evolution of Account with Constant A_w, A_l, M, b

The Evolution Equation and the C++ Program Consider a variable T possessing a value T_i at each point in time i. This variable inherits the denomination from the word *trade*. It takes on the values −1 (loss), 0 (no trading), 1 (gain). This allows us to write the following recursive equation for A_{i+1}:

$$A_{i+1} = A_i + \text{int}(bA_i/M)\, [A_w T_i (T_i + 1) - A_l T_i (T_i - 1)]/2 \quad \textit{(account evolution equation)} \tag{4.20}$$

where T_i is the trading result after i trades have been completed. All values of T_i and A_i can be collected into two vectors $\boldsymbol{T}$ and $\boldsymbol{A}$. The vector $\boldsymbol{A}$ contains one more element compared to the vector $\boldsymbol{T}$; the last additional entry holds the final account value. Given A_0, A_w, A_l, M, b, and $\boldsymbol{T}$ the following C++ algorithm computes the evolution of the account. Most of the code in the header file `AccountAlg.h` checks multiple error conditions and creates necessary diagnostics.

```
#ifndef __AccountAlg_h__
#define __AccountAlg_h__

#include <vector>
#include <sstream>
#include <stdexcept>
using namespace std;

namespace PPBOOK {

    typedef vector<int>      Trades;
    typedef vector<double>   Account;

    inline  Account
    evolve_account(double initialValue, double win, double loss,
        double margin, double fraction, const Trades& trades)
    {
        if(initialValue < 0.0) {
            ostringstream   s;
            s    << "evolve_account: initialValue " << initialValue
                << " must be >= 0";
            throw   invalid_argument(s.str());
        }
        if(win < 0.0) {
            ostringstream   s;
            s    << "evolve_account: win " << win << " must be >= 0";
            throw   invalid_argument(s.str());
        }
        if(loss < 0.0) {
            ostringstream   s;
            s    << "evolve_account: loss " << loss << " must be >= 0";
            throw   invalid_argument(s.str());
        }
        if(margin <= 0.0) {
            ostringstream   s;
            s    << "evolve_account: margin " << margin << " must be > 0";
            throw   invalid_argument(s.str());
        }
```

```
        if(fraction < 0.0 || fraction > 1.0) {
            ostringstream  s;
            s  << "evolve_account: fraction " << fraction
               << " must be from the interval [0, 1]";
            throw  invalid_argument(s.str());
        }
        Account a(1, initialValue);
        for(unsigned int i = 0; i < trades.size(); i++) {
            if(trades[i] == 1)
                a.push_back(a[i] + win * int(fraction * a[i] / margin));
            else if(trades[i] == -1)
                a.push_back(a[i] - loss * int(fraction * a[i] / margin));
            else if(trades[i] == 0)
                a.push_back(a[i]);
            else {
                ostringstream  s;
                s  << "evolve_account: trades[" << i << "] = "
                   << trades[i] << "must be equal to -1 or 0 or 1";
                throw  invalid_argument(s.str());
            }
        }
        return  a;
    }

} // PPBOOK

#endif /* __AccountAlg_h__ */
```

The program from the file `account.cpp` reuses this algorithm, collecting data from the standard input:

```
#include <iostream>
#include <iomanip>
using namespace std;

#include "AccountAlg.h"
using namespace PPBOOK;

int main(int, char*[])
{
    try {
        double  initialValue, win, loss, margin, fraction;
        cin >> initialValue >> win >> loss >> margin >> fraction;
        Trades  trades;
        int tr;
        while(cin >> tr)
```

```
            trades.push_back(tr);
        Account a(evolve_account(initialValue, win, loss, margin,
                        fraction, trades));
        cout    << setw(5) << "#" << " "
                << setw(10) << "Account" << " "
                << setw(2) << "TR" << " "
                << setw(5) << "Contr" << " "
                << setw(10) << "P&L" << " "
                << setw(10) << "Ratio"
                << endl;
        unsigned int    i = 0;
        for(; i < trades.size(); i++) {
            double  r = fraction * a[i] / margin;
            int     n = r <= 0.0 ? 0 : static_cast<int>(r);
            double  pl = (trades[i] * (trades[i] + 1) * win -
                trades[i] * (trades[i] - 1) * loss) * n * 0.5;
            cout    << setw(5) << i << " "
                    << setw(10) << a[i] << " "
                    << setw(2) << trades[i] << " "
                    << setw(5) << n << " "
                    << setw(10) << pl << " "
                    << setw(10) << (r != 0.0 ? n / r : 0)
                    << endl;
        }
        cout    << setw(5) << i << " "
                << setw(10) << a[i]
                << endl;
    }
    catch(const exception& e) {
        cerr    << e.what() << endl;
    }
    catch(...) {
        cerr    << "Unknown exception" << endl;
    }
    return  0;
}
```

Simulation This program can now be run with the following parameters: A_0 = \$5,000, A_w = \$1,000, A_l = \$900, M = \$1,400, and b = 0.373(3). The last value was computed using Equation (4.14) for the optimal b^* with the assumption that $W/L = 3/2$. This W/L ratio implies the hypothetical values $p_w = 3/(3+2) = 0.6$ and $p_l = 2/(3+2) = 0.4$. We will also assume that there are exactly five trades. The three gains and two losses are distributed among these five trades as (1, 1, 1, −1, −1) or (1, −1, 1, −1, 1) or (−1, −1, 1, 1, 1) and so on to include all combinations. Recalling the formula for combinations, we find that the total number of combinations is equal to $5!/(2!3!) = 10$, where the exclamation sign denotes factorial. If we are permitted to use a fractional number of contracts and an account with fractions of a penny, then Equation

(4.09) gives the final account value of $\$5{,}000 \times 1.26(6)^3 \times 0.76^2 = \$5{,}869.27$. This value does not depend on the order of transactions and is the same for any of the 10 combinations. A sequence of five losses would leave the account with the value $1,267.00. A sequence of five gains would increase the account to the value $16,303.53. The program `account.cpp` helps to evaluate each combination separately. The following two results show how real life may differ from the results of Equations (4.09) and (4.14):

```
echo 5000 1000 900 1400 0.37333333 1 1 1 -1 -1 | account
   #     Account TR Contr          P&L        Ratio
   0        5000  1     1         1000         0.75
   1        6000  1     1         1000        0.625
   2        7000  1     1         1000     0.535714
   3        8000 -1     2        -1800       0.9375
   4        6200 -1     1         -900     0.604839
   5        5300
```

```
echo 5000 1000 900 1400 0.37333333 -1 -1 1 1 1 | account
   #     Account TR Contr          P&L        Ratio
   0        5000 -1     1         -900         0.75
   1        4100 -1     1         -900     0.914634
   2        3200  1     0            0            0
   3        3200  1     0            0            0
   4        3200  1     0            0            0
   5        3200
```

We see first that the account size indeed depends on the order of wins and losses even if the ratio and the total number of trades are the same. The final account value for each of the ten combinations becomes: 1 – (1 1 1 –1 –1) = $5,300, 2 – (1 1 –1 1 –1) = $6,200, 3 – (1 –1 1 1 –1) = $6,200, 4 – (–1 1 1 1 –1) = $6,200, 5 – (–1 1 1 –1 1) = $6,200, 6 – (–1 1 –1 1 1) = $6,200, 7 – (–1 –1 1 1 1) = $3,200, 8 – (1 1 –1 –1 1) = $6,200, 9 – (1 –1 –1 1 1) = $6,200, 10 – (1 –1 1 –1 1) = $6,200.

Second, the trading can be terminated once the amount to be allocated is less than the margin requirement. This happens in combination 2. Indeed, $\$3{,}200 \times 0.373 = \$1{,}194.67 < \$1{,}400$ and the third transaction cannot be executed. If the account shrinks, then the number of contracts to be purchased decreases.

The third observation shows that the average final account size obtained from the 10 combinations is equal to $(8 \times \$6{,}200 + \$5{,}300 + \$3{,}200)/10 = \$5{,}810$, which is not far from $5,869.27—the result found using Equations (4.09) and (4.14). The operator `int()` always reduces the amount of money to be allocated compared with the recommended fractional amount. This is good when a trade is a loss and bad when it is a profit. The reduction depends on the ratio $\mathrm{int}(bA_i/M)/(bA_i/M)$. This ratio is given in the output of the program.

The fourth observation can be made after reviewing the sequence of 5 wins:

```
echo 5000 1000 900 1400 0.37333333 1 1 1 1 1 | account
   #     Account TR Contr          P&L        Ratio
   0        5000  1     1         1000         0.75
```

```
1        6000  1    1        1000      0.625
2        7000  1    1        1000   0.535714
3        8000  1    2        2000     0.9375
4       10000  1    2        2000       0.75
5       12000
```

The value \$12,000 is < \$16,303.53 obtained from Equations (4.09) and (4.14). The ratio of these numbers is 12000/16303.53 = 0.736. We can then solve the equation $0.736 = (1+x)^5/1.26^5$. $x = 1.26 \times 0.736^{1/5} - 1 = 0.18$. The ratio 0.18/0.26 = 0.694 can be viewed as an approximation of the average ratio (0.75 + 0.625 + 0.535714 + 0.9375 + 0.75)/5 = 0.719. This may have a bias because x is not a constant value but depends on the account size in the previous step. If the account grows, then the number of contracts purchased gradually increases.

The fifth conclusion comes after increasing the initial account to \$10,000, with other conditions remaining the same:

```
echo 10000 1000 900 1400 0.37333333 -1 -1 1 1 1 | account
#     Account TR Contr         P&L      Ratio
0       10000 -1    2        -1800       0.75
1        8200 -1    2        -1800   0.914634
2        6400  1    1         1000   0.585938
3        7400  1    1         1000   0.506757
4        8400  1    2         2000   0.892857
5       10400
```

A trader with a \$10,000 account survived and realized a net gain after the two consecutive losses, which would have wiped out a trader with only a \$5,000 account. It is important that both traders allocated the same optimal fractional amount 0.373. Money loves big money!

How else can we use Equation (4.20) and the corresponding program `account.cpp`? It can help to estimate the maximum number of losing trades in one sequence. For instance, for a \$5,000 account this number is equal to 2. For the \$10,000 account, it is equal to 5. Alternatively, one can estimate the account size needed to survive a certain number of consecutive losses with other conditions being equal. For instance, in order to survive three losses and still be able to enter a fourth trade of one contract, it is necessary to have begun with at least \$6,450 plus 1 cent. Additionally, one can estimate the *account surviving b* (not the optimal b^*), if the account size and the number of consecutive losses are specified and other parameters are the same.

Controlling A_l Selecting the expression int(bA_i/M) instead of bA_i/M to decide the number of traded futures contracts leads to a much more realistic evolution of a trading account. However, the assumption that A_w and A_l are constant is far from realistic. A partial repair of Equation (4.20) may come from using the average per trade, specifically the average profit per contract and the average loss per contract $\langle A_w \rangle$ and $\langle A_l \rangle$. A more conservative trader may apply the maximum drawdown per contract or maximum loss per contract instead of the average loss $\langle A_l \rangle$. How can one reduce fluctuations of A_l to some extent without having to make A_l a constant? And if the average loss $\langle A_l \rangle$ is determined after a few preliminary trades, how can one use this value and control new individual losses A_l?

If a trading system does not assume the use of stop-loss orders and has transactions solely based on its buy and sell signals, then there is a little control over either $<A_l>$ or the maximum drawdown per contract. If, instead, a trading system includes the use of stop-loss orders as a part of the system, then there is usually better control of the individual losses, A_l, and consequently the average loss, $<A_l>$, the maximum drawdown per contract, and maximum loss per contract. For instance, if one found that average loss is equal to $<A_l>$ after multiple applications of a system, then a stop-loss order based on that value may help control future losses to some extent and reduce the average loss of the system. Of course, intraday slippage and, to a greater extent, slippage from holding positions overnight may increase the size of the losses. If stop-loss orders were added to an optimized trading system, then they can cause the returns to drop considerably and affect the average profitability $<A_w>$. Because risk control is important, a system must contain the necessary stop-loss logic (or an alternative risk control) at the beginning in order to limit the size of $<A_l>$, the maximum drawdown per contract, and the maximum loss per contract.

Controlling A_w: Objectives Individual gains can be as variable as individual losses when there are no controls. One known way to capture additional profits and reduce the variability of the individual gains A_w as well as the average gain $<A_w>$ is by using a trailing stop-loss order. As the equity in the account grows, the initial stop-loss order is gradually moved up for a long position and down for a short one. Before initiating a trade, a trader should have clear understanding of:

- Why he is doing it. The answer "in order to make money" is not enough. It may be better to write the reasons on paper. For a discretionary trading approach, instead of a fully automated one, these reasons should justify why the price should go higher or lower. If this cannot be written or clearly formulated, then it may indicate that the decision is primarily emotional. Emotions are most often providing bad guidelines for trading.
- How much can be lost without dramatically damaging an account so that a reasonable number of transactions can be executed after the loss to allow new opportunities to be realized.
- What profit can be expected from the trade.

Let's say that one uses the *market setup* approaches, *timing signals*, *patterns*, and/or *swing* techniques described by some recognized traders who represent that they actively uses their own recommendations for trading. A few easily identified candidates are Larry Williams (1999), Gary Smith (2000), and Laurence Connors and Linda Raschke (1996). Perhaps decisions are made based on your own system and a diligent market research and a systematic approach (not necessarily automated) that you have developed. Or you may be satisfied with the results of some commercially available trading system after a careful review. This would answer the first point—why you have made the decision to enter the market. We should also consider the words of Noble Prize winner Dr. William F. Sharpe (Dugan 2005):

Past average experience may be a terrible predictor of future performance.

Of course, this may simply be a response to a bad trading experience by the famous economist. But suppose that a trader decides that $500 is a reasonable amount to lose on the proposed trade based on the account value. This loss would be small enough to leave enough capital to make an additional series of new transactions. By studying the market, the trader finds that the historic price fluctuations tend to be $500 is a single day in only 1 out of 20 days. This can be found by analyzing the *true range* (the largest of the price move from the previous closing price to the high or low of the next day). This means that the initial stop-loss order of $500 is in agreement with both his money management requirements and the natural market volatility. Literally, the ratio 1/20 can be treated as a 5 percent probability that within the next day the market will go against the position and trigger the stop-loss order. This approach to risk control will give the trader extra time to rethink the position, not to mention the ability to sleep well throughout the night. Then $500 is a reasonable answer to the second point. Often, it is an undercapitalized account that prevents the trader from finding a sensible compromise between the money management requirements and the natural price volatility of the market.

The trader might have experience with a specific market. It is generally agreed that it is better to trade a market for which you have some experience or learn about it before beginning actual trading. The trader may know that in this market it is reasonable to expect profits of $750 per trade for one contract. The trader may also express the profits in terms of a multiple of the formulated losses that have already been assessed. For instance, the profit objective can be equal to 1.5 of loss = 1.5 × $500 = $750. The loss-and-profit objective should at least include the known costs, such as commissions and fees, and an estimate of the intraday slippage (if nothing more than a few ticks) for entering and exiting transactions. Then the loss and profit should be translated into price changes to make a list of the key price objectives that should be monitored during the current trade. So $750 is the answer on the third point.

Controlling A_w: Trailing Stop-Loss A trailing stop-loss is a method of risk control often used by experienced traders. A trailing stop-loss order recipe may take many forms. One that corresponds to the objectives formulated in the previous section may be constructed as follows:

1. Set the initial stop-loss order to $500.
2. Raise the stop-loss level to the breakeven price (no loss, no profit) once the price reaches the level representing half of the unit profit objective ($375 = $750/2).
3. If the price reaches the level of 1 profit unit objective ($750), raise the stop-loss level to a price preserving two-thirds ($500) of the unrealized profit.
4. Every time a new high price occurs in the interval between one and two profit unit objectives [$750, $1,500], recalculate and raise the trailing stop-loss level using this new high price to preserve two-thirds of the highest unrealized profit.
5. Move the stop order to preserve three-fourths of the maximum profit reached once the existing profit achieves between two and three profit unit objectives [$1,500, $2,250].
6. If there are more than three profit units ($2,250), then increase stop price to capture 90 percent of maximum profit.

It is tedious to make these computations, but a simple program `goal.cpp` (only the program specifications are shown, the program is not developed for this book) can accomplish it if we assume the following input from a command line:

```
goal
Usage: goal price tick tickvalue fees loss ratio contracts
    price     - entry price
    tick      - price tick
    tickvalue - value of one tick
    fees      - comissions plus fees per contract
    loss      - maximum stop loss amount
    ratio     - objective profit to loss ratio
    contracts - positive/negative number of contracts for long/short position
```

Then a typical run of the program corresponding to the example above might look as follows:

```
goal 609.25 0.25 12.5 22.34 500 1.5 1
Entry price          : 609.25
Tick                 : 0.25
Tick value           : 12.5
Fees                 : 22.34
Stop Loss Amount     : 500
Profit to Loss Ratio: 1.5
Number of contracts : 1
LONG POSITION
3.0*P      654.75   2252.66
90%*P      650.25   2027.66
2.0*P      639.75   1502.66
75%*P      632.25   1127.66
1.0*P      624.75    752.66
66%*P      619.75    502.66
0.5*P      617.25    377.66
B.E.P      609.75      2.66
ENTRY      609.25    -22.34
STOP       599.75   -497.34
```

The program rounds prices, resulting in decreasing the losses and increasing the profits. It does not include any slippage, and it does not produce intermediate prices for any local maximum prices that have already been reached. However, when there are fast market moves, it is useful to have continuous output to facilitate making quicker decisions about the price of a new trailing stop-loss order.

Controlling *M* There is not much we can do about margin. The initial margin changes infrequently. In many practical situations, it is reasonable to make the assumption of constant margin.

Equation (4.20) implies that before initiating a new trade, the previous one must be completed. An active trader can decide to enter a new trade in one market when some of previous positions in another market have not been closed. The ability to enter new positions depends on the current total equity in the account and the sum of margin requirements on all open positions. The difference between these two (total equity minus margin) is known as *trading power*. If some positions are open, then in using Equation (4.20) the account value A_i (which can be considered the equivalent of the current total equity) can make the number of new trading contracts bigger than allowed by the trading power of the account. At the same time, applying the product of the allocation fraction b and the current trading power amount instead of bA_i is out of the scope of Equations (4.09), (4.14), and (4.20). The complexity dealing with trading power, total equity, open equity, and complex positions will be addressed in later chapters.

Controlling b A trader must control the allocation fraction until the equity in the account and margin requirements allow further trading. The assumption that a single constant optimal value b^* can be applied to every new trade is based on the assumption that a strategy continues to gain and lose the same amounts and with the same probabilities. The last assumption cannot be true in general because it depends on the market conditions and not only the strategy.

Evolution of Account with Nonconstant A_w and A_l

Stochastic Version of the Equation The next step toward a more realistic process is to continue to use A_w and A_l but treat them as random variables, where each is characterized by its own distribution function $f_w(a_w)$ and $f_l(a_l)$, respectively. In this notation, the random variable is denoted by using an uppercase A and its values by the lowercase a characters. By definition, a win A_w has only positive values. Alternatively, one can allow A_w to take on any values (positive and negative), forgetting for a moment what the subscript w means, but then the $f_w(a_w)$ must have a shape prohibiting nonpositive values of A_w. This implies that $f_w(a_w) = 0$ for all $a_w \leq 0$. Similarly, in the definition of a loss including breakeven trades, A_l takes only nonpositive values. If one thinks that A_l can take any value, then the function $f_l(a_l)$ must have a shape prohibiting positive values of A_l. This implies that $f_l(a_l) = 0$ for all $a_l > 0$.

While splitting P&L results into profits and losses is natural, working with two variables and two distributions is more complicated than with one. Because of that, one can introduce a single random variable A_{pl} having a distribution function $f_{pl}(a_{pl})$, allowing both positive and negative P&L values. Then Equation (4.20) is translated into:

$$A_{i+1} = A_i + A_{pl}\,\mathrm{int}(bA_i/M) \quad \textit{(account evolution equation with random P\&L)} \qquad (4.21)$$

This equation looks simpler than Equation (4.20) but is now stochastic because it contains the random variable A_{pl}. There is also a hidden randomness in the variable A_i. Of course, at any given moment i, when the history is known (information is filtered), A_i is not random. However, taking into account that at the beginning of trading one knows only A_0, it becomes clear why all A_i ($i > 0$) are random at that starting point. The A_{i+1} in Equation (4.21) is random because it depends on A_{pl}. If A_i is realized and known, then the mathematical expectation (E) of A_{i+1} in the next trade is given by:

$$\begin{aligned} E(A_{i+1}) &= E(A_i + A_{pl}\,\text{int}(bA_i/M)) = A_i + E(A_{pl}\,\text{int}(bA_i/M)) \\ &= A_i + \text{int}(bA_i/M)E(A_{pl}) \end{aligned} \tag{4.22}$$

To create these derivations, it is necessary to use properties of mathematical expectation: $E(constant) = constant$, $E(constant + x) = E(constant) + E(x)$, $E(constant * x) = constant * E(x)$, where $E(A_{pl})$ is given by

$$E(A_{pl}) = \int a_{pl} f(a_{pl}) da_{pl} \tag{4.23}$$

where integration boundaries change from $-\infty$ to $+\infty$.

Equation (4.23) works if a_{pl} is continuous. Equations (4.22) and (4.23) imply that a certain scenario leading to A_i has been realized. The attempt to write a more generic equation would require working with mathematical conditional expectation $E(A_{i+1} \mid A_i)$. In that case we could apply $E(A_{pl})$ instead of $E(A_{pl} \mid A_i)$ only if $f(a_{pl})$ is independent with respect to A_i and i.

How can we get $f(a_{pl})$? Do we need to know the entire function so that we can estimate the expectation $E(A_{pl})$? If we do know the entire function, what kind of useful information is available to us? Let us consider a simple hypothetical example.

Example: Getting Distribution of A_{pl} A trading system that is applied 10 times generated the following P&L: –17, 45, 99, 70, –30, –40, 190, 120, –90, and 80. The average P&L is $<A_{pl}> = (-17 + 45 + 99 + 70 - 30 - 40 + 190 + 120 - 90 + 80)/10 = 42.7$. The average win is $<A_w> = (45 + 99 + 70 + 190 + 120 + 80)/6 = 100.6(6)$. The average loss is $<A_l> = (17 + 30 + 40 + 90)/4 = 44.25$. (Note that positive numbers are used for the loss, but for clarity the correct sign will be written where it is needed.) The ratios $W/N = 6/10 = 0.6$ and $L/N = 4/10 = 0.4$ approximate the probabilities p_w and p_l, respectively. The mathematical expectation is $p_w <A_w> - p_l <A_l> = 0.6 \times 100.6(6) - 0.4 \times 44.25 = 42.6(9)$. Clearly, this is the same number as $<A_{pl}> = 42.7$. We get an estimate of the number without any distribution function. Additionally, we see that $<A_{pl}> = p_w <A_w> - p_l <A_l>$. What about the distribution function $f(a_{pl})$?

Now divide the interval that includes all P&L values [–100, 200] into subintervals of length 50 and put alongside each subinterval the number of times that a P&L occurred in it. The 6 subintervals and their counts should be: [–100, –50] 1, [–50, 0] 3, [0, 50] 1, [50, 100] 3, [100, 150] 1, [150, 200] 1. This can be depicted as the histogram

```
 x| x
 x| x
xx|xxxx
-------
```

Now assign to each subinterval the value equal to the average of its boundaries and associate each value with its frequency. This can be calculated as the count/10: –75, 0.1; –25, 0.3; +25, 0.1; +75, 0.3; +125, 0.1; +175, 0.1. Treating these frequencies as probabilities of the six values brings us to an estimate of a mathematical expectation in a discrete case:

$E(A_{pl}) = -75 \times 0.1 - 25 \times 0.3 + 25 \times 0.1 + 75 \times 0.3 + 125 \times 0.1 + 175 \times 0.1 = 40$. This is another way of estimating the mathematical expectation $E(A_{pl})$. Note that the answer 40 is close to 42.7. Clearly, the value 40 depends on how the intervals are selected. Because the sample number of 10 is very small, the shape of the distribution function $f_{pl}(a_{pl})$ (which we just found) is very approximate. For our small sample, the estimation of the average is much more precise than estimation of the function tails. However, as the number of P&L entries increases, the intervals can be divided into finer sets and a better estimate will be obtained, provided the distribution of A_{pl} remains the same from trade to trade.

Chapter 8 is used to develop the class `Distribution` and the program-filter `distrib.cpp`. This last program takes a sequence of numbers separated by white spaces (a space, tab, or new line character) from the standard input and a width specified in the command line and computes basic statistics for the sequence. It uses the width for building an empirical distribution of the numbers. The results of applying it to the previous example are:

```
echo -17 45 99 70 -30 -40 190 120 -90 80 | distrib 50
Mean           = 42.7
Sample size    = 10
Variance       = 7364.68
Std. deviation = 85.8177
Maximum value  = 190
Minimum value  = -90
All values [-17, 45, 99, 70, -30, -40, 190, 120, -90, 80]
Width          = 50
0 (-100, -50] 1
1 (-50, 0] 3
2 (0, 50] 1
3 (50, 100] 3
4 (100, 150] 1
5 (150, 200] 1
```

The numbers separated by white spaces can be also input from a file. If the file name is `data.txt`, then the result is obtained after running `distrib 50 < data.txt`. Each bucket interval listed at the end of the output is opened from the left side (it does not include the left boundary) and closed from the right side (which does include the right boundary). The number of occurrences follows each interval. The sum of occurrences is equal to the total number of observations. Dividing the number of occurrences by the sample size gives a probability that an observation is within a corresponding interval.

Maximum Loss, Maximum Drawdown, and Tails of the Distribution Most books estimating the performance of trading systems report information about the largest winning and largest losing trades, the average winning and average losing trades, and the maximum drawdown over the entire sequence of trades, all on a *per contract basis*. Information about the average profit and loss $E(A_{pl})$ is important for estimating the average account value $E(A_{i+1})$ at each step of the account evolution, as seen in Equation (4.22). However, the actual risk of trading greatly depends on the distribution function $f_{pl}(a_{pl})$. Given a probability of loss the distribution function $f_{pl}(a_{pl})$, the ratio of the allocation fraction b to the margin M, and the current account value A_i are the factors in Equation (4.21) that determine the absolute and relative amount of money that can be lost at the next step.

The largest losing trade can be found simply by comparing the realized losses of all trades in a sample. These trades may deal with complex positions consisting of different number of contracts traded at different prices. Under these conditions one way to come to a result is to compare losses on a per-contract basis. Let's say we have made two trades (four transactions) and the strategy vector (of actions) is (1, −1, 2, −2). The first trade created a long one-contract position, then exited it. After that, the second trade resulted in a long position consisting of two contracts, then closed it. If we divide P&L values of both trades by the size of the position (the number of contracts), then we can compare the results on a per-contract basis. This looks simple.

However, the process can become less obvious. Consider the strategy vector (1, 2, −1, −2). Given prices for all four transactions, we shall easily compute the final profit and/or loss. However, how can we combine such transactions into trades, and what would it mean to compare such trades on a per-contract basis? The answer depends on a set of *position offsetting rules*, and in general these rules are not unique. There is no standard here, but some practices accepted will be discussed and applied in later chapters. Intuitively, it is easier to operate by a notion of transaction (an individual action) than by a notion of trade (a combination of transactions). It may be helpful to review the definitions of the terms *transaction* and *trade* given in Chapter 2.

For the maximum potential profit strategy, the largest losing trade has no sense as a concept because such a strategy excludes both losing and breakeven trades. We shall return to this in the next chapter. The probability of a losing trade is equal to zero for any potential profit strategy.

Similar difficulties arise for drawdown, maximum drawdown, and average drawdown, if we want to compute them on a per-contract basis. In general, a drawdown is associated with a loss of equity (Jones 1999). Naturally, the total equity falls after a losing trade is completed. This is a drawdown. A sequence of consecutive losses is another form of drawdown. The fall of equity happens when a position is open and the price moves against it. It is very possible that the trade that created such a position will ultimately be profitable; however, during that trade, the total account equity falls because of the decreasing open position equity. This temporary loss of equity can be recorded as a drawdown and is very important for risk estimates. But even for a profitable trade, where the price moves only in a favorable direction, the total equity drops if a part of commissions and/or other fees is paid at the moment the first transaction is entered. Then this drop is also a drawdown. In Chapter 9, we consider more precise definitions of drawdown, and maximum and average drawdowns (Jones 1999), and apply them in writing the program `evaluate.cpp`. Here, it is enough to note that for the maximum potential profit strategy, if transaction cost is not zero, a drawdown can be negative.

If a trading system essentially reinvests profits, and creation of complex positions is a natural part of it, then reporting only the maximum drawdown on a per-contract basis is an inadequate way of judging the risk and performance of such a system. In such cases, it is very reasonable to report both the maximum drawdawn (as a maximum equity loss) and similar parameters on a per-contract basis when the computation algorithm is clearly defined.

Let's return now to the distribution function $f_{pl}(a_{pl})$. If the function is known, then we can compute how much money can be lost on the next trade within a specified probability. For instance, in the previous example using the interval [–100, –50], the probability of a loss is equal to 0.1. This means that 1 in 10 trades can result in a loss within this interval. However, the maximum loss per trade in this sample is –\$90. Let's assume that in a performance report we only see the largest losing trade with the value –\$90 and we do not know the distribution of profits and losses. Then we know that this loss interval can be reached but we do not know how often it may have happened. It is possible that every second trade had a loss from the interval [–100, –50]. Let's evaluate the two systems separately, where one experiences a –\$90 loss one time during 10 trades, and another shows a loss of –\$90 on every second trade.

In order to estimate the extreme values better and associate them with reasonable probabilities, there will need to be an adequate amount of sample data in the tails of the distribution function.

A complete distribution of profits and losses and similar information about maximum drawdown will be needed to evaluate corresponding probabilities of gaining or losing a specific amount of money. This information is more valuable than the average win, average loss, maximum loss, and maximum drawdown. Ironically, whenever the last four statistics are reported, a complete set of information was available or could easily have been produced with some minor programming changes.

Relationship to Value at Risk Once a position has been entered, until a trader undertakes some new action regarding the position, the evolution of profits and losses of this position is solely in hands of the market. Under these conditions, the calculation of *value at risk* (VaR) attempts to answer the question: "How bad can things get?" (Hull 1997). VaR is tenaciously calculated every day by most institutions that have market exposure in order to estimate their short-term risk exposure. The approach is based on the assumptions that a stochastic process determines price moves and the distribution of random variables driving this process is known. Very often, price changes dP are assumed to follow a lognormal distribution during a short time interval dt. This implies that the asset returns dP/P have a normal distribution during the same time interval. This corresponds to the expectation that, on average, higher prices should result in higher absolute returns or the same relative return on price. This also ensures that price is positive. If the distribution of random variables is known at some moment, then it is possible to give a definite answer to two questions: (1) "What is the probability that a price move will be of a certain size at that moment?" and (2) "What is the largest loss that can occur for a given probability level?" Both questions are complementary. It is easy to convert VaR into a price change using the dollar value of a one-point move. Because the entry price of an open position is known, we can now find the price level that may be hit with a specified probability.

Clearly, the VaR estimated as described does not depend on trader's activity. At the same time, the maximum loss per trade and the probability of reaching it deal with a trading system. The profits and losses as emphasized in Chapter 1 depend on both the trading system and the conditions of the market to which it was applied. This may make one think that the VaR is a more objective characteristic of the market than the empirical distribution of profits and losses highly dependent on the nature of the trading system. However, remember that the application of VaR requires the assumption of a model process for prices. The last is not very objective and introduces what is called *model risk.* For instance, since 1960 it has been known that asset returns do not obey a normal (Gaussian) distribution (Mandelbrot and Hudson 2004). The pioneering research in cotton and wheat prices completed by Benoit Mandelbrot (1963), followed by Eugene Fama's analysis of the blue-chip stocks constituting the Dow Jones index, and subsequent investigations of U.S. dollar/Japanese yen, and U.S. dollar/deutschemark exchange rates, and the monitoring of the Standard and Poor's (S&P) 500 index show that the markets are much riskier than explained by the ordinary assumption of Brownian motion (Mandelbrot, 2004). However, profits and losses are empirical and have no model risk. Both approaches imply a suffering assumption that stochastic behavior of the future repeats stochastic behavior of the past. Nevertheless, I think both approaches are complementary and can be useful.

Optimizing *b* We can now state that the variable A_{pl} is random. Additionally, the stochastic Equation (4.21) includes the cast operator `int()`. These realistic assumptions complicate evaluation. How can we get an optimal allocation fraction b^* under these conditions? Should the allocation fraction b be a constant? If not, then on which parameters should it depend? How do we find this dependence or function?

The optimal b^* given by the Equation (4.14) is conceptually close to *optimal f* introduced by Ralph Vince (1992). At the same time, both b^* and f are inherited from Kelly's approach (1956). In deriving Equation (4.14) from the beginning, the margin parameter M was used to determine the maximum number of contracts to be traded, based on the amount of money that could be allocated for a given trade. This is why optimal b^* depends on M. How can we obtain the optimal b^* if the allocated fraction b is fixed for all trades but A_{pl} is random and `int()` is used?

The following fragment of C++ code is equivalent to the iterative application of Equation (4.21):

```
...
vector<double> storage_for_G;
for(unsigned int j = 0; j < EXPERIMENTS; j++) {
    double A = A0;
    for(unsigned int i = 0; i < N; i++) {
        A += AplRandom() * int(b * A / M);
        if(A <= 0.0)
            throw ivalid_argument("Account is destroyed!");
    }
    double G = log(A / A0) / N;
    storage_for_G.push_back(G);
}
...
```

It is assumed that A_0, M, N (see the section "Denominations" above) are positive numbers; therefore, all essential checkups implemented prior to this block have specifically prevented division by zero and the evaluation of the log of nonpositive numbers. The growth function G is evaluated right after the inner for-loop completing N iterations. G is random because each iteration A_{pl} is random. After making N iterations, the first random value G_0 is obtained and stored in the vector `storage_for_G`. The outer for-loop is applied `EXPERIMENTS` number of times collecting G values. Finally, all values of G from the vector can be added to an object of the class `Distribution` (see Chapter 8). The last can estimate the average value of G for given b, A_0, M, and N. Under other equal conditions, the average value of G is a function of b. If we change b, then we get a new average value of G. Our task is to determine the value of b^* that maximizing average value of G.

This is a task for a class `Optimizer`, which goes beyond the scope of this book. Useful algorithms and code suitable for optimizers and solvers are described in Press et al. (1992). Instead of using a more efficient optimizer, we can arrive at the same solution by creating values of b from a systematic incrementation using small steps within the interval [0, 1]. The step 0.001 would mean a 0.1 percent allocation. Clearly, in this way, one or more b values maximizing the average value G can be found in the interval. This looks simple. However, where do we get the random values A_{pl}?

Random A_{pl} Building a random numbers generator with a distribution the same as the empirical distribution found in the example above will be a significant diversion from the main focus of this book. Because of that, I will not develop the framework for this process; however, I will describe one way in which this can be achieved.

First, we need a uniform random number generator that returns fractional numbers within the interval [0, 1] (any other interval with known boundaries can be created with a simple transformation). The algorithms are described in Knuth (1998). The C code for four suitable functions ran0, ran1, ran2, and ran3 generating uniformly distributed numbers can be found in Press et al. (1992). Particularly, the function ran2 is supplied with the following comment:

> *. . . ran2 provides perfect random numbers; a practical definition of "perfect" is that we will pay $1000 to the first reader who convinces us otherwise (by finding a statistical test that ran2 fails in a nontrivial way, excluding the ordinary limitations of a machine's floating-point representation).*

Second, one needs to transform uniformly distributed numbers into random numbers with a given distribution. In terms of the example building the A_{pl} distribution and described a few sections earlier, this means that (1) the numbers are generated randomly and (2) the numbers, for instance, from the interval (50, 100] are generated three times more often than the numbers from the interval (–100, –50]. The ratios of occurrences for other intervals must also correspond to the empirical estimation. Donald Knuth (1998) describes several algorithms and discusses the efficiency of different implementations. The following is an illustration suitable for our case:

Write the intervals and corresponding probabilities as a row of pairs (–100, –50], 1/10; (–50, 0], 3/10; (0, 50], 1/10; (50, 100], 3/10; (100, 150], 1/10; (150, 200], 1/10. Note that the sum of the probabilities is equal to 1. Following the example, we take the average values of two corresponding boundaries of an interval and associate them with increasing sums of probabilities (cumulative probabilities). This gives a new row –75, 1/10; –25, 4/10; 25, 5/10; 75, 8/10; 125, 9/10; 175, 1. The cumulative probabilities divide the interval [0, 1] into subintervals

–75, [0, 1/10); –25, [1/10, 4/10); 25, [4/10, 5/10); 75, [5/10, 8/10); 125, [8/10, 9/10); 175, [9/10, 1]. A random number generator then works as follows: Get a random number uniformly distributed in the interval [0, 1] using, let's say, the function ran2. Let's say that the random number is 0.543. Find an interval of cumulative probabilities to which this number belongs. This turns out to be [5/10, 8/10). Return the corresponding value of $A_{pl} = 75$. Obtain a new random number from ran2, say 0.2327. Find an interval of cumulative probabilities to which this number belongs [1/10, 4/10). Return the corresponding value of $A_{pl} = -25$. Generate the necessary number of A_{pl} values. Use them for getting G as shown in the sample code above.

Instead of working with discrete probabilities and P&L values, one could apply interpolation (linear is the simplest) and/or approximation techniques. This can replace a distribution histogram with a smoother curve. It is necessary to be sure that the integral (area) under such a curve is equal to 1. For a cumulative distribution function represented above by discrete intervals of cumulative probabilities, a smoothing algorithm must preserve the monotonic nondecreasing properties of the dependence. These methods (Press et al. 1992; Dierckx 1995; De Boor 1978) are also beyond the scope of this book.

The result is that a constant optimal b^* can be estimated for an empirically built distribution of random P&L values. It is hard to believe that this value is independent of the market conditions (i.e., the potential profit) and is determined solely by a trading system.

Allocation Fraction *b* as a Function of Other Parameters The method described above will produce a fixed optimal value b^*. The idea behind this trading style is to increase the number of contracts traded when equity grows and decrease it when equity falls. This is achieved by allocating a constant fraction of the currently available equity for each new trade. Using a single fixed value of b can still lead to an undesirable sequence of large or quick losses. Such an unsuccessful real-life experience may denote changing market conditions (instability) and the inability of trading system to adapt to these changes. Persisting with the same system may result in a long sequence of losses. If money management is applied independently of the system, then the trading signals are generated by the system but the number of contracts (the position size) is determined by money management. It could then be possible and desirable to reduce the number of contracts on the next trade faster than dictated by b^*.

Several sources (Vince 1992; Jones 1999; Williams 1999) discuss interesting allocation strategies with variable fractional allocations. They consider faster and slower rates for increasing and/or decreasing the number of contracts for a next trade based on the results of trading. The same authors also consider situations where the number of contracts should be less than the maximum permitted by margin and measured by the drawdown, multiples of drawdown, or combinations of drawdown and margin. Such assumptions applied to our case would mean that b^* is a function of some variable. But how could we determine this function?

For the first step, it is most useful to get b^* values as a function of initial conditions $b^* = b^*(A_0, M, N)$ by applying the method already described. For trading a given market with constant M the function depends only on the two variables A_0 and N and represents a surface, which can be visualized. The influence of A_0 and N will be determined by how flat that surface appears.

The results obtained in this chapter are sufficient to consider the application of money management to a potential profit strategy. This will be done in the next chapter.

CONCLUSIONS

For an artificial case with constant trading results and a fractional number of contracts and account size, the following are formulas corresponding to futures trading:

- The best allocation fraction is $b^* = (p_w - (1 - p_w)A_l/A_w)\, M/A_l$.
- The maximum growth rate is $G^* = p_w \ln(p_w) + p_l \ln(p_l) + p_w \ln(1 + A_w/A_l) + p_l \ln(1 + A_l/A_w)$.
- The condition making b^* reachable is $0 < p_w A_w - p_l A_l < A_w A_l/M$.

  The relationship of these formulas to the Kelly and Shannon formulas is shown.

- The Equation $A_{i+1} = A_i + \text{int}(bA_i/M)\,[A_w T_i (T_i + 1) - A_l T_i (T_i - 1)]/2$ is suggested to represent the evolution of an account, where the number of contracts is an integer. A corresponding C++ program is written. It can evaluate results from a row of profits and losses under more realistic conditions.
- The stochastic version $A_{i+1} = A_i + A_{pl}\, \text{int}(bA_i/M)$ is suggested. The way to estimate the distribution of the random variable A_{pl} and create simulations is proposed.

CHAPTER 5

Money Management for Potential Profit Strategy

The r- and l-algorithms from Chapter 3 produce a potential profit strategy that properly handles transaction costs and generates the maximum profit and loss (P&L) under the conditions that each trade has the same number of contracts. In this chapter, we will apply the money management results obtained in the previous chapter to a potential profit strategy. The goal is to increase the P&L further under the restriction of a *self-financing account*, one that does not use capital other than the initial investment and subsequent profits and loss. In order to achieve an increased P&L, we must first be able to trade a greater number of contracts at times recommended by the r- or l-algorithm and within limits allowed by the total equity currently in the account. The second step is to optimally increase positions during the intervals between the times recommended by the r- or l-algorithm as allowed by the increased trading power of the account. Both steps represent a level of P&L optimization based on the total equity and trading power. This optimization achieves the maximum P&L and answers the question: "What is a minimum investment required to achieve a targeted P&L?" At this point, we will consider only the results of trading a single market and a portfolio of a single instrument. However, each long or short position may now include several contracts bought or sold at different times and at different prices. This chapter introduces the classes `Position`, `Trade`, and `Trades`, and illustrates how the two types of P&L improvements can be achieved. The two corresponding algorithms are the subject of the next chapter.

THE BEST ALLOCATION FRACTION FOR POTENTIAL PROFIT STRATEGY

A potential profit strategy must reverse its positions one or more times after it enters in order to exit that market. Each reversal transaction can be decomposed into a transaction that offsets the previous position and one that initiates an opposite position. A pair of transactions initiating and offsetting a position is called a round-trip trade. If a potential profit strategy is not a "do nothing strategy," then it includes at least one round-trip trade and each of them is profitable (see property 1 in Chapter 2). A potential profit strategy does not contain breakeven trades (P&L = 0). This implies that, for potential profit strategy, pl = 0. At first glance we would need to postulate that for such a strategy Al = 0. However, to be precise we should say that such a strategy simply does not contain trades for which P&L ≲ 0. In other words, for this type of strategy, the concept Al makes no sense. At the same time, statements pw = 1 and Aw > 0 do make sense. The relationship pw + pl = 1 remains valid. However, in general, Aw is not constant. For a given price and cost time interval, all values Aw are well determined. Nevertheless, Aw can be viewed as a random variable obeying some distribution function fw(aw). Similar to the P&L and potential profit strategy, this function becomes a market characteristic under given transaction costs.

If we are allowed to trade a fractional number of contracts and perform that accounting with fractional penny amounts, then setting $p_l = 0$ in Equation (4.14) gives:

$$b_{pps}{}^* = p_w\, M / A_l = M / A_l \tag{5.01}$$

The subscript *pps* says that this is for a potential profit strategy. The term A_l in Equation (5.01) makes no sense under our conditions. Instead of removing the notion of A_l completely, we will pretend that it quickly goes to zero. Then the best allocation fraction quickly reaches infinity $b_{pps}{}^* = +\infty$.

Another way to come to the same conclusion is to set $L = 0$ (no losing or breakeven trades). Then the relative change in the account value after $N = W$ trades are completed is obtained from Equation (4.10).

$$A_N / A_0 = (1 + bA_w / M)^W = (1 + bA_w / M)^N \tag{5.02}$$

This does not involve the senseless constant A_l. The growth function built from this equation becomes:

$$G_{pps} = \lim_{N\to\infty} (\ln(A_N / A_0) / N) = p_w \ln(1 + bA_w / M) = \ln(1 + bA_w / M) \tag{5.03}$$

Considered as a function of b, the value of G_{pps} has no maximum. Indeed,

$$dG_{pps} / db = A_w / (M + bA_w) \tag{5.04}$$

Because all terms involved in Equation (5.04) are positive, the right side of the equation is never equal to zero. It moves quickly to zero, as b moves quickly to positive infinity. If one were able to follow this approach to create a potential profit strategy, then the best tactic would be to allocate everything available to each new trade.

In real life, the allocation of all resources for a "sure deal" is not always possible (or desirable) because financial obligations may require that the allocated money be recalled before the profit is realized. Such circumstances are out of the scope of this discussion.

SELF-FINANCING RESTRICTION

As has just been shown, the optimal allocation fraction can be > 1. Similar conditions may arise in cases other than the potential profit strategy. Ralph Vince (1992) has shown that optimal f can be ≥ 1. It follows from Equation (4.14) that the condition $b^* \geq 1$ is equivalent to:

$$p_w A_w - p_l A_l \geq A_w A_l / M \qquad (5.05)$$

Comparing this with Inequality (4.19), let $p_w = 0.6$, $p_l = 0.4$, $A_w = 1000$, $A_l = 900$, and $M = 5000$. Then Inequality (5.05) is satisfied because $240 \geq 180$. Under these conditions, Equation (4.14) gives $b^* = 1.2 > 1$. Then 20 percent of the current account should be taken from an outside source; otherwise, the best allocation fraction cannot be used. What does this result mean?

The margin requirement is specified by exchanges and brokerage firms and becomes the operational requirement for all traders. Consider a strategy that has average loss of $900, which is much less than the required margin of $5,000. When formulating a strategy, a trader may pretend to have privileged conditions that allows lower margin, but in real life the voice is not heard: the trader must obey the same rules as other participants. Even though a trader creates a "proprietary" strategy that systematically maintains losses much lower than margin, the regulatory agencies do not take this into account and reduce margin requirements on a case-by-case basis. The required margin is important because it impacts both financing and rate of return.

The self-financing account requirement is $b \leq 1$. The optimal $b^* = +\infty$ cannot be realized because margin is fixed; therefore, the maximum reachable b must be selected. If only the self-financing requirement is applied, then the maximum value of b for a potential profit strategy is equal to 1. Maintenance margin restrictions may further reduce the value of b.

MINIMAL A_0

Let the r- or l-algorithms generate a potential profit strategy that is not a "do nothing" strategy. What is the minimal account cash balance A_0 required to buy or sell U number of contracts at the same time that the strategy enters the first futures position? First, the account must have U times the initial margin M or $A_0 \geq UM$. Once the position is open, in order to avoid a margin call the total equity of the account must not drop below U times maintenance margin M_m amount, typically 75% of UM. A realistic assumption is $M \geq M_m$. The total equity is the sum of a current cash balance and *open futures position equity* (unrealized profits or losses, which we will also call *open position equity*).

At the moment of the first transaction, we will assume that the cash balance is reduced because of the transaction fee payment. This cost will be calculated as U times one-half the sum of the commissions and other fees per contract based on a round-trip trade. At the time the first trade is entered, the *open futures trade equity* is zero because the entry price and the market price are the same. For instance, if the round-trip cost, C, is split into two equal portions $C/2$ to be applied to the two transactions forming the first round-trip trade, then right after the first transaction the total equity must drop to $A_0 - UC/2$ due entirely to posting of transaction costs reducing the *cash balance* but not the open position equity. The immediate maintenance margin requirement is that $A_0 - UC/2 \geq UM_m$. The relevant intersection of inequalities is $A_0 \geq U(M_m + C/2) \cap A_0 \geq UM$. If $M - M_m > C/2$, then the condition $A_0 \geq UM$ prevails. Otherwise, the inequality $A_0 \geq U(M_m + C/2)$ must be obeyed. These inequalities are sufficient for the determination of A_0 only if the absolute transaction cost is the same at each point in time. The last property ensures that the *r*- or *l*-algorithms select the best buy or sell points on the *s*-interval at price extremes. Hence, further price changes on the *s*-interval may only increase the open position equity and leave initial transaction costs as the only factor reducing the total equity. Under these conditions the moment of a transaction is the moment of maximum decline in total equity for a potential profit strategy.

In general, elements of the cost vector $\boldsymbol{C}$ can be different. Then transactions on the *s*-interval must be executed at prices and costs minimizing the value $kP_i + C_i$ for a buy or maximizing the value $kP_i - C_i$ for a sell, respectively (see property 5 in Chapter 2 and related explanations in Chapter 3). For example, after taking a long position, the price may immediately decrease at the next point $i + 1$. That point is not selected as the best buy point if the cost C_{i+1} is too high and the value $kP_{i+1} + C_{i+1}$ is not a local minimum on the *s*-interval. However, in terms of maintaining the amount UM_m only the price P_{i+1} but not the cost C_{i+1} is relevant for determining the decline in the open position equity and, as a result, the total account equity. Advancing from point i to $i + 1$, under a lower-price scenario, the total equity drops to $A_0 - UC_i + kU(P_{i+1} - P_i)$, where the difference in the parentheses is negative. It is this value that must be $\geq UM_m$. Let's use point $i + 1$ as an illustration, although it can be any point between the first and second transactions. In order to avoid a margin call, we need to find A_0 such that it will compensate for the total equity drop in advance. To accomplish this, it is essential to search for both the minimums of $kP_i + C_i$ and P_i for a buy trade and both maximums of $kP_i - C_i$ and P_i for a sell trade on an interval between the two transactions.

Why in practice is C_{i+1} irrelevant for maintaining enough account equity to hold a position? The only possible explanation is that the cost of each transaction is substantially less than the initial and maintenance margins. This ensures that closing a position in the case of a margin call does not result in a negative account balance because there was enough capital preserved to pay all fees. If the last condition is not assumed, then it is necessary to track both price and costs in order to determine the potential total equity drop. Following the practices accepted by the futures industry, we will also consider only effects of price change on the open position equity.

For the first trade, if the best buy point is designated as the index value *buy* and the lowest price between *buy* and the next transaction is found at the index value *lowest*, where *lowest* $\geq$ *buy*, then the maximum drop in the total equity for the long position between the two transactions is equal to $U[k(P_{lowest} - P_{buy}) - C_{buy}]$. Then $A_0 \geq U[M_m + C_{buy} + k(P_{buy} - P_{lowest})] \cap A_0 \geq UM$ and the minimum starting account cash balance is determined as:

$$\text{If } M_m + C_{buy} + k(P_{buy} - P_{lowest}) \geq M, \\ \text{then } A_0 = U[M_m + C_{buy} + k(P_{buy} - P_{lowest})] \text{ else } A_0 = UM \tag{5.06}$$

Similarly, if the best selling point is found at index value *sell* and the highest price between *sell* and the next transaction is found at index value *highest*, where $highest \geq sell$, then the maximum drop in total equity for the short position between the two transactions is equal to $U[k(P_{sell} - P_{highest}) - C_{sell}]$. Then $A_0 \geq U[M_m + C_{sell} + k(P_{highest} - P_{sell})] \cap A_0 \geq UM$ and the minimum starting account cash balance is determined as

$$\text{If } [M_m + C_{sell} + k(P_{highest} - P_{sell})] \geq M, \\ \text{then } A_0 = U[M_m + C_{sell} + k(P_{highest} - P_{sell})] \text{ else } A_0 = UM \quad (5.07)$$

The C++ implementation of this method is shown in the header file: `PotentialProfit-MinAccountAlg.h`

```
#ifndef __PotentialProfitMinAccountAlg_h__
#define __PotentialProfitMinAccountAlg_h__

#include <cmath>
#include <vector>
#include <sstream>
#include <stdexcept>
using namespace std;

#include "Prices.h"
#include "Cost.h"
#include "SpecCost.h"
#include "Strategy.h"
#include "PotentialProfitAlg.h"
using namespace PPBOOK;

namespace PPBOOK {

    inline  double
    potential_profit_min_account_alg(const Prices& prices,
        const vector<Cost<SpecAbsoluteCost> >& costs,
        unsigned int nContracts, double imargin, double mmargin,
        Strategy& pps)
    {
        // Checks input
        if(imargin <= 0.0) {
            ostringstream   s;
            s   << "potential_profit_min_account_alg: imargin "
                << imargin << " (initial margin) must be positive";
            throw   invalid_argument(s.str());
        }
```

```
if(mmargin <= 0.0) {
    ostringstream  s;
    s << "potential_profit_min_account_alg: mmargin "
        << mmargin << " (maintenance margin) must be positive";
    throw  invalid_argument(s.str());
}
if(mmargin > imargin) {
    ostringstream   s;
    s   << "potential_profit_min_account_alg: mmargin "
        << mmargin << " must be less than or equal to imargin "
        << imargin;
    throw  invalid_argument(s.str());
}
// Builds potential profit strategy
pps = potential_profit_ralg(prices, costs, nContracts);
// Computes initial minimal account cash balance
if(pps.size() == 0)
    return  0.0;
unsigned int    buy, sell;
buy = sell = (unsigned int)pps.size();
for(unsigned int j = 0; j < pps.size(); j++) {
    if(pps[j] > 0) {
        buy = j;
        break;
    }
    else if(pps[j] < 0) {
        sell = j;
        break;
    }
}
if(buy != pps.size()) {
    unsigned int    lowest = buy;
    for(unsigned int j = buy + 1; pps[j] == 0; j++)
        if(prices[j] < prices[lowest])
            lowest = j;
    double  v = mmargin + costs[buy].cost() +
            (prices[buy] - prices[lowest])
            * prices.tickValue() / prices.tick();
    return  nContracts * ((v < imargin) ? imargin : v);
}
else if(sell != pps.size()) {
    unsigned int    highest = sell;
    for(unsigned int j = sell + 1; pps[j] == 0; j++)
        if(prices[j] > prices[highest])
            highest = j;
```

```
            double  v = mmargin + costs[sell].cost() +
                    (prices[highest] - prices[sell])
                    * prices.tickValue() / prices.tick();
            return  nContracts * ((v < imargin) ? imargin : v);
        }
        return  0.0;
    }

} // PPBOOK

#endif /* __PotentialProfitMinAccountAlg_h__ */
```

The function `potential_profit_min_account_alg` uses an object of prices and a vector of costs, the number of contracts, initial margin, maintenance margin, and a nonconstant reference to an object of the class `Strategy`. After checking the consistency of margin values, it reuses the *r*-algorithm's `potential_profit_ralg` for building a potential profit strategy returned via the input-output parameter `pps`. Then it computes and returns A_0. In order to accomplish this, the function searches for the first (entry) and second (exit or reversal) transactions recommended by the potential profit strategy. It also keeps track of the times of the maximum and minimum prices, which were dependent on a buy or sell type of entry transaction. The rest is the C++ code for Statements (5.06) and (5.07). The function returns 0 for a "do nothing" potential profit strategy.

ACTIONS AND POSITIONS TEST4.CPP

The vector $\boldsymbol{U}$ represented by the class `Strategy` introduced in Chapter 2 and shows how many contracts are bought or sold in a single transaction. It will contain zeros for "do nothing" actions. This vector of actions can be converted into a vector of open long or short contracts using the C++ standard algorithm `partial_sum`. For instance, the vector of actions (0, 0, 1, 0, 0, –2, 1, 0) corresponds to the vector of opened contracts (0, 0, 1, 1, 1, –1, 0, 0). Another C++ standard algorithm `adjacent_difference` is able to convert the vector of opened contracts back to vector of actions. The following program from the source file `test4.cpp` illustrates this:

```
#include <iostream>
#include <numeric>
using namespace std;

#include "Strategy.h"
using namespace PPBOOK;

typedef vector<int> Position;
typedef ostream_iterator<int, char, char_traits<char> > IntOutput;
```

```
int main(int, char*[])
{
    try {
        // Initializes Strategy vector by a built-in array saving
        // on for-loop and push_back calls.
        const Strategy::value_type  v[] = {0, 0, 1, 0, 0, -2, 1, 0};
        Strategy s(v + 0, v + sizeof(v) / sizeof(Strategy::value_type));

        // Outputs initial strategy to cout saving on for-loop
        IntOutput   out(cout, " ");
        copy(s.begin(), s.end(), out);
        cout    << endl;

        // Converts Strategy to Position containing current number of
        // contracts. Avoids for-loop by reusing partial_sum.
        Position    p;
        partial_sum(s.begin(), s.end(), back_inserter(p));

        // Outputs positions to cout saving on for-loop
        copy(p.begin(), p.end(), out);
        cout    << endl;

        // Confirms that adjacent_difference recovers Strategy
        // from Position. Directly outputs result to cout.
        adjacent_difference(p.begin(), p.end(), out);
        cout    << endl;
    }
    catch(const exception& e) {
        cerr    << e.what() << endl;
    }
    catch(...) {
        cerr    << "Unknown exception" << endl;
    }
    return  0;
}
```

It is amazing how C++ can be expressive. Modern C++ features are not only able to provide industrial strength software but confer aesthetic enjoyment. The program above applies the constructor of a `vector` from range iterators, the template class `ostream_iterator`, the adapter `back_inserter`, and the algorithms `copy`, `partial_sum`, and `adjacent_difference`. It outputs the predicted result:

```
0 0 1 0 0 -2 1 0
0 0 1 1 1 -1 0 0
0 0 1 0 0 -2 1 0
```

The `typedef` definition of the class `Position` is suitable if each long or short position contains contracts bought or sold at one price (*simple positions*). The class `Strategy` representing actions has been applied for the development of the *r*- and *l*-algorithms. Similar algorithms can be designed using the notion of a simple position and the class `Position` defined in the example. This follows from the relationship between simple positions and actions shown above.

The class `Position` should also be sufficient for the second of the major three algorithms developed in this book to maximize profits. This second algorithm is referred to as the *first P&L reserve algorithm*. What does the word *reserve* mean in this context? It means a *reserve of improvement* or *capital available for additional trading* of the potential profit strategy. Where may this reserve come from so that it increases the profit of a potential profit strategy? It may come from increasing the number of contracts traded at times recommended by a potential profit strategy, that is, trading a larger number of contracts at times when reversal transactions occur and when permitted by the increased trading power resulting from accumulated profits. Hence, the first P&L reserve algorithm reinvests profits at times recommended by a potential profit strategy. This algorithm is more complicated than the *r*- and *l*-algorithms. However, it does not have to be built from scratch but can be created on top of the *r*- and *l*-algorithms. This algorithm is a child of the potential profit strategy.

Although the first P&L reserve algorithm outperforms its parent, the potential profit strategy, there is additional potential for improvement. This leads to the *second P&L reserve algorithm* that can generate even larger profits. In the second reserve, the size of the position can be increased selectively at times between the points recommended by the *r*- and *l*-algorithms. This leads to a notion of a complex position where transactions of one type are done at different times and most likely at different prices. Because of the complications, the use of the position `vector<int>` for the development of the second P&L reserve algorithm is inconvenient. Complex positions require a more intelligent class. In order to estimate the change in the total equity of a complex position and calculate the current cash balance that might be the result of the partial offsetting of a position, we need to know the rules set by the futures industry. How these positions are handled is shown in the next section followed by a section describing the rules for offsetting positions.

THE FIRST AND SECOND P&L RESERVES

Using an example of gold (GC) prices (429, 428, 443, 455, 449) and transaction costs (50, 50, 50, 50, 50), the output from the `maxprof` program shown in Chapter 3 is:

```
echo GC 50 429 428 443 455 449 | maxprof
   #        GC      Cost     R     L
   0        429       50     0     0
   1        428       50     1     1
   2        443       50     0     0
   3        455       50    -2    -2
   4        449       50     1     1
R-P&L = 3100 L-P&L = 3100
```

The vector of positions is (0, 1, 1, –1, 0). Clearly, if each action is multiplied by a positive integer, then the P&L increases proportionally. Because the cost is the same for each transaction the maximum total equity drop between the first and second transactions (indices 1 and 3) is observed at the moment of the first transaction and explained by the fee payment. Under these conditions, Statement (5.06) determines A_0. Initial M and maintenance M_m margins for GC are set at $1,350 and $1,000 per contract, respectively. As previously explained, $P_{buy} = P_{lowest}$, then $M_m + C_{buy} + 0 = 1000 + 50 = 1050 < M = 1350$, and $A_0 = UM = 1 \times 1350 = 1350$. This amount is needed in order to enter the market with one contract. This amount should not be confused with the cash needed to open an account at a particular brokerage firm. A brokerage firm may require from $5,000 to $10,000 or more based on their perception of risk, or simply to qualify the customer. There is no contradiction here. One may open the account, satisfying the broker's requirements, but later withdraw part of deposit. Or the account value may decline due to losses from unsuccessful trades. Some firms may charge a maintenance fee, if the account drops below certain level or is not active.

The current cash balance immediately after the first transaction is $1,350 – $50 = $1,300. The open position equity is 0. The total equity is $1,300. The price then increases to the level indicated at point 3, $455/oz., so the open position equity becomes 100 × (455 – 428) = $2,700. The total equity is then equal to $1,300 + $2,700 = $4,000. The short sell action –2 is split into (–1, –1) where the first –1 offsets the long position. The offsetting action causes a charge of the $50 transaction fee and, at the same time, credits the trade profit of $2,700 to the current cash balance giving $1,300 – $50 + $2,700 = $3,950. This is the balance before entering the next trade, a short sale of an additional one contract, corresponding to taking the short position –1 at the point 3. Of course, both contracts are sold at the same price 455. However, with initial margin of $1,350 and the cash balance of $3,950, we have enough funds to sell two (the total action of –3 liquidates one and enters two new trades) but not one (total action –2) contract at point 3. This is the case of the first reserve where the excess P&L at the point of new transaction is used for adding a contract. The *r*- or *l*-algorithm points are used, but we sell short more contracts because the total equity has grown and the unused funds exceed the additional margin requirement.

The strategy that recognizes the first P&L reserve case is (0, 1, 0, –3, 2). Adding money management, the ability to change the number of contracts, to the potential profit strategy (0, 1, 0, –2, 1) creates the new strategy (0, 1, 0, –3, 2) which outperforms the parent. Indeed, P&L = –$50 [cost of initiating long position 1] + $100 × (455 – 428) [profit offsetting long position 1] – $50 [cost of offsetting long position 1] – 2 × $50 [cost of initiating short position –2] – 2 × $100 × (449 – 455) [profit offsetting short position –2] – 2 × $50 [cost of offsetting short position –2] = –$50 + $2,700 – $50 – $100 + $1,200 – $100 = $3,600. This is $3,600 – $3,100 = $500 greater. The extra gain comes from one more additional contract sold short at the point 3 as –1 × $100 × (449 – 455) = $600. The last amount is reduced by the initiating cost of $50 and the offsetting cost of $50 for this extra position.

In order to see where the second reserve case may be applied, we check the total equity at point 2. The current open position equity is equal to $100 × (443 – 428) = $1,500. The total equity is equal to $1,350 – $50 + $1,500 = $2,800. Because the position is still open the trading power of the account is determined as total equity less the total initial margin on all open positions. The trading power $2,800 – $1,350 = $1,450 permits us to buy one more contract than the one we already have. As events develop further this clearly makes sense. The first part of the strategy becomes (0, 1, 1,...). Right after this second transaction the cash balance drops to the value \$1,250 = \$1,300 – \$50 because of the additional fee payment. The open position equity on two contracts is still \$1,500 = \$1,500 (the first position) + 0 (the additional contract). Because the price rises at the point 3 the net returns from this more complex long position, now consisting of two contracts one bought at 428 at point 1 and the second bought at 443 at point 2, increase the total equity to \$1,350 – \$50 + \$100 × (443 – 428) – \$50 + 2 × \$100 × (455 – 443) – 2 × \$50 = \$1,300 + \$1,500 – \$50 + \$2,400 – \$100 = \$2,750 + \$2,400 – \$100 = \$5,050. This total equity now permits us to go short int(5050 / 1350) = 3 contracts. Hence, the final strategy is (0, 1, 1, –5, 3). This corresponds to the vector of positions (0, 1, 2, –3, 0). The P&L is computed as –\$50 + \$1,500 – \$50 + \$2,400 – \$100 – 3 × \$50 [the cost of going short three contracts] – 3 × \$100 × (449 – 455) [the profit from offsetting the short position of three contracts] – 3 × \$50 = \$3,700 – \$150 + \$1,800 – \$150 = \$5,200. The following are the profits and final cash balances for the three strategies in increasing order:

```
(0, 1, 0, -2, 1) 3100 4450 potential profit strategy
(0, 1, 0, -3, 2) 3600 4950 potential profit strategy + 1st P&L reserve
(0, 1, 1, -5, 3) 5200 6550 potential profit strategy + 2nd P&L reserve
```

All three start from the same initial cash balance \$1,350, the minimum required for buying a single contract. In this example, the second P&L reserve case also includes the first P&L reserve case.

What is the relationship between these three strategies? The use of the first P&L reserve case does not differ much from the potential profit strategy. It is a reversal system. It executes the same buy and sell order at the same points as the corresponding potential profit strategy. The only difference is that the size of transactions may gradually increase.

The second P&L reserve case is not a reversal system as seen at points 2, where the long position grows in size. This is not a point where transactions occurred in the potential profit strategy or in applying the reserve case 1. How can this be consistent with property 4 and its corresponding proof in Chapter 2? Property 4 works with positions of the same size. In fact, the proof of property 4 indicates that buying one contract at point 1 and one contract at point 2, at 428 and then 443, respectively, causes us to give up part of the profit that would have been achieved by buying two contracts at the first price of 428. This implies that a true basis for maximum profit is the potential profit strategy. However, this ignores the fact that transactions must occur based on the trading power of an account. Yes, buying two contracts at 428 would be better *if it were possible*, but with an initial cash balance of \$1,350, only one could be bought. The second P&L reserve strategy exploits these situations.

Another feature of the second P&L reserve strategy is that between the two consecutive reversal points suggested by *r*- or *l*-algorithm, positions are added only so that the already established positions are increased. There are no other good reversal points between those proposed by the *r*- or *l*-algorithms.

- The potential profit strategy applied to a single market has a fundamental meaning and is the basis for the first and second P&L reserve strategies.
- The first and second P&L reserve strategies are extensions of the corresponding potential profit strategy. They take into account the self-financing account restriction, a limited

initial cash balance, and the initial and maintenance margins required by futures regulatory agencies and brokerage firms.

RULES FOR OFFSETTING POSITIONS

The potential profit strategy and the first P&L reserve strategy consist of simple positions where all contracts are bought or sold at one moment based on one price occurrence and with one cost applied. The second P&L reserve strategy may contain complex positions where each position may have more than one contract, each bought or sold at different times and most likely at different prices and costs. Estimating the open position equity needed to build corresponding algorithms becomes more complicated. One way to accomplish this is to create a weighted average of prices using the number of contracts. But this can lead to average prices that do not correspond to minimum tick value given in the contract specifications.

Another is to follow prescribed rules for offsetting complex positions. These rules are based on the trade entry date and the trade price. In Chapter 1, the classes for date and time were intentionally not introduced. When working with a single market (a stream of prices), dates can be tracked by one integer index and the time within a day can be tracked by a second integer index. The first index simply increases as each day changes. The second index increases for each new intraday transaction, while the first remains unchanged. Once the first index increases, the second restarts from its initial value. This is as complex as we need for a single market. However, a portfolio of several types of contracts requires the synchronization of events, that is, we would like all the time stamps associated with every price in one market to also appear in every other market. While very fine integer indices might help, a better way would be to rely on classes for date and time. Developing such classes of good quality is out of the scope of this book.

It is a standard practice that long and short transactions executed within one day (one trading session) are offset before those transactions held from a previous day. Typically, the buy order with the lowest price is matched with the sell order of the lowest price. Then the next lowest priced buy is matched with the next lowest priced sell, and so on. Depending on the number and type of transactions, some of them can be left unmatched. These unresolved transactions are matched against the oldest open positions from previous dates. This is similar to the queuing process called *First In, First Out*, known as *FIFO* in computer science literature. This is analogous to the behavior of persons "standing in line." When several open positions exist on the previous date, then offsetting is done using the lowest-priced buy or the lowest-priced sell, depending on the position currently being matched. While nuances can be different (for instance, *last in, first out [LIFO] accounting* can be applied to match positions). I will rely on these three offsetting rules in the future.

CLASSES TRADE AND TRADES

Two opposite transactions of the same size can be grouped as one trade, where the second transaction completely offsets the first one. This offsetting shifts open position equity to realized equity and changes the cash balance existing in an account prior to the trade by adding the profit or subtracting the loss. Additionally, both transaction costs reduce the available cash balance. Finally, applying the rules for offsetting positions allows us to subdivide all transactions into a sequence of completed trades and possibly the remaining complex open position consisting of one type of transaction (a buy or sell) with a different number of contracts entered at different prices and at different costs. For analysis of individual trades, it is convenient to have a dedicated class `Trade` and a class aggregating several trades. The following is the header file `Trade.h` containing both classes:

```
#ifndef __Trade_h__
#define __Trade_h__

#include <cmath>
#include <sstream>
#include <stdexcept>
#include <vector>
using namespace std;

namespace PPBOOK {

    class Trade {
    public:
        // Absolute (not fractional) entry and exit costs must be given
        // per contract. Entry and exit indices should correspond to
        // prices in an object of the class Prices.
        Trade(double entryPrice, double entryCost, int entrySize,
            size_t entryIndex, double exitPrice, double exitCost,
            size_t exitIndex, double pricePointValue)
            : entryPrice_(entryPrice), entryCost_(entryCost),
            entrySize_(entrySize), entryIndex_(entryIndex),
            exitPrice_(exitPrice), exitCost_(exitCost),
            exitIndex_(exitIndex), pricePointValue_(pricePointValue)
        {
            if(!entrySize)
                throw invalid_argument(
                        "Trade entry size must be non-zero.");
            if(entryPrice <= 0.0) {
                ostringstream   s;
                s   << "Trade entry price " << entryPrice
                    << " must be positive.";
                throw   invalid_argument(s.str());
            }
            if(entryCost < 0.0) {
                ostringstream   s;
                s   << "Trade entry cost " << entryCost
```

```
                << " must be non-negative.";
            throw   invalid_argument(s.str());
        }
        if(exitPrice <= 0.0) {
            ostringstream   s;
            s   << "Trade exit price " << exitPrice
                << " must be positive.";
            throw   invalid_argument(s.str());
        }
        if(exitCost < 0.0) {
            ostringstream   s;
            s   << "Trade exit cost " << exitCost
                << " must be non-negative.";
            throw   invalid_argument(s.str());
        }
        if(entryIndex > exitIndex) {
            ostringstream   s;
            s   << "Trade entry index " << (unsigned int) entryIndex
                << " must be less than or equal to exit index "
                << (unsigned int) exitIndex;
            throw   invalid_argument(s.str());
        }
        if(pricePointValue <= 0.0) {
            ostringstream   s;
            s   << "Trade price point value " << pricePointValue
                << " must be positive.";
            throw   invalid_argument(s.str());
        }
    }

    double  entryPrice() const {return entryPrice_;}
    double  entryCost() const {return entryCost_;}
    int     entrySize() const {return entrySize_;}
    size_t  entryIndex() const {return entryIndex_;}
    double  exitPrice() const {return exitPrice_;}
    double  exitCost() const {return exitCost_;}
    size_t  exitIndex() const {return exitIndex_;}
    double  pricePointValue() const {return pricePointValue_;}

    // Does not include transaction costs.
    double  equityChange() const {return (exitPrice() - entryPrice())
                * entrySize() * pricePointValue();}
    // Does not include equity change.
    double  totalCost() const {return (entryCost() + exitCost())
                * abs(entrySize());}
```

```
        // Returns profit & loss value.
        double  pl() const {return equityChange() - totalCost();}
        // Returns profit & loss per unit (contract, share).
        double  plPerUnit() const {return pl() / abs(entrySize());}

    private:
        double  entryPrice_;
        double  entryCost_;
        int     entrySize_;
        size_t  entryIndex_;
        double  exitPrice_;
        double  exitCost_;
        size_t  exitIndex_;
        double  pricePointValue_;
    };

    typedef vector<Trade>                           Trades;

} // PPBOOK

#endif /* __Trade_h__ */
```

The class `Trade` was not defined as a template dependent on price and/or cost specifications. Instead, it accepts arbitrary positive prices and non-negative costs. In addition to the entry price and cost, and exit price and cost combinations, it records an entry size for each trade. The exit size of a trade is equal to its negative entry size. The entry and exit indices reference an object from which prices are obtained. This can be an object of the class `Prices`. Only the basic consistency of prices, costs, and indices can be checked without access to specification classes. It is a responsibility of classes using the class `Trade` to ensure the desirable consistency. The class `Trade` applies default copy and assignment semantics.

A simple `typedef` introducing a `vector` of trades is sufficient for our purpose. The class `Trades` helps to build a P&L distribution and collect other interesting statistics. This class can be used not only with potential profit but also other strategies. My task now is to write a class suitable for handling complex trading positions.

CLASS POSITION

The following is the definition of the class `Position` from the header file `Position.h` that is suitable for our needs:

```
#ifndef __Position_h__
#define __Position_h__
```

```
#include <deque>
#include <vector>
#include <ostream>
#include <sstream>
#include <stdexcept>
#include <numeric>
using namespace std;

#include "Trade.h"
using namespace PPBOOK;

namespace PPBOOK {

    struct PriceCostContractsIndex {
        // DOES NOT CHECK INPUT.
        PriceCostContractsIndex(double p, double c, int n, size_t i)
            : price_(p), cost_(c), contracts_(n), index_(i){}
        double  price_;
        double  cost_;
        int     contracts_;
        size_t  index_;
    };
    typedef deque<PriceCostContractsIndex>      ComplexPosition;

    class Position {
    public:
        // Constructor(s)
        // Creates empty position.
        Position(){}

        // Creates a position using transaction price, cost per contract,
        // number of contracts, index, and price point value. Positive or
        // negative sign of contracts means respectively buy or sell
        // action. Index must correspond to price in object of Prices.
        Position(double price, double cost, int contracts, size_t index,
            double pricePointValue)
        {
            Trades  ts; // Not filled, when new position is established.
            change(price, cost, contracts, index, pricePointValue, ts);
        }

        // If position is open returns true. Otherwise returns false.
        bool    isOpen() const {return cp_.size() > 0;}

        // Returns 1 for long, -1 for short, and 0 for closed position.
```

```
int     longClosedShort() const
{
    if(!cp_.size()) return 0;
    return  cp_[0].contracts_ > 0 ? 1 : -1;
}

// Returns total number of open contracts. Positive or negative
// numbers mean long or short position respectively. Returns 0,
// if position is not open.
int     contracts() const
{
    int n = 0;
    for(ComplexPosition::size_type i = 0; i < cp_.size(); i++)
        n += cp_[i].contracts_;
    return  n;
}

// Returns total cost of establishing position.
double  cost() const
{
    double  c = 0;
    for(ComplexPosition::size_type i = 0; i < cp_.size(); i++)
        c += cp_[i].cost_ * abs(cp_[i].contracts_);
    return  c;
}

// Returns open equity counted for all transactions using
// current price and price point value.
double  openEquity(double price, double pricePointValue) const
{
    // Checks input.
    if(price <= 0.0) {
        ostringstream   s;
        s   << "Position::openEquity: current price "
            << price << " must be positive.";
        throw   invalid_argument(s.str());
    }
    if(pricePointValue <= 0.0) {
        ostringstream   s;
        s   << "Position::openEquity: price point value "
            << pricePointValue << " must be positive.";
        throw   invalid_argument(s.str());
    }
    double  oe = 0.0;
    for(ComplexPosition::size_type i = 0; i < cp_.size(); i++)
```

```
        oe += (price - cp_[i].price_) * cp_[i].contracts_
                * pricePointValue;
    return  oe;
}

// Outputs position to a stream for diagnostics.
void    output(ostream& o) const
{
    o   << "Is open   " << isOpen() << endl;
    o   << "Contracts " << contracts() << endl;
    o   << "[";
    for(ComplexPosition::size_type i = 0; i < cp_.size(); i++)
        o   << cp_[i].price_ << ", " << cp_[i].cost_ << ", "
            << cp_[i].contracts_ << ", "
            << (unsigned int) cp_[i].index_ << ";";
    o   << "]" << endl;
}

// Given transaction price, cost per contract, number of
// contracts, index, and price point value returns open
// equity difference before and after transaction. Positive or
// negative sign of contracts means respectively buy or sell
// action. Index must correspond to price in object of Prices.
// If current position is offset at least partly, then adds
// corresponding trades to ts.
double  change(double price, double cost, int contracts,
            size_t index, double pricePointValue, Trades& ts)
{
    // Checks input.
    if(price <= 0.0) {
        ostringstream   s;
        s   << "Position::change: transaction price "
            << price << " must be positive.";
        throw   invalid_argument(s.str());
    }
    if(cost < 0.0) {
        ostringstream   s;
        s   << "Position::change: transaction cost per contract "
            << cost << " must not be negative.";
        throw   invalid_argument(s.str());
    }
    if(pricePointValue <= 0.0) {
        ostringstream   s;
        s   << "Position::change: price point value "
            << pricePointValue << " must be positive.";
```

```
            throw   invalid_argument(s.str());
        }
        // Does not record "do nothing" action.
        if(!contracts) return 0.0;
        // Determines type of transaction (buy or sell).
        int sgn = contracts > 0 ? 1 : -1;
        if(!isOpen() || longClosedShort() == sgn) {
            // Either establishes new or increases existing position.
            cp_.push_back(PriceCostContractsIndex(price, cost,
                contracts, index));
            return  0.0;
        }
        // Needs to offset at least partly existing position.
        double  eqBeg = openEquity(price, pricePointValue);
        int     n = contracts;
        while(cp_.size() != 0) {
            if(abs(cp_[0].contracts_) == abs(n)) {
                ts.push_back(Trade(cp_[0].price_, cp_[0].cost_,
                    cp_[0].contracts_, cp_[0].index_, price, cost,
                    index, pricePointValue));
                cp_.pop_front();
                return  eqBeg - openEquity(price, pricePointValue);
            }
            else if(abs(cp_[0].contracts_) > abs(n)) {
                ts.push_back(Trade(cp_[0].price_, cp_[0].cost_, -n,
                    cp_[0].index_, price, cost, index,
                    pricePointValue));
                cp_[0].contracts_ += n;
                return  eqBeg - openEquity(price, pricePointValue);
            }
            else {
                ts.push_back(Trade(cp_[0].price_, cp_[0].cost_,
                    cp_[0].contracts_, cp_[0].index_, price, cost,
                    index, pricePointValue));
                n += cp_[0].contracts_;
                cp_.pop_front();
            }
        } // while(cp_.size() != 0)
        cp_.push_back(PriceCostContractsIndex(price, cost, n,
            index));
        return  eqBeg;
    }
private:
    ComplexPosition cp_;
};
```

```
} // PPBOOK

#endif /* __Position_h__ */
```

The structure PriceCostContractsIndex keeps track of the price, cost per contract, number of contracts, and the price index of a single transaction. It uses default copy and assignment semantics and allows public access to its data members. The class Position encapsulates a deque of such structures. The deque is selected instead of a vector because the initial element in the applied algorithm will need to be erased. Removing the initial element from a deque is much more efficient than from a vector. A position is open if it contains at least one transaction record. The only way to affect a position is to call the operation change(). The last prohibits records with a zero number of contracts; therefore, the "do nothing" action does not change a position and is not recorded. This operation returns the difference in the open equity from before to after a transaction. This difference increases or decreases the cash balance. If a position contains more than one record, then a sign of contracts for all records is the same. The operation change() takes care to properly offset contracts that have been bought and sold. Because classes Date and Time are not involved, and the two integer indices described in the previous section are not applied, a simplified version of offsetting can be selected. Each new transaction offsets the oldest transaction first, then the next one, and so on. The order of offsetting does not affect the account value. The results of these offsetting are recorded in an external object of the class Trades. The operations isOpen(), longClosedShort(), contracts() report the open status, the type, and the total number of contracts in a position, respectively. The operation cost() returns the total cost of the complex position. The class Position does not apply contract price specification classes for price validation or for getting the dollar value of a price point. The class must be used carefully in combination with those classes testing prices.

USING POSITION AND TRADES TEST5.CPP

In order to get a better feeling for the classes Position and Trades, consider the following testing program, test5.cpp, which implements the example described in the section "The First and Second P&L Reserves":

```
#include <iostream>
#include <iomanip>
using namespace std;

#include "Prices.h"
#include "SpecCost.h"
#include "Cost.h"
#include "Strategy.h"
#include "Position.h"
```

```
using namespace PPBOOK;

int main(int, char*[])
{
    try {
        Prices      price("GC");
        price.append(429);
        price.append(428);
        price.append(443);
        price.append(455);
        price.append(449);

        vector<Cost<SpecAbsoluteCost> > cost(price.size(), 50.0);

        Strategy    strat;
        strat.push_back(0);
        strat.push_back(1);
        strat.push_back(0);
        strat.push_back(-2);
        strat.push_back(1);

        Strategy    stratPL1;
        stratPL1.push_back(0);
        stratPL1.push_back(1);
        stratPL1.push_back(0);
        stratPL1.push_back(-3);
        stratPL1.push_back(2);

        Strategy    stratPL2;
        stratPL2.push_back(0);
        stratPL2.push_back(1);
        stratPL2.push_back(1);
        stratPL2.push_back(-5);
        stratPL2.push_back(3);

        double      total = 1350.0;
        double      totalPL1 = 1350.0;
        double      totalPL2 = 1350.0;
        double      cash = total;
        double      cashPL1 = totalPL1;
        double      cashPL2 = totalPL2;

        double      k = price.tickValue() / price.tick();
        Position    pos;
        Position    posPL1;
```

```
Position    posPL2;
Trades      ts;
Trades      tsPL1;
Trades      tsPL2;

int width = 6;
cout    << setw(width) << "TOTAL" << " "
        << setw(width) << "CASH" << " "
        << setw(width) << "OPEN" << " "
        << setw(width) << "TOTAL1" << " "
        << setw(width) << "CASH1" << " "
        << setw(width) << "OPEN1" << " "
        << setw(width) << "TOTAL2" << " "
        << setw(width) << "CASH2" << " "
        << setw(width) << "OPEN2" << " "
        << endl;

for(size_t i = 0; i < price.size(); i++) {
    if(strat[i] != 0) {
        cash -= abs(strat[i]) * cost[i].cost();
        cash += pos.change(price[i], cost[i].cost(),
                    strat[i], i, k, ts);
    }
    if(stratPL1[i] != 0) {
        cashPL1 -= abs(stratPL1[i]) * cost[i].cost();
        cashPL1 += posPL1.change(price[i], cost[i].cost(),
                    stratPL1[i], i, k, tsPL1);
    }
    if(stratPL2[i] != 0) {
        cashPL2 -= abs(stratPL2[i]) * cost[i].cost();
        cashPL2 += posPL2.change(price[i], cost[i].cost(),
                    stratPL2[i], i, k, tsPL2);
    }
    total = cash + pos.openEquity(price[i], k);
    totalPL1 = cashPL1 + posPL1.openEquity(price[i], k);
    totalPL2 = cashPL2 + posPL2.openEquity(price[i], k);
    cout    << setw(width) << total << " "
            << setw(width) << cash << " "
            << setw(width) << pos.openEquity(price[i], k) << " "
            << setw(width) << totalPL1 << " "
            << setw(width) << cashPL1 << " "
            << setw(width) << posPL1.openEquity(price[i], k)
            << " "
            << setw(width) << totalPL2 << " "
```

```
                << setw(width) << cashPL2 << " "
                << setw(width) << posPL2.openEquity(price[i], k)
                << endl;
        }
        Trades::size_type   j;
        cout    << "Potential profit = " << total << endl;
        for(j = 0; j < ts.size(); j++) {
            cout    << (unsigned int)j
                    << " P&L = " << setw(4) << ts[j].pl()
                    << " Equity = " << setw(4) << ts[j].equityChange()
                    << " Cost = " << setw(3) << ts[j].totalCost()
                    << " P&L/Size = " << setw(4) << ts[j].plPerUnit()
                    << " Size = " << setw(2) << ts[j].entrySize()
                    << endl;
        }
        cout    << "Reserve 1 = " << totalPL1 << endl;
        for(j = 0; j < tsPL1.size(); j++) {
            cout    << (unsigned int)j
                    << " P&L = " << setw(4) << tsPL1[j].pl()
                    << " Equity = " << setw(4) << tsPL1[j].equityChange()
                    << " Cost = " << setw(3) << tsPL1[j].totalCost()
                    << " P&L/Size = " << setw(4) << tsPL1[j].plPerUnit()
                    << " Size = " << setw(2) << tsPL1[j].entrySize()
                    << endl;
        }
        cout    << "Reserve 2 = " << totalPL2 << endl;
        for(j = 0; j < tsPL2.size(); j++) {
            cout    << (unsigned int)j
                    << " P&L = " << setw(4) << tsPL2[j].pl()
                    << " Equity = " << setw(4) << tsPL2[j].equityChange()
                    << " Cost = " << setw(3) << tsPL2[j].totalCost()
                    << " P&L/Size = " << setw(4) << tsPL2[j].plPerUnit()
                    << " Size = " << setw(2) << tsPL2[j].entrySize()
                    << endl;
        }
    }
    catch(const exception& e) {
        cerr    << e.what() << endl;
    }
    catch(...) {
        cerr    << "Unknown exception" << endl;
    }
    return  0;
}
```

The reader should recognize the set of GC contract prices and the corresponding lists of transactions for the potential profit strategy and the first and second P&L reserves strategies. There are no algorithms used; we need to rely on the strategies obtained "manually" in the section mentioned. The program illustrates how the difference in open equity returned by the operation `change()` and transaction costs adjust a current cash balance, how the open position equity is calculated, and how the total equity is computed. The example also breaks down transactions by trades. This is done in parallel for all three strategies, and the comparative results are output. They agree with the numbers from the previous analysis:

```
TOTAL   CASH   OPEN TOTAL1  CASH1  OPEN1 TOTAL2  CASH2  OPEN2
  1350   1350      0   1350   1350      0   1350   1350      0
  1300   1300      0   1300   1300      0   1300   1300      0
  2800   1300   1500   2800   1300   1500   2750   1250   1500
  3900   3900      0   3850   3850      0   4900   4900      0
  4450   4450      0   4950   4950      0   6550   6550      0
Potential profit = 4450
0 P&L = 2600 Equity = 2700 Cost = 100 P&L/Size = 2600 Size =  1
1 P&L =  500 Equity =  600 Cost = 100 P&L/Size =  500 Size = -1
Reserve 1 = 4950
0 P&L = 2600 Equity = 2700 Cost = 100 P&L/Size = 2600 Size =  1
1 P&L = 1000 Equity = 1200 Cost = 200 P&L/Size =  500 Size = -2
Reserve 2 = 6550
0 P&L = 2600 Equity = 2700 Cost = 100 P&L/Size = 2600 Size =  1
1 P&L = 1100 Equity = 1200 Cost = 100 P&L/Size = 1100 Size =  1
2 P&L = 1500 Equity = 1800 Cost = 300 P&L/Size =  500 Size = -3
```

CONCLUSIONS

- Money management has been applied for a potential profit strategy.
- Examples clearly show that two additional P&L optimizations of the potential profit strategy are possible. The first P&L reserve strategy increases the size of reversal positions at those times recommended by *r*- or *l*-algorithm, if the growth in the trading power of an account permits. The second P&L reserve strategy adds positions *between those times* recommended by *r*- or *l*-algorithm, but also if the trading power of an account permits. The second P&L reserve strategy achieves the maximum profit attainable trading a single market under the condition of a specific initial capital investment.
- C++ classes `Trade`, `Trades`, and `Position` are developed.
- Two new algorithms for the first and second P&L reserves can now be introduced.

CHAPTER 6

Best to Better

Now we have everything ready to squeeze out additional profits from a potential profit strategy. This chapter presents two profit-and-loss reserve algorithms and a program computing the market offer. Forward!

ALGORITHM FOR THE FIRST PROFIT-AND-LOSS RESERVE STRATEGY

The natural input for building the first and second profit-and-loss (P&L) reserve strategies includes vectors of prices $\boldsymbol{P}$ and costs $\boldsymbol{C}$, initial margin M, maintenance margin M_m, and the initial number of contracts traded U. It is simpler, however, to build both strategies assuming that a potential profit strategy $\boldsymbol{U_{pps}}$ and its initial cash balance A_0 are known in advance. The function `potential_profit_min_account_alg` previously described helps us get both items. Given the vectors $\boldsymbol{P}$, $\boldsymbol{C}$, $\boldsymbol{U_{pps}}$, and values A_0, M, and M_m, the following steps represent the first algorithm:

1. Scan $\boldsymbol{U_{pps}}$ and find the first buy or sell action. This is the market entry point. The absolute value of this action is U. If the action is found and $U \neq 0$, then go to the step 2. If no such action is found, then the first P&L reserve strategy is a "do nothing" strategy. Return the value zero and STOP.
2. Depending on the sign of the first action, enter a long or short position with U contracts at the current price. Record this action in a collector, which has been initially filled by zeros, for the first P&L reserve strategy. Reduce the initial cash balance A_0 by the current cost times U (the total transaction cost). Go to step 3.

3. Continue scanning U_{pps} from left to right following the transaction point. Once the next buy or sell action is found, go to step 4.
4. Offset the current position using the current price and add the equity change to the current cash balance. Reduce the account balance by the current cost times the absolute size of the offset position. If the absolute value of the current action from U_{pps} is equal to U, then the final exit point has occurred. This is because the potential profit strategy is a true reversal system. Under these conditions, only the entry and exit points have the number of contracts equal to the absolute value of U. All other actions are either "do nothing" or have a bigger size needed to exit one trade and enter an opposite position. The algorithm building the potential profit strategy ensures the last property. Record the exit point in the collector for the first P&L reserve strategy and return the current cash balance. STOP. If it is not the final exit point, then go to step 5.
5. Because a position is offset and the trading power of the account is equal to the current cash balance, determine the number of contracts for a new and opposite position using Equation (4.03). There is no reason to check whether the equity in the new position will satisfy the maintenance margin because the transaction is executed at the point found by the r-algorithm for a potential profit strategy. After entering the position using the same offsetting price, reduce the cash balance by the related transaction costs. Record the transaction that offsets the old trade and enter a new position as one action occurring at one price in the collector for the first P&L reserve strategy. Go to step 3.

This algorithm does not apply the concept of open position equity. At any transaction time, the open position equity is treated as zero. Instead, the current cash balance will reflect the total account value normally equal to the sum of the current cash balance and open position equity. Because of that, the operation `Position::openEquity()` was not used. The last operation will be essential when building the algorithm for the second P&L reserve strategy. The C++ implementation of the algorithms `first_pl_reserve_prime_alg` and `first_pl_reserve_alg` from the header file `FirstPLReserveAlg.h` follows:

```
#ifndef __FirstPLReserveAlg_h__
#define __FirstPLReserveAlg_h__

#include <cmath>
#include <vector>
#include <sstream>
#include <algorithm>
#include <functional>
#include <stdexcept>
using namespace std;

#include "Prices.h"
#include "Cost.h"
#include "SpecCost.h"
#include "Strategy.h"
```

```
#include "Trade.h"
#include "Position.h"
#include "PotentialProfitAlg.h"
#include "PotentialProfitMinAccountAlg.h"
using namespace PPBOOK;

namespace PPBOOK {

    // The function first_pl_reserve_prime_alg does not check the input.
    // The initial cash balance a0 and potential profit strategy pps must
    // be computed by the function potential_profit_min_account_alg from
    // the same prices, costs, imargin, and mmargin. This ensures the
    // input consistency. A corresponding number of contracts used by
    // potential_profit_min_account_alg is the absolute value of the
    // first non zero element of pps. The function returns the first P&L
    // reserve value. A corresponding strategy is returned via the
    // input-output parameter plr1s. If pps is a "do nothing" strategy,
    // then P&L is equal to zero.
    inline  double
    first_pl_reserve_prime_alg(const Prices& prices, const
        vector<Cost<SpecAbsoluteCost> >& costs, const Strategy& pps,
        double a0, double imargin, double mmargin, Strategy& plr1s,
        Trades& ts)
    {
        // STEP 1. Evaluates entry point and initial number of contracts.
        Strategy::const_iterator    ep = find_if(pps.begin(), pps.end(),
                                        bind2nd(not_equal_to<int>(), 0));
        Strategy        s1(pps.size(), 0); // temporary actions collector
        if(ep == pps.end()) {
            plr1s.swap(s1); // "Do nothing" strategy is found.
            return  0.0;    // STOP.
        }
        unsigned int    nContracts = abs(*ep);
        size_t          j = ep - pps.begin();

        // STEP 2. Enters the market.
        double          k = prices.tickValue() / prices.tick();
        Position        pos(prices[j], costs[j].cost(), pps[j], j, k);
        double          cash = a0 - nContracts * costs[j].cost();
        s1[j] = pps[j];

        j++;
        for(; j < pps.size(); j++) {
            // STEP 3. Searching for a next transaction.
            if(pps[j] == 0) continue;
```

```
            // STEP 4. Offsets the current position.
            int curPos = pos.contracts();
            cash += pos.change(prices[j], costs[j].cost(), -curPos, j,
                        k, ts);
            cash -= abs(curPos) * costs[j].cost();

            if(abs(pps[j]) == nContracts) {
                s1[j] = -curPos;    // Market exit point.
                break;              // STOP.
            }
            // STEP 5. Enters a reverse position.
            int n = int(cash / imargin) * pps[j] / abs(pps[j]);
            cash -= abs(n) * costs[j].cost();
            cash += pos.change(prices[j], costs[j].cost(), n, j, k, ts);
            s1[j] = -curPos + n;
        }
        plr1s.swap(s1);
        return  cash - a0;
    }

    // This version reuses potential_profit_min_account_alg and
    // first_pl_reserve_prime_alg. It ensures that pps and a0 needed
    // to first_pl_reserve_prime_alg are computed from the same input
    // also used by first_pl_reserve_prime_alg. The function returns
    // P&L value. The potential profit and first P&L reserve strategies
    // are returned via input-output parameters pps and plr1s
    // respectively.
    inline  double
    first_pl_reserve_alg(const Prices& prices, const
        vector<Cost<SpecAbsoluteCost> >& costs, unsigned int nContracts,
        double imargin, double mmargin, double& a0, Strategy& pps,
        Strategy& plr1s, Trades& ts)
    {
        a0 = potential_profit_min_account_alg(prices, costs, nContracts,
            imargin, mmargin, pps);
        return  first_pl_reserve_prime_alg(prices, costs, pps, a0,
                imargin, mmargin, plr1s, ts);
    }

} // PPBOOK

#endif /* __FirstPLReserveAlg_h__ */
```

The comments in the code above should provide sufficient explanations.

ALGORITHM FOR THE SECOND P&L RESERVE STRATEGY

An algorithm for the second P&L reserve strategy must take care of additional transactions executed between those consecutive transactions recommended by a potential profit strategy. These additional transactions, if any, must increase the size of a position that is already established. At which times these new trades occur and with how many additional contracts depends on the original position, the current price and cost, the price and cost at the next reversal or exit points, the growing trading power of the account, and the ability to gain additional profit.

Let j_1 and j_2 be indices of two neighboring transactions recommended by a potential profit strategy. If j_1 corresponds to a buy point, then the next buy point j_b, $j_1 < j_b < j_2$ (between j_1 and j_2 if any) must be executed at the lowest possible sum of $k\boldsymbol{P}[j_b] + \boldsymbol{C}[j_b]$, where k is the dollar equivalent of a one-point price move. Buying an additional n contracts is possible if the current trading power of the account is sufficient for buying n contracts at j_b. This makes sense only if buying at point j_b is profitable at the time j_2. The current trading power of the account is determined as the current cash balance plus open position equity at price $\boldsymbol{P}[j_b]$ minus the position size times the initial margin. Hence, the number of additional contracts n that can be added is:

$$n = \text{int}((\text{cash} + \text{open position equity} - |\text{position size}| \times \text{initial margin}) / \text{initial margin}) \tag{6.01}$$

Similarly, if j_1 is a sell point, then the sale at point, j_s, $j_1 < j_s < j_2$ (if any) must be executed at the highest possible difference $k\boldsymbol{P}[j_s] - \boldsymbol{C}[j_s]$. Selling an additional n contracts is possible if a current trading power of the account is sufficient for selling n contracts at j_s. This makes sense only if selling at point j_s is profitable at time j_2. The same Equation (6.01) can be used to determine n, as shown in the following example. Then $\boldsymbol{P} = \boldsymbol{P}(400.5, 400, 400.1, 415, 414.5, 420, 410, 405)$; $\boldsymbol{C} = \boldsymbol{C}(50, 50, 50, 50, 50, 50, 50, 50)$; $\boldsymbol{U_{pps}} = \boldsymbol{U_{pps}}(0, 1, 0, 0, 0, -2, 0, 1)$.

```
echo GC 50 400.5 400 400.1 415 414.5 420 410 405 | maxprof
  #        GC      Cost     R     L
  0     400.5        50     0     0
  1       400        50     1     1
  2     400.1        50     0     0
  3       415        50     0     0
  4     414.5        50     0     0
  5       420        50    -2    -2
  6       410        50     0     0
  7       405        50     1     1
R-P&L = 3300 L-P&L = 3300
```

Let the initial and maintenance margins be equal to \$1,350 and \$1,000, respectively. Under these conditions, Equation (5.06) gives A_0 = \$1,350. Scanning $\boldsymbol{U_{pps}}$ from left to right the first pair of indices is $j_1 = 1$ and $j_2 = 5$. The minimum value of $k\boldsymbol{P}[j] + \boldsymbol{C}[j]$ for $1 < j < 5$ is at point 2. It is equal to $k\boldsymbol{P}[2] + \boldsymbol{C}[2]$ = \$100 × 400.1 + \$50 = \$40,060. However, at this point, the trading power is not enough for buying additional contracts. Indeed, \$1,350 [initial cash] – \$50 [transaction cost] + \$100 [dollars value of one point] × 1 [position size] × (400.1 – 400) – 1 [position size] × \$1,350 [initial margin] = \$1,300 [current cash] + \$10 [open position equity] – \$1,350 [total initial margin] = \$1,310 [total equity] – \$1,350 = –\$40. We must have a trading power of at least \$1,350 in order to buy one additional contract. At this point, there is no margin call because \$1,310 [total equity] > \$1,000 [maintenance margin]. At point 3 the trading power is equal to \$1,350 – \$50 + \$100 × 1 × (415 – 400) – 1 × \$1,350 = \$1,300 + \$1,500 – \$1,350 = \$1,450 which is enough to buy an additional contract. However, it is better to buy the contract at point 4 with the lower sum \$100 × $\boldsymbol{P}[4] + \boldsymbol{C}[4]$ = \$41,450 + \$50 = \$41,500 compared to the sum at point 3, \$100 × $\boldsymbol{P}[3] + \boldsymbol{C}[3]$ = \$41,500 + \$50 = \$41,550. The trading power at point 4 is equal to \$1,350 – \$50 + \$100 × 1 × (414.5 – 400) – 1 × \$1,350 = \$1,300 + \$1,450 – \$1,350 = \$1,400, which is also enough reserves for buying one contract. Hence, the position should be increased at point 4 but not at 3. Does it make sense to increase it at all? Yes, because it is a profitable transaction – \$50 + \$100 × 1 × (420 – 414.5) – \$50 = \$550 – \$100 = \$450. The next point is the reversal point $j_2 = 5$. If we offset the position consisting of two contracts bought at 400.0 and 414.5, respectively, we get the total cash value = \$1,350 – \$50 + \$100 × 1 × (420 – 400) – \$50 [the closing transaction cost for the first contract] – \$50 [the initiating transaction cost for the second contract] + \$100 × 1 × (420 – 414.5) – \$50 [the closing transaction cost for the second contract] = \$1,300 + \$2,000 – \$100 + \$550 – \$50 = \$3,700. This is enough value to sell two contracts at 420. The beginning of the second P&L reserve strategy is then (0, 1, 0, 0, 1, – 4, . . .).

The next pair of indices needs to be determined at the reversal point recommended by a potential profit strategy. We can see in the sample data that the pair becomes $j_1 = 5$ and $j_2 = 7$. There is only one intermediate point 6. The trading power at this point is \$3,700 – 2 × \$50 – \$100 × 2 × (410 – 420) – 2 × \$1,350 = \$3,600 + \$2,000 – \$2,700 = \$2,900. Yes, this is sufficient for selling two additional contracts because \$2,900 > 2 × \$1,350 = \$2,700, the required margin. But does it make sense? If we check the potential profit for one contract we find –\$50 – \$100 × 1 × (405 – 410) – \$50 = – \$50 + \$500 – \$50 = \$400, then the return is positive and it certainly does make sense. But the strategy extends further (0, 1, 0, 0, 1, – 4, – 2, . . .), and point $j_2 = 7$ is the exit point. The final short position, consisting of four contracts, where two were initially sold at 420 and an extra two sold at 415, now needs to be closed out. This gives the second P&L reserve strategy a final cash balance of \$3,700 – 2 × \$50 [initiating cost for two contracts] – \$100 × 2 × (405 – 420) [profit from two contracts] – 2 × \$50 [closing cost for two contracts] – 2 × \$50 [initiating cost for two extra contracts] – \$100 × 2 × (405 – 410) [profit from two extra contracts] – 2 × \$50 [closing cost for two extra contracts] = \$3,600 + \$3,000 – \$100 – \$100 + \$1,000 – \$100 = \$7,300. We see that the second P&L reserve strategy is (0, 1, 0, 0, 1, – 4, – 2, 4).

Let's summarize. The potential profit strategy (0, 1, 0, 0, 0, – 2, 0, 1) has generated the profit \$3,300 and increased the account value from \$1,350 to \$4,650. We got this result using the program `maxprof.cpp`. The second P&L reserve strategy (0, 1, 0, 0, 1, – 4, – 2, 4) has created the profit \$5,950. The account has grown in value from \$1,350 to \$7,300. We found this result "manually." What about the first P&L reserve strategy applied under the same conditions? We now have enough information and the tools for computing the first P&L reserve strategy using C++ results from the previous section. The file `test6.cpp` illustrates how this can be accomplished:

```
#include <iostream>
#include <iomanip>
#include <vector>
using namespace std;

#include "SpecCost.h"
#include "Prices.h"
#include "Cost.h"
#include "FirstPLReserveAlg.h"
using namespace PPBOOK;

typedef ostream_iterator<int, char, char_traits<char> > IntOutput;

int main(int, char*[])
{
    try {
        const size_t    N = 8;
        const double    p[N] = {400.5, 400, 400.1, 415, 414.5, 420,
                            410, 405};
        Prices  prices("GC");
        for(size_t j = 0; j < N; j++)
            prices.append(p[j]);
        vector<Cost<SpecAbsoluteCost> > costs(prices.size(), 50.0);

        const double        imargin = 1350; // initial margin
        const double        mmargin = 1000; // maintenance margin
        const unsigned int  nContracts = 1;

        Strategy    pps;    // collector for potential profit strategy
        Strategy    plr1s;  // collector for first P&L reserve strategy
        double      a0;     // collector for initial cash balance
        Trades      ts;
        double      pl1 = first_pl_reserve_alg(prices, costs,
                        nContracts, imargin, mmargin, a0, pps, plr1s,
                        ts);
        IntOutput   out(cout, " ");
        cout    << "(" << flush;
        copy(plr1s.begin(), plr1s.end(), out);
        cout    << ")" << endl;
        cout    << "A0 = " << a0 << " PL1 = " << pl1 << " Total = "
                << a0 + pl1 << endl;
    }
```

```
    catch(const exception& e) {
        cerr    << e.what() << endl;
    }
    catch(...) {
        cerr    << "Unknown exception" << endl;
    }
    return  0;
}
```

The output for the first P&L reserve strategy is generated automatically:

```
(0 1 0 0 0 -3 0 2 )
A0 = 1350 PL1 = 4700 Total = 6050
```

Buying at point 4 instead of point 3 introduces a complication into the algorithm. How can this be handled? I propose to sort the indices between j_1 and j_2 using the sum $k\boldsymbol{P}[j] + \boldsymbol{C}[j]$ as a criteria. For each pair of indices, only one sorting is needed. For instance, indices (2, 3, 4) correspond to the values ($40,060, $41,550, $41,500). After sorting the values in ascending order those vectors become (2, 4, 3) and ($40,060, $41,500, $41,550). The next step is to scan the vector of indices from left to right. The determination of the two values is important at each point in time. The first value is the trading power of the account based on the open position and current price. By referring to the margin, we can know whether adding to the position is possible. The second value is the potential profit between the current time and the time of the next reversal (or exit). If the P&L value adjusted by cost is positive, then buying makes sense. In order to maximize the profit, it is necessary to act at the left-most value of the sorted vector of indices where the two conditions are true. Once a contract is added, there is no reason to sort the remaining indices and values before reaching point j_2.

For selling, the process is similar except that the differences $k\boldsymbol{P}[j] - \boldsymbol{C}[j]$ and corresponding reordering indices are sorted in descending order. Again the two conditions (sufficient trading power and positive potential P&L) must occur at the left-most sorted index in order to add new short contracts. The algorithm for the inputs $\boldsymbol{P}$, $\boldsymbol{C}$, $\boldsymbol{U_{pps}}$, A_0, M_m, and M is given below. For the second P&L reserve strategy, the vector $\boldsymbol{U_{pl2}}$ is a collector and is initially filled with zeros. At the beginning, an empty object of the class `Position` is constructed.

1. Using index j scan $\boldsymbol{U_{pps}}$ from left to right until $\boldsymbol{U_{pps}}[j] \neq 0$. This is the market entry point. The entry number of contracts is $U = |\boldsymbol{U_{pps}}[j]|$. If $U \neq 0$, then go to step 2. If all $\boldsymbol{U_{pps}}[j] = 0$, then the second P&L reserve strategy is a "do nothing" strategy. Return P&L = 0 and STOP.
2. Set $j_1 = j$. Update the object of the class `Position` using the operation `change()` with the price $\boldsymbol{P}[j_1]$, the cost $\boldsymbol{C}[j_1]$, and the number of contracts $\boldsymbol{U_{pps}}[j_1]$. The newly entered position is long if $\boldsymbol{U_{pps}}[j_1] > 0$ or short if $\boldsymbol{U_{pps}}[j_1] < 0$. Record this action in the vector $\boldsymbol{U_{pl2}}$ at the current value of index j. Reduce the initial cash balance A_0 by $U \times \boldsymbol{C}[j_1]$. Go to step 3.
3. Increment j by one until the next transaction $\boldsymbol{U_{pps}}[j] \neq 0$ is found. Set $j_2 = j$, $j_2 > j_1$. If $j_2 > j_1 + 1$, then go to step 4; otherwise, go to step 8.

4. Create the vector $\boldsymbol{J}$ of size $j_2 - j_1 - 1$ containing index values $j_1 + 1, j_1 + 2, \ldots, j_2 - 1$ and the vector of adjusted prices $\boldsymbol{AP}$ of the same size as $\boldsymbol{J}$. If the current position is long then fill the vector $\boldsymbol{AP}$ with the values $k\boldsymbol{P}[\boldsymbol{J}[i]] + \boldsymbol{C}[\boldsymbol{J}[i]]$, where index i takes on all values from the interval $[0, j_2 - j_1 - 2]$. Then sort the vector $\boldsymbol{AP}$ in ascending order and synchronously reorder the elements of the vector $\boldsymbol{J}$. If the current position is short, then fill the vector $\boldsymbol{AP}$ with the values $k\boldsymbol{P}[\boldsymbol{J}[i]] - \boldsymbol{C}[\boldsymbol{J}[i]]$, where index i takes on all values from the interval $[0, j_2 - j_1 - 2]$. Then sort the vector $\boldsymbol{AP}$ in descending order and synchronously reorder the elements of the vector $\boldsymbol{J}$. Go to step 5.
5. Set index $i = 0$. Go to step 6.
6. Increment i until it is less than $j_2 - j_1 - 1$, and for each iteration compute the open position equity using the operation `Position::openEquity()` and price $\boldsymbol{P}[\boldsymbol{J}[i]]$. For each i compute the total equity as the sum of the current cash balance and open position equity. Use these values in Equation (6.01) for getting the number of contracts n that is to be added to the open position. If n is zero or the P&L value $-type \times k \times (\boldsymbol{P}[\boldsymbol{J}[i]] - \boldsymbol{P}[j_2]) - \boldsymbol{C}[\boldsymbol{J}[i]] - \boldsymbol{C}[j_2]$ is not positive (type = +1 for long and −1 for short positions), then go to step 6. If $n > 0$ and the P&L is positive, then go to step 7. If $i = j_2 - j_1 - 1$, then go to step 8.
7. Increase the current position by $type \times n$ contracts using the price $\boldsymbol{P}[\boldsymbol{J}[i]]$. Reduce the current cash balance by $n \times \boldsymbol{C}[\boldsymbol{J}[i]]$. Record the action $type \times n$ in $\boldsymbol{U}_{pl2}$. Go to step 6.
8. Offset the current position with price $\boldsymbol{P}[j_2]$. Reduce the current cash balance by $|offset\ position\ size| \times \boldsymbol{C}[j_2]$. Add the equity change caused by the position offset to the current cash balance. If $|\boldsymbol{U}_{pps}[j_2]| \neq U$, then go to step 9. Otherwise, this is the exit point. Record the action *–offset position size* in $\boldsymbol{U}_{pl2}$. Return the current total equity minus A_0 as the P&L. STOP.
9. Use the positive or negative sign of $\boldsymbol{U}_{pps}[j_2]$ to determine whether to go long or short. At this time the position is offset and the total equity is equal to the current cash balance. Using Equation (6.01) determine the required value of n. Set the next transaction *type* equal to +1 if $\boldsymbol{U}_{pps}[j_2] > 0$ and −1 if $\boldsymbol{U}_{pps}[j_2] < 0$. Update the object of the class `Position` with the price $\boldsymbol{P}[j_2]$, the cost $\boldsymbol{C}[j_2]$, and the number of contracts equal to $type \times n$. Reduce the current cash balance by $n \times \boldsymbol{C}[j_2]$. Record $type \times (|offset\ position\ size| + n)$ as a combined single reversal action in $\boldsymbol{U}_{pl2}$. Use $|offset\ position\ size|$ obtained on step 8. Set $j_1 = j_2$. Go to step 3.

The following functions `second_pl_reserve_prime_alg` and `second_pl_reserve_alg` is the C++ implementation from the header file: `SecondPLReserveAlg.h`

```
#ifndef __SecondPLReserveAlg_h__
#define __SecondPLReserveAlg_h__

#include <cmath>
#include <vector>
#include <algorithm>
```

```
#include <functional>
#include <sstream>
#include <stdexcept>
using namespace std;

#include "Prices.h"
#include "Cost.h"
#include "SpecCost.h"
#include "Strategy.h"
#include "Trade.h"
#include "Position.h"
#include "PotentialProfitAlg.h"
#include "PotentialProfitMinAccountAlg.h"
using namespace PPBOOK;

namespace PPBOOK {

    // Comparators needed for ascending and descending sorting.
    typedef pair<unsigned int, double>  IndexValue;
    class   IndexValueAscending {
    public:
        bool operator()(const IndexValue& a, const IndexValue& b) const
        {
            return  a.second < b.second;
        }
    };

    class   IndexValueDescending {
    public:
        bool operator()(const IndexValue& a, const IndexValue& b) const
        {
            return  a.second > b.second;
        }
    };

    // The function second_pl_reserve_prime_alg does not check input. The
    // initial cash balance a0 and potential profit strategy pps must be
    // computed by the function potential_profit_min_account_alg from the
    // same prices, costs, imargin (initial), and mmargin (maintenance).
    // This ensures input consistency. The corresponding number of
    // contracts used by potential_profit_min_account_alg is the absolute
    // value of the first non zero element of pps. The function returns
    // the second P&L reserve value. A corresponding strategy is returned
    // via the input-output parameter plr2s. If pps is a "do nothing"
    // strategy, then P&L is equal to zero.
```

```
inline  double
second_pl_reserve_prime_alg(const Prices& prices, const
    vector<Cost<SpecAbsoluteCost> >& costs, const Strategy& pps,
    double a0, double imargin, double mmargin, Strategy& plr2s,
    Trades& ts)
{
    // STEP 1. Evaluates entry point and initial number of contracts.
    Strategy::const_iterator    ep = find_if(pps.begin(), pps.end(),
                                    bind2nd(not_equal_to<int>(), 0));
    Strategy        s2(pps.size(), 0); // temporary actions collector
    if(ep == pps.end()) {
        plr2s.swap(s2); // "Do nothing" strategy is found. STOP.
        return  0.0;
    }
    unsigned int    nContracts = abs(*ep);
    size_t          j1 = ep - pps.begin();

    // STEP 2. Enters the market.
    double          k = prices.tickValue() / prices.tick();
    Position        pos(prices[j1], costs[j1].cost(), pps[j1],
                        j1, k);
    double          cash = a0 - nContracts * costs[j1].cost();
    s2[j1] = pps[j1];

    size_t          j = j1 + 1;
    for(; j < pps.size(); j++) {
        // STEP 3. Searching for a next transaction.
        if(pps[j] == 0) continue;
        size_t  j2 = j;
        if(j2 > j1 + 1) {
            // STEP 4. Helper vector of indices and adjusted prices.
            vector<IndexValue>  jpv;
            size_t              i = j1 + 1;
            for(; i < j2; i++)
                jpv.push_back(IndexValue(i, k * prices[i]
                    + pos.longClosedShort() * costs[i].cost()));
            if(pos.longClosedShort() > 0)
                stable_sort(jpv.begin(), jpv.end(),
                    IndexValueAscending());
            else if(pos.longClosedShort() < 0)
                stable_sort(jpv.begin(), jpv.end(),
                    IndexValueDescending());
            // STEP 5.
            i = 0;
            // STEP 6.
```

```
        size_t  t = j1;
        for(; i < jpv.size(); i++) {
            if(jpv[i].first <= t) continue;
            double  equity = pos.openEquity(prices[jpv[i].first],
                                    k);
            double  total = cash + equity;
            // Additional number of contracts.
            int     n = int((total - imargin *
                        abs(pos.contracts())) / imargin);
            if(n < 1) continue;
            // potential P&L of increasing position by 1.
            double  pl = -pos.longClosedShort() * k *
                (prices[jpv[i].first] - prices[j2])
                - costs[jpv[i].first].cost() - costs[j2].cost();
            if(pl <= 0.0) continue;
            // STEP 7. Increase current position.
            cash -= abs(n) * costs[jpv[i].first].cost();
            cash += pos.change(prices[jpv[i].first],
                costs[jpv[i].first].cost(), pos.longClosedShort()
                * n, jpv[i].first, k, ts);
            s2[jpv[i].first] = pos.longClosedShort() * n;
            t = jpv[i].first;
        }
    } // if(j2 > j1 + 1)

    // STEP 8. Offsets the current position.
    int curPos = pos.contracts();
    cash -= abs(curPos) * costs[j2].cost();
    cash += pos.change(prices[j2], costs[j2].cost(), -curPos,
            j2, k, ts);
    if(abs(pps[j2]) == nContracts) {
        s2[j2] = -curPos;   // Market exit point.
        break;              // STOP
    }
    // STEP 9. Enters a reverse position.
    int n = int(cash / imargin) * pps[j2] / abs(pps[j2]);
    cash -= abs(n) * costs[j2].cost();
    cash += pos.change(prices[j2], costs[j2].cost(), n,
            j2, k, ts);
    s2[j2] = -curPos + n;
    j1 = j2;
}
// Swaps temporary and permanent collector. STOP.
plr2s.swap(s2);
return  cash - a0;
```

```
    }

    // This version reuses potential_profit_min_account_alg and
    // second_pl_reserve_prime_alg. It ensures that pps and a0 needed
    // to second_pl_reserve_prime_alg are computed from the same input
    // also used by second_pl_reserve_prime_alg. The function returns
    // P&L value. The potential profit and second P&L reserve strategies
    // are returned via input-output parameters pps and plr2s
    // respectively.
    inline  double
    second_pl_reserve_alg(const Prices& prices, const
        vector<Cost<SpecAbsoluteCost> >& costs, unsigned int nContracts,
        double imargin, double mmargin, double& a0, Strategy& pps,
        Strategy& plr2s, Trades& ts)
    {
        a0 = potential_profit_min_account_alg(prices, costs, nContracts,
            imargin, mmargin, pps);
        return  second_pl_reserve_prime_alg(prices, costs, pps, a0,
                    imargin, mmargin, plr2s, ts);
    }

} // PPBOOK

#endif /* __SecondPLReserveAlg_h__ */
```

The following is the testing program from the file test7.cpp:

```
#include <iostream>
#include <iomanip>
#include <vector>
using namespace std;

#include "SpecCost.h"
#include "Prices.h"
#include "Cost.h"
#include "SecondPLReserveAlg.h"
using namespace PPBOOK;

typedef ostream_iterator<int, char, char_traits<char> > IntOutput;

int main(int, char*[])
{
    try {
        const size_t    N = 8;
```

```
        const double    p[N] = {400.5, 400, 400.1, 415, 414.5, 420,
                                410, 405};
        Prices  prices("GC");
        for(size_t j = 0; j < N; j++)
            prices.append(p[j]);
        vector<Cost<SpecAbsoluteCost> > costs(prices.size(), 50.0);

        const double        imargin = 1350; // initial margin
        const double        mmargin = 1000; // maintenance margin
        const unsigned int  nContracts = 1;

        Strategy    pps;    // collector for potential profit strategy
        Strategy    plr2s;  // collector for first P&L reserve strategy
        double      a0;     // collector for initial cash balance
        Trades      tsPL2;
        double      pl2 = second_pl_reserve_alg(prices, costs,
                          nContracts, imargin, mmargin, a0, pps, plr2s,
                          tsPL2);
        IntOutput   out(cout, " ");
        cout    << "(" << flush;
        copy(plr2s.begin(), plr2s.end(), out);
        cout    << ")" << endl;
        cout    << "A0 = " << a0 << " PL2 = " << pl2 << " Total = "
                << a0 + pl2 << endl;
    }
    catch(const exception& e) {
        cerr    << e.what() << endl;
    }
    catch(...) {
        cerr    << "Unknown exception" << endl;
    }
    return  0;
}
```

The correct output is:

```
(0 1 0 0 1 -4 -2 4 )
A0 = 1350 PL2 = 5950 Total = 7300
```

PROGRAM APPLYING THREE ALGORITHMS

For convenience, it is best to complete the development of the three individual algorithms with the program in the file `maxprof3.cpp`, which uses all of them.

```
#include <iostream>
#include <iomanip>
#include <string>
#include <cmath>
using namespace std;

#include "Prices.h"
#include "PotentialProfitAlg.h"
#include "ProfitAndLossAlg.h"
#include "FirstPLReserveAlg.h"
#include "SecondPLReserveAlg.h"
using namespace PPBOOK;

int main(int argc, char*[])
{
    try {
        // Reads input
        string          market;
        unsigned int    nContracts;
        double          imargin, mmargin;
        cin >> market >> nContracts >> imargin >> mmargin;

        Prices                          prices(market);
        vector<Cost<SpecAbsoluteCost> > costs;
        double  cost, price;
        // Fills prices and costs dependently on the requested format
        if(argc > 1) {
            while(cin >> price && cin >> cost) {
                prices.append(price);
                costs.push_back(cost);
            }
        }
        else {
            cin >> cost;
            while(cin >> price) {
                prices.append(price);
                costs.push_back(cost);
            }
        }
        // Computes A0 and pps
        Strategy    pps;
        double      a0 = potential_profit_min_account_alg(prices, costs,
                            nContracts, imargin, mmargin, pps);
        double      pl = profit_and_loss(prices, pps, costs);
```

```
Strategy    plr1s;
Trades      tsplr1s;
double      pl1 = first_pl_reserve_prime_alg(prices, costs,
                    pps, a0, imargin, mmargin, plr1s, tsplr1s);
Strategy    plr2s;
Trades      tsplr2s;
double      pl2 = second_pl_reserve_prime_alg(prices, costs,
                    pps, a0, imargin, mmargin, plr2s, tsplr2s);

// Reports results
double  k = prices.tickValue() / prices.tick();
cout    << setw(4) << "#" << " "
        << setw(9) << prices.name() << " "
        << setw(5) << "Cost" << " "
        << setw(4) << "PPS" << " "
        << setw(6) << "PPS1" << " "
        << setw(6) << "PPS2" << " "
        << setw(6) << "Pos2" << " "
        << setw(8) << "Cash2" << " "
        << setw(8) << "Equity2" << " "
        << setw(8) << "Total2"
        << endl;

tsplr2s.clear();
Position    pos2;
double      cash2 = a0;
for(unsigned int i = 0; i < prices.size(); i++) {
    if(plr2s[i] != 0) {
        cash2 -= abs(plr2s[i]) * costs[i].cost();
        cash2 += pos2.change(prices[i], costs[i].cost(),
                    plr2s[i], i, k, tsplr2s);
    }
    double  equity2 = pos2.openEquity(prices[i], k);
    double  total2 = cash2 + equity2;
    cout    << setw(4) << i << " "
            << setw(9) << setprecision(9) << prices[i] << " "
            << setw(5) << costs[i].cost() << " "
            << setw(4) << pps[i] << " "
            << setw(6) << plr1s[i] << " "
            << setw(6) << plr2s[i] << " "
            << setw(6) << pos2.contracts() << " "
            << setw(8) << cash2 << " "
```

```
                    << setw(8) << equity2 << " "
                    << setw(8) << total2
                    << endl;
        }
        cout    << "A0 = " << a0 << " "
                << "P&L = " << pl << " "
                << "P&L1 = " << pl1 << " "
                << "P&L2 = " << pl2 << " "
                << "IM = " << imargin << " "
                << "MM = " << mmargin
                << endl;
    }
    catch(const exception& e) {
        cerr    << e.what() << endl;
    }
    catch(...) {
        cerr    << "Unknown exception" << endl;
    }
    return  0;
}
```

This program assumes that the standard input contains the contract descriptor, the initial number of contracts, initial margin, maintenance margin, and either a single cost followed by a sequence of prices or a sequence of pairs of cost and price values. The following example shows how it can be called:

```
echo GC 1 1350 1000 50 400.5 400 400.1 415 414.5 420 410 405 | maxprof3
  #       GC  Cost  PPS    PPS1    PPS2    Pos2    Cash2  Equity2   Total2
  0    400.5    50    0       0       0       0     1350        0     1350
  1      400    50    1       1       1       1     1300        0     1300
  2    400.1    50    0       0       0       1     1300       10     1310
  3      415    50    0       0       0       1     1300     1500     2800
  4    414.5    50    0       0       1       2     1250     1450     2700
  5      420    50   -2      -3      -4      -2     3600        0     3600
  6      410    50    0       0      -2      -4     3500     2000     5500
  7      405    50    1       2       4       0     7300        0     7300
A0 = 1350 P&L = 3300 P&L1 = 4700 P&L2 = 5950 IM = 1350 MM = 1000
```

Together with prices, costs, and the minimum initial account size, the program outputs the actions of the three strategies and the corresponding P&L. Additionally, the right-most four columns contain the current position, cash balance, open position equity, and total equity for the second P&L reserve strategy.

CONCLUSIONS

- Two algorithms have been proposed that work under the self-financing restriction to maximize potential profit. Both are based on the fundamental properties of a potential profit strategy. The first algorithm creates a strategy increasing the size of reversal positions at the times recommended by the r- or l-algorithms, if permitted by the growth of trading power in the account. The second algorithm produces a strategy that adds to positions between the times indicated as reversal points recommended by r- or l-algorithms, again if the trading power of the account permits. The second algorithm creates a strategy achieving maximum profit trading a single market under the condition that the initial capital is restricted.
- A C++ framework including the classes `Prices`, `Trades`, `Position`, `Cost` and the three best profit algorithms is applied to a program that accepts prices, costs, the initial number of contracts traded, and the initial and maintenance margins. It reports the maximum profits and the comparative results of the corresponding strategies.

CHAPTER 7

Direct Applications

Whether traders just dream about big profits or actually set them as personal goals, they should know what "big" is—the limit that can be achieved. The three variations of the best profit strategy developed on the road to this chapter uncovers what the market can offer. It answers the question: "What is possible?" In this chapter, the strategies will be applied to real market data.

ONLY IN THE PAST

The potential profit and corresponding strategy are market properties. As with any other market property, they can be obtained only over a past time interval.

What Are Traders Actually Doing and How Are They Doing It?

When a trader calculates moving averages of historic prices; builds support, resistance, and trend lines; analyzes price gaps; observes the appearance of *trading patterns* (Elder 1993); follows the Commitments of Traders Reports (Williams 2005); rationalizes the usefulness of volume and open interest (Shaleen 1991); or works in accordance with Fibonacci retracement levels, he always applies these calculations and techniques on past data. This past may include today's date—but only after the market closes!

From time to time there are markets that show a strong correlation between the closing price direction and a price move at a different time. For example, the "wild card play" (Hull 1997) is a situation in which an "option" is given to the party holding the short position based on the fact that the pit session for Chicago Board of Trade (CBOT) Treasury bond futures ends at 2 P.M., while electronic trading of Treasury bonds continues for an additional two hours, until 4 P.M. Additionally, the party holding a short position has until 8 P.M. to decide whether to issue a notice of intention to deliver to the clearinghouse. If delivery is decided, then the settlement price from the previous 2 P.M. close is applied for the purpose of determining the invoice price. If bond prices decline after 2 P.M., then the party can buy the cheapest-to-deliver bonds and issue the delivery notice. If the bond prices do not decline, the position can be left open and the party will wait until the next day, repeating the same strategy. Although this sounds like free money, the wild card option is not free, and the price differential has usually been discounted in advance and is reflected in the 2 P.M. close.

The belief that market properties uncovered from the past will be repeated and can help in making the right trading decisions in the future is a common thread uniting many speculators. If we believe the widely accepted premise that the majority (90 percent) of traders lose money, then we can conclude that either the right properties are not determined or not followed or there is no repetition of patterns. Of course, traders are not interested in the last possibility, and the fact that others have not successfully capitalized on these patterns does not mean they do not exist; therefore, the search continues. The following was written in 1923 (Lefevre 1923) and attributed to Jesse Livermore (pseudonym Larry Livingstone):

> *... there is nothing new in Wall Street. There can't be because speculation is as old as the hills. Whatever happens in the stock market to-day has happened before and will happen again.*

By developing indicators based on the past and current prices, which then generate trading signals, traders can view the same price data from different angles. They believe that changing the angle of view will help to catch something hidden in the original price flow. Changing the angle of view or the conditions of observation in order to study an object better is a standard approach in scientific research. However, many academicians have been very skeptical about the world of *technical analysis* applied to market prices. The ability to draw lines and patterns has been classified as an art (Elder 1993). This art component, when applied to the decision-making process, which cannot be replicated by a computer program, leaves the fields open for the application of human *intuition* and skills. In fact, a new field has been named *behavioral finance* to recognize and study the way in which traders make nontechnical decisions and the way large groups react to market events and price movement. Perry Kaufman has recently upgraded a very good encyclopedic overview of technical analysis and trading systems in the new edition of his book (2005).

A Word on Human Intuition

Is human intuition important? You may have noticed that, from time to time, advertisements in financial magazines and newspapers show images of a chessboard or chessmen. I believe this symbolizes the intellectual aspect of making decisions, and *chess* seems a good and respectful candidate for drawing parallels. In the most recent history of chess, we find that advances in computer hardware and software have radically changed our views about the uniqueness of human reasoning and intuition. Thirty years ago, any serious chess player could hardly believe that a computer program could challenge human intuition or even consider it to be a reasonable technical substitute. At that time, the small memory and lack of computing speed were such severe limitations that the normal rules of the game could not be used. For instance, in some earlier software applications, all four bishops were taken off the board and the board itself was given the size 6 by 6 instead of 8 by 8 (Newborn 1975). In Chapter 4, we saw the relationship between Equation (4.16) derived for a growth function using futures contracts and the famous Claude Shannon Equation (4.17). Shannon also contributed a fundamental algorithm for the computerized simulation of chess (Shannon 1950). Modern chess programs inherit many of his ideas, resulting in significant advances. The program Deep Blue won a chess match over Garry Kasparov—the best human player at the time of the competition. It has been demonstrated that while computers and humans work very differently to achieve a goal, sufficient computation power, a good database for opening and end-game positions, and algorithms that have a practical objective can give the same results in chess as the best human intuition. When it comes to intricate patterns, the computer has the advantage.

Can programs trade better than the best humans? Maybe not in some venues, but even now there is trading that can be done only by computers and not humans. The most obvious of these is high-frequency trading, where positions are entered in selected stocks at key points, then liquidated within seconds. The object is to strip off very small gains (optimistically, about 1 cent per share) hundreds of times each day. We also know that many large, professional trading companies use fully automated programs to trade long-, medium-, and short-term strategies. It would be interesting to know how these computerized programs compare to the results of discretionary trading in competitions such as the Robbins World Cup. The only reason that may influence the participation of such programs in competitions is the following: why share information about a program that continues to make money? Two of these approaches, *genetic programming* (Koza 1992) and *neural nets* (Chester 1993; Gallant 1993), have been intensively investigated worldwide since the 1980s. The increase in electronic markets has facilitated the need to increase the execution speed in order to beat others in reacting to news and other market events. Computerized trading, as well as investor preference, has been a primary force that has been driving the development of all aspects of electronic trading.

In the near future, automated text processing and analyzing tools, which can recognize the semantics of human manuscripts, will routinely evaluate billions of Internet messages in order to rank the bullish or bearish sentiment of the information.

What and How Are Academicians Doing?

Are the academicians having a better loss rate than 90 percent? Certainly, there are several areas of finance, especially in the realm of pricing derivatives, that have a very solid academician foundation. The Nobel Prize awarded to Myron Scholes and Robert Merton (only his sudden death prevented Fisher Black from receiving this award) demonstrates the clear respect of the community (Black 1987, ; Black 1973; Merton 1990) for these achievements. The solutions provided in this area do not pretend to predict the future. The "modest" task of pricing required enormous computer power, and the algorithms that were developed bordered on "art." They can be described as follows: Given a set of prices of tradable investment assets, what would be a reasonable price for another financial instrument that is dependent on some of the assets at given point in time? In order to formulate suitable models in this area, it is necessary to make assumptions about the relationships of price, short-term interest rates, forward rates, cost of carry, and distributions at any given moment. The principles of (1) self-financing strategies or portfolios replicating all cash flows of an instrument and (2) no arbitrage, are the basis of modern pricing (Harrison and Pliska 1981). Ironically, while we cannot predict the future, we can combine certain quantities of dependent assets (a simple example is a stock and a call option on that stock) and create a market-neutral relationship, where the entire portfolio will not change its value regardless of any price change in that stock. Then such portfolio must have the same value as some risk-free instrument, such as a Treasury note.

Modern pricing has come far from the original Black and Scholes assumptions about constant short-term interest rates and *volatility*, as well as the nature of price distributions. New approaches that assume short-term interest rates or forward rates follow stochastic processes and volatility itself is a stochastic process are able to increase the *degrees of freedom* of a model and improve its fitting properties. This allows the results to replicate such effects as the so-called volatility skews and smiles (Rebonato 2004). There is an interesting attempt to draw a deeper analogy between the stochastic description of prices and quantum mechanics and quantum field theory (Baaquie 2004). Again we are fitting known prices of similar instruments in an attempt to obtain the current price of another similar instrument from the calibrated model. This is useful for hedging and the evaluation of arbitrage situations in which the trader attempts to remove all risks from the process. Is it useful for predicting the future price change?

Not especially. In fact, in the instant following the calibration of a model and pricing the derivative, you would need to recalibrate many of the modern models and reprice the derivative in accordance with changing economy and the prices of other similar instruments. This accumulates the information but does not predict the future. Moreover, the *drift* parameter (a candidate for predicting the direction of prices) used in the log-normal process and responsible for constant contribution into price changes of the underlying security is reduced from the final *Black-Sholes formula* based on the *risk-neutral valuation*. The theoretical call and put option prices, obtained from the Black-Scholes formula, do not depend on the drift but only on the volatility and other parameters. In terms of trading goals, if the drift is associated with the trend, then it seems quite reasonable not to eliminate but to know and apply it. This would be consistent with the statement "the trend is your friend." Predicting the trend is a major goal in trading, but elusive for almost everyone.

One of the problems is that it is not so easy to say what a trend is. Consider a standard *Brownian motion* B_t, where the time t variable takes values from the interval $[0, T]$. This is often applied as a building element for the simulation of price changes. By definition the process begins at $B_0 = 0$ and has stationary and independent increments. It is continuous at time t. The increments $B_{t2} - B_{t1}$ between any two points $t1$ and $t2$ are random and have a normal distribution with mean zero and variance $|t2 - t1|$, where the vertical lines denote the absolute value. The well-known *Levy theorem* states that there is no difference between a Brownian motion and a Wiener process (Neftci 1996). This implies that Brownian motion is a *martingale process*. A martingale in simple terms is a *driftless stochastic process* (Rogers 2000 covers the subject with comprehensive mathematical details). This means that with respect to the probability P specified by the probability density function of a normal distribution, the expected value is given by the equality $E^P[B_{t2}|I_{t1}] = B_{t1}$ for all $t2 > t1$. The symbol I_{t1} denotes summarized information available at time $t1$. Theoretically, B_t can reach any value. Many snapshots of the evolution of this process will look the same as local trends. At the same time, zero drift characterizing Brownian motion implies that the expected value of any future price following to this process is equal to a current price. This illustrates that what is visible by eye as a trend is not necessarily associated with the drift, which is zero in this example.

For pricing derivatives, finding a probability measure under which ratios of prices of all instruments to a price of some trading asset used as a common denominator follow martingale processes is an elegant way to get the final result—the price of a derivative (Geman et al. 1995). Let me then ask the question: If academicians try to eliminate the trend, which "is a friend," are the results obtained friendly to trading? Instead, they are actually solving a different problem, and in that arena they seem to be doing better. However, there are no evidences that the 10 percent belonging to the winning camp consists of academicians.

The Bridge

Academicians do make assumptions about the price distribution of underlying assets. For instance, we may expect that volatility (the square root of variance) during a short time interval is proportional to the square root of the time interval (Hull 1997). This is the power ½. Other evidence (Mandelbrot 2004) shows that the power can be between ½ and 1. This is useful for finding more realistic VaR (value at risk) estimations. But wait, if one suggests a stochastic process driven by random variables of known distributions, then other observable characteristics such as trend lines, price patterns, and moving averages values are all deduced from this information and can be simulated. For instance, the probability that two moving averages with different calculation periods will cross becomes quite certain, as will the probability that the price will penetrate some trend channel line.

Elements of technical analysis, which sometimes causing skepticism among academicians, can be a natural consequence of the same stochastic processes applied by academicians. This idea can be used for navigating bridges between what is often considered, two opposing worlds.

For instance, if one selects the price behavior of *geometric Brownian motion* $dP/P = m \times dt + s \times dz$, which has been mentioned in previous chapters, then it is clearly possible to simulate and observe whether certain trendlines and support and resistance lines appear and with what frequency. For practical applications, this process is considered too simple and more realistic models should be selected (Mandelbrot 2004).

It is interesting to read how those traders with many years of experience describe trends and volatility (Williams 2000):

> *I doubt that anyone fully understood how the markets work until the mid-1980s. Sure, we knew about trend; about overbought and oversold markets; about a few patterns, seasonal influences, fundamentals, and the like. But we really did not know what caused trend or, more correctly put, how it began and ended. We do now [...]. Trends*

are set in motion by what I call "explosions of price activity." Succinctly, if price, in one hour, day, week, month (pick your time frame for trend identification) has an explosive move up or down, the market will continue in that direction until there is an equal or greater explosive move in the opposite direction. This has come to be known as an expansion in volatility and is verbally captured by the phrase Doug Brie coined, "volatility breakout," based on my early 1980 work.

This qualitative description contains interesting elements of price changes that have been observed in the markets and would therefore argue for the use of sophisticated quantitative statistical tools. Modern theoretical and revolutionary approaches (Mandelbrot 2004) recognize the following features observed empirically in prices:

- The existence of fat tails—relatively frequent big price changes ("*explosive move up or down*")—that contradict Gaussian distributions
- Volatility clustering—regions or bands of low and high price changes ("*explosions of price activity,*" "*an expansion in volatility*")
- Scaling of distribution moments leading to a similarity in price charts observed over different time frames ("*price, in one hour, day, week, month [pick your time frame for trend identification]*")
- Long memory of price changes ("... the market will continue in that direction ...")

From these points it would seem that there is a psychological foundation for building a bridge that spans the opposing worlds of fundamental and technical analysis, and substituting a common view.

We should recognize at this time that whether we deal with real or simulated prices, the meaning of the potential profit and the corresponding strategy is unchanged because these properties are computed from any series of prices and costs. It does not matter how these data are obtained. However, the statistical properties of the market offering (potential profit) essentially deal with the statistical properties of prices and costs. If one simulates multiple price paths following a certain stochastic process, then the potential profit can be evaluated separately for each path. The obtained multiple values that are found on these unique paths can then be subjected to the statistics tools to yield an evaluation of a distribution of the market offering.

Collapse of the Theory?

Following the thought process of Benoit Mandelbrot (2004), it is fair to say that modern financial theory is based on three significant efforts, each punctuated by a Nobel Prize. The three points that form the plane that serves as a foundation of "the house of modern finance" are the Modern Portfolio Theory of Harry Markowitz (1999), the Capital Asset Pricing Theory of William Sharpe (1964), and the Black-Scholes (1973) and Merton (1990) approach for pricing derivatives. Mandelbrot underlines two facts: (1) all three approaches are substantially based on Bachelier's original 1900 assumption that price changes obey the Bell curve, the normal Gaussian distribution that drives Brownian motion; and (2) experimental evidence shows that price changes are much riskier and wilder and do not correspond to this assumption. The actual distributions fall somewhere between the Gauss and Cauchy distributions. Since the famous analysis of cotton prices (Mandelbrot 1963), the financial industry has accumulated the intriguing observations (Mandelbrot 2004) that (1) price changes do not follow a Gaussian distribution (cotton, wheat, Dow, Standard and Poor's 500, Japanese yen/U.S. dollar exchange rate, deutschemark/U.S. dollar exchange rate) but have fat tails; (2) the *kurtosis* (the fourth central moment divided by standard deviation raised to the fourth power) of experimental distributions is often significantly higher than 3—the value followed from the Gaussian distribution; and (3) the longer memory effect indicates non-Markov properties of prices and contradicts the efficient price theory which is based in the historical independence of prices.

If we try to place the three fundamental theoretical points stated in the previous paragraph into some coordinate system of only two dimensions, then one dimension should correspond to the underlying distribution of price changes. This dimension can get its scale from the kurtosis of the distribution, where the kurtosis of value 3 based on a Gaussian distribution would indicate the pivotal point (a line) in this coordinate system. Because all three approaches are based on the Gaussian bell curve distribution, all three points must be placed on one line corresponding to the kurtosis value 3. Three points, which are not on one line, constitute a triangle—a shape that is quite stable and rigid from an engineering point of view. A unique foundation plane can be drawn using these three points. However, our points are on one line. The plane can rotate around this line. An entire building can easily turn upside down. In addition, the evidence summarized by Mandelbrot and Hudson (2004) means that our line can vibrate! This is because the common denominator—Brownian motion, ingeniously selected by Louis Bachelier (1900) as the first theoretical vehicle—is the basis of all three approaches and can cause the entire line to shift at one time. The building is on a shaking plane, which can rotate! Can we think of this as a stable foundation?

If we consider a market as a system, then ignorance of the differences between theoretical assumptions and actual price changes can be viewed as factors acting on the system. The behavior of a system normally works contrary to the factors affecting it. This is reminiscent of the principle that Le Shatel'e applied to thermodynamic systems. How can a system reduce the factor of ignorance? It can wipe out all traders who rely on wrong assumptions. The stock market crash on October 19, 1987, is a reminder. When we measure lengths of objects, we can make bigger or smaller errors, but we are never exact. The deviation between the measured amount and true length is the error. But when we observe a big price change between yesterday and today's closing prices, this is no error. This change is a fact.

Recognizing the limitations of "Bachelier's legacy" (Mandelbrot and Hudson 2004), there are new approaches that try to capture the most significant features of price changes. Among those are:

- Variations of ARCH models (Robert Engle's 2003 Nobel Prize in Economics) such as FIGARCH (Baillie et al. 1996)
- Multiple *stochastic volatility* models (Rebonato 2004)
- Models using fatter distributions based on the *Levy alpha-skew stable distribution* and parametric variations of the *generalized hyperbolic distribution* (Barndorff-Nielsen and Stelzer 2005)
- Models using *Poisson distribution* simulating rare events and diffusion jumps (Neftci 1996)

- And, of course, the very rich *multifractal model of asset returns* based on *fractional Brownian motion* dependent on *random multifractal trading times* (Mandelbrot and Hudson 2004).

These models optimistically hint that a collapse can theoretically be prevented. Increased computational power and more advanced design power of programming languages can establish a good base for the implementation of these models. This book, however, cannot even briefly describe the alternatives existing in this area. The theoretical basis for price models is a different subject. This book is about the potential profit and corresponding strategy properties, which can be computed given real prices and costs, or prices simulated by any of those models.

A Word on Potential Profit and Strategy

Why "a word" if it is already the entire book? The potential profit and the strategy that creates it are fundamental market properties. Similar to other properties, they require a flow of prices as input in order to be calculated. What distinguishes them from other pure price indicators is that they need additional information such as transaction costs and standardized accounting rules. However, what distinguishes them even more is their ultimate objective. These properties are explicitly bound to the final goal and the most important part of speculative trading—the monetary gain.

Potential profit and its corresponding strategy are the most goal-oriented market properties. They will continue to have meaning as long as speculative trading exists.

SLEEPING BEAUTY

Let us look at the style of the best trader—the one who knows the future.

Application to Tick Price Data

A complete history of tick price data is able to allow exhaustive calculation of potential profit values and strategies. For this example, we will use tick-by-tick prices for the January 2006 CBOT soybean contract. Data for Friday, October 21, 2005, have been selected arbitrarily. These daily data are supplied in the home page of CBOT and publicly available (Data source: www.cbot.com). The prices are given in the traditional form 5894, where the last digit, which can be 0, 2, 4, or 6, is the whole number representing eighths of 1 cent. This requires the conversion from 5894 to $589.5 = 589 + 4 \times 1/8$. At the same time, the original source contains the time of the price and some associated information. Because times and dates are not used in any of our calculations, they are not shown; therefore, the final file is suitable for the application of the program `maxprof3` developed in Chapter 6. The number of points in the original data file is quite large. While C++ is a good choice for the scale of this project, for simple text-processing tasks, other languages such as AWK (Aho et al. 1988) and related programs (awk, sed, etc.) are publicly available through CYGWIN GNU software and are quite efficient and convenient. The file that we'll use is named `CBOT_20051021_SF06_DATA.txt`. The SF06 is a standard name of the contract, where S denotes soybean, F is for the delivery month January, and 06 is the year 2006. A brief sample of the data appears:

```
S 1 1080 800 13
589.00
590.00
589.50
...
```

An extensive part of the data is given in the program output that follows. The initial and maintenance margins are $1,080 and $800, respectively. The program will work under Windows or UNIX as `maxprof3 < CBOT_20051021_SF06_DATA.txt`. The complete output is given so that you can study the results and compare your own implementation.

#	S	Cost	PPS	PPS1	PPS2	Pos2	Cash2	Equity2	Total2
0	589	13	1	1	1	1	1067	0	1067
1	590	13	0	0	0	1	1067	50	1117
2	589.5	13	0	0	0	1	1067	25	1092
3	589.75	13	0	0	0	1	1067	37.5	1104.5
4	590	13	0	0	0	1	1067	50	1117
5	589.5	13	0	0	0	1	1067	25	1092
6	590	13	0	0	0	1	1067	50	1117
7	590.5	13	0	0	0	1	1067	75	1142
8	591	13	-2	-2	-2	-1	1141	0	1141
9	590.5	13	0	0	0	-1	1141	25	1166
10	590	13	2	2	2	1	1165	0	1165
11	590.5	13	0	0	0	1	1165	25	1190
12	590.25	13	0	0	0	1	1165	12.5	1177.5
13	590	13	0	0	0	1	1165	0	1165
14	590.5	13	0	0	0	1	1165	25	1190
15	590	13	0	0	0	1	1165	0	1165
16	590.5	13	0	0	0	1	1165	25	1190
17	591	13	-2	-2	-2	-1	1189	0	1189
18	590.5	13	0	0	0	-1	1189	25	1214
19	590	13	0	0	0	-1	1189	50	1239
20	590.5	13	0	0	0	-1	1189	25	1214
21	589	13	2	2	2	1	1263	0	1263
22	590	13	0	0	0	1	1263	50	1313
23	590	13	0	0	0	1	1263	50	1313
24	590.5	13	-2	-2	-2	-1	1312	0	1312
25	590	13	0	0	0	-1	1312	25	1337
26	589.75	13	0	0	0	-1	1312	37.5	1349.5
27	589.5	13	0	0	0	-1	1312	50	1362
28	590	13	0	0	0	-1	1312	25	1337

29	589.5	13	0	0	0	-1	1312	50	1362
30	589.25	13	2	2	2	1	1348.5	0	1348.5
31	589.5	13	0	0	0	1	1348.5	12.5	1361
32	590	13	0	0	0	1	1348.5	37.5	1386
33	589.5	13	0	0	0	1	1348.5	12.5	1361
34	590	13	0	0	0	1	1348.5	37.5	1386
35	590.25	13	0	0	0	1	1348.5	50	1398.5
36	590	13	0	0	0	1	1348.5	37.5	1386
37	590.5	13	-2	-2	-2	-1	1385	0	1385
38	590	13	0	0	0	-1	1385	25	1410
39	589.5	13	0	0	0	-1	1385	50	1435
40	590	13	0	0	0	-1	1385	25	1410
41	589.5	13	0	0	0	-1	1385	50	1435
42	590	13	0	0	0	-1	1385	25	1410
43	589.5	13	0	0	0	-1	1385	50	1435
44	589.25	13	0	0	0	-1	1385	62.5	1447.5
45	589	13	0	0	0	-1	1385	75	1460
46	588.75	13	0	0	0	-1	1385	87.5	1472.5
47	588.5	13	0	0	0	-1	1385	100	1485
48	588	13	0	0	0	-1	1385	125	1510
49	587.5	13	0	0	0	-1	1385	150	1535
50	587	13	2	2	2	1	1534	0	1534
51	587.5	13	0	0	0	1	1534	25	1559
52	588	13	0	0	0	1	1534	50	1584
53	589	13	-2	-2	-2	-1	1608	0	1608
54	588.5	13	0	0	0	-1	1608	25	1633
55	589	13	0	0	0	-1	1608	0	1608
56	588	13	0	0	0	-1	1608	50	1658
57	588.5	13	0	0	0	-1	1608	25	1633
58	588	13	0	0	0	-1	1608	50	1658
59	588.5	13	0	0	0	-1	1608	25	1633
60	588	13	0	0	0	-1	1608	50	1658
61	587.5	13	0	0	0	-1	1608	75	1683
62	588	13	0	0	0	-1	1608	50	1658
63	587.5	13	0	0	0	-1	1608	75	1683
64	588	13	0	0	0	-1	1608	50	1658
65	587.5	13	0	0	0	-1	1608	75	1683
66	587.25	13	2	2	2	1	1669.5	0	1669.5
67	587.5	13	0	0	0	1	1669.5	12.5	1682
68	587.25	13	0	0	0	1	1669.5	0	1669.5
69	587.5	13	0	0	0	1	1669.5	12.5	1682
70	588	13	-2	-2	-2	-1	1681	0	1681
71	587.5	13	0	0	0	-1	1681	25	1706
72	588	13	0	0	0	-1	1681	0	1681
73	587.5	13	0	0	0	-1	1681	25	1706

74	588	13	0	0	0	-1	1681	0	1681
75	587.5	13	0	0	0	-1	1681	25	1706
76	588	13	0	0	0	-1	1681	0	1681
77	587.5	13	0	0	0	-1	1681	25	1706
78	588	13	0	0	0	-1	1681	0	1681
79	587.5	13	0	0	0	-1	1681	25	1706
80	587	13	0	0	0	-1	1681	50	1731
81	586.75	13	0	0	0	-1	1681	62.5	1743.5
82	586.5	13	0	0	0	-1	1681	75	1756
83	587	13	0	0	0	-1	1681	50	1731
84	586.5	13	0	0	0	-1	1681	75	1756
85	586	13	0	0	0	-1	1681	100	1781
86	586.25	13	0	0	0	-1	1681	87.5	1768.5
87	586	13	0	0	0	-1	1681	100	1781
88	585.5	13	2	2	2	1	1780	0	1780
89	586	13	0	0	0	1	1780	25	1805
90	586.5	13	0	0	0	1	1780	50	1830
91	587	13	0	0	0	1	1780	75	1855
92	586.5	13	0	0	0	1	1780	50	1830
93	587	13	0	0	0	1	1780	75	1855
94	586.5	13	0	0	0	1	1780	50	1830
95	587	13	0	0	0	1	1780	75	1855
96	587.25	13	0	0	0	1	1780	87.5	1867.5
97	587.5	13	-2	-2	-2	-1	1854	0	1854
98	586.5	13	0	0	0	-1	1854	50	1904
99	587	13	0	0	0	-1	1854	25	1879
100	586.5	13	0	0	0	-1	1854	50	1904
101	586	13	0	0	0	-1	1854	75	1929
102	585.5	13	2	2	2	1	1928	0	1928
103	586	13	0	0	0	1	1928	25	1953
104	586.5	13	-2	-2	-2	-1	1952	0	1952
105	586	13	0	0	0	-1	1952	25	1977
106	586.5	13	0	0	0	-1	1952	0	1952
107	586	13	0	0	0	-1	1952	25	1977
108	586.25	13	0	0	0	-1	1952	12.5	1964.5
109	586	13	0	0	0	-1	1952	25	1977
110	586.5	13	0	0	0	-1	1952	0	1952
111	586	13	0	0	0	-1	1952	25	1977
112	586.5	13	0	0	0	-1	1952	0	1952
113	586	13	0	0	0	-1	1952	25	1977
114	586.5	13	0	0	0	-1	1952	0	1952
115	586	13	0	0	0	-1	1952	25	1977
116	586.5	13	0	0	0	-1	1952	0	1952
117	586	13	0	0	0	-1	1952	25	1977
118	586.25	13	0	0	0	-1	1952	12.5	1964.5

119	586	13	0	0	0	-1	1952	25	1977
120	585.75	13	0	0	0	-1	1952	37.5	1989.5
121	585.5	13	2	2	2	1	1976	0	1976
122	586	13	0	0	0	1	1976	25	2001
123	585.5	13	0	0	0	1	1976	0	1976
124	586	13	0	0	0	1	1976	25	2001
125	585.5	13	0	0	0	1	1976	0	1976
126	586	13	0	0	0	1	1976	25	2001
127	585.5	13	0	0	0	1	1976	0	1976
128	586	13	0	0	0	1	1976	25	2001
129	585.5	13	0	0	0	1	1976	0	1976
130	586	13	0	0	0	1	1976	25	2001
131	586.25	13	-2	-2	-2	-1	1987.5	0	1987.5
132	586	13	0	0	0	-1	1987.5	12.5	2000
133	585.75	13	0	0	0	-1	1987.5	25	2012.5
134	586	13	0	0	0	-1	1987.5	12.5	2000
135	586.25	13	0	0	0	-1	1987.5	0	1987.5
136	586	13	0	0	0	-1	1987.5	12.5	2000
137	585.5	13	2	2	2	1	1999	0	1999
138	586	13	0	0	0	1	1999	25	2024
139	585.5	13	0	0	0	1	1999	0	1999
140	586	13	0	0	0	1	1999	25	2024
141	585.5	13	0	0	0	1	1999	0	1999
142	586	13	0	0	0	1	1999	25	2024
143	585.5	13	0	0	0	1	1999	0	1999
144	586	13	0	0	0	1	1999	25	2024
145	586.25	13	0	0	0	1	1999	37.5	2036.5
146	586.5	13	-2	-2	-2	-1	2023	0	2023
147	586.25	13	0	0	0	-1	2023	12.5	2035.5
148	586	13	0	0	0	-1	2023	25	2048
149	585.5	13	0	0	0	-1	2023	50	2073
150	585.25	13	2	2	2	1	2059.5	0	2059.5
151	586	13	-2	-2	-2	-1	2071	0	2071
152	585.5	13	0	0	0	-1	2071	25	2096
153	585	13	0	0	0	-1	2071	50	2121
154	584.25	13	2	2	2	1	2132.5	0	2132.5
155	584.5	13	0	0	0	1	2132.5	12.5	2145
156	584.75	13	0	0	0	1	2132.5	25	2157.5
157	585	13	-2	-2	-2	-1	2144	0	2144
158	584.5	13	0	0	-1	-2	2131	25	2156
159	584.25	13	0	0	0	-2	2131	50	2181
160	584	13	0	0	0	-2	2131	75	2206
161	583.5	13	0	0	0	-2	2131	125	2256
162	583.25	13	0	0	0	-2	2131	150	2281
163	583.5	13	0	0	0	-2	2131	125	2256

164	583	13	2	3	4	2	2254	0	2254
165	583.5	13	0	0	0	2	2254	50	2304
166	584	13	0	0	0	2	2254	100	2354
167	583.5	13	0	0	0	2	2254	50	2304
168	584	13	0	0	0	2	2254	100	2354
169	583.5	13	0	0	0	2	2254	50	2304
170	584	13	0	0	0	2	2254	100	2354
171	583.75	13	0	0	0	2	2254	75	2329
172	583.5	13	0	0	0	2	2254	50	2304
173	584	13	0	0	0	2	2254	100	2354
174	583.5	13	0	0	0	2	2254	50	2304
175	584	13	0	0	0	2	2254	100	2354
176	584.5	13	0	0	0	2	2254	150	2404
177	584	13	0	0	0	2	2254	100	2354
178	584.5	13	0	0	0	2	2254	150	2404
179	585	13	-2	-4	-4	-2	2402	0	2402
180	584.5	13	0	0	0	-2	2402	50	2452
181	585	13	0	0	0	-2	2402	0	2402
182	584	13	2	4	4	2	2450	0	2450
183	584.5	13	0	0	0	2	2450	50	2500
184	584	13	0	0	0	2	2450	0	2450
185	584.25	13	0	0	0	2	2450	25	2475
186	584.5	13	0	0	0	2	2450	50	2500
187	584.25	13	0	0	0	2	2450	25	2475
188	584.5	13	0	0	0	2	2450	50	2500
189	585	13	0	0	0	2	2450	100	2550
190	584.5	13	0	0	0	2	2450	50	2500
191	585	13	0	0	0	2	2450	100	2550
192	584.5	13	0	0	0	2	2450	50	2500
193	584.75	13	0	0	0	2	2450	75	2525
194	585	13	0	0	0	2	2450	100	2550
195	584.75	13	0	0	0	2	2450	75	2525
196	584.5	13	0	0	0	2	2450	50	2500
197	584.75	13	0	0	0	2	2450	75	2525
198	585	13	0	0	0	2	2450	100	2550
199	585.5	13	-2	-4	-4	-2	2548	0	2548
200	585.25	13	0	0	0	-2	2548	25	2573
201	585	13	0	0	0	-2	2548	50	2598
202	585.5	13	0	0	0	-2	2548	0	2548
203	585	13	0	0	0	-2	2548	50	2598
204	585.5	13	0	0	0	-2	2548	0	2548
205	585	13	0	0	0	-2	2548	50	2598
206	584.75	13	0	0	0	-2	2548	75	2623
207	584.5	13	0	0	0	-2	2548	100	2648
208	584	13	2	4	4	2	2646	0	2646

209	584.5	13	0	0	0	2	2646	50	2696
210	585	13	-2	-4	-4	-2	2694	0	2694
211	584.5	13	0	0	0	-2	2694	50	2744
212	585	13	0	0	0	-2	2694	0	2694
213	584.75	13	0	0	0	-2	2694	25	2719
214	584.5	13	0	0	0	-2	2694	50	2744
215	585	13	0	0	0	-2	2694	0	2694
216	584.5	13	0	0	0	-2	2694	50	2744
217	584.25	13	0	0	0	-2	2694	75	2769
218	584	13	0	0	0	-2	2694	100	2794
219	583.75	13	2	4	4	2	2767	0	2767
220	584	13	0	0	0	2	2767	25	2792
221	584.5	13	0	0	0	2	2767	75	2842
222	584	13	0	0	0	2	2767	25	2792
223	584.5	13	0	0	0	2	2767	75	2842
224	585	13	-2	-4	-4	-2	2840	0	2840
225	584.5	13	0	0	0	-2	2840	50	2890
226	584	13	2	4	4	2	2888	0	2888
227	584.5	13	0	0	0	2	2888	50	2938
228	585	13	-2	-4	-4	-2	2936	0	2936
229	584	13	2	4	4	2	2984	0	2984
230	584.5	13	0	0	0	2	2984	50	3034
231	584	13	0	0	0	2	2984	0	2984
232	584.25	13	0	0	0	2	2984	25	3009
233	584.5	13	0	0	0	2	2984	50	3034
234	585	13	-2	-4	-4	-2	3032	0	3032
235	584.5	13	0	0	0	-2	3032	50	3082
236	585	13	0	0	0	-2	3032	0	3032
237	584.5	13	0	0	0	-2	3032	50	3082
238	584	13	0	0	0	-2	3032	100	3132
239	584.5	13	0	0	0	-2	3032	50	3082
240	584	13	0	0	0	-2	3032	100	3132
241	583.75	13	0	0	0	-2	3032	125	3157
242	584	13	0	0	0	-2	3032	100	3132
243	583.75	13	0	0	0	-2	3032	125	3157
244	583.5	13	2	4	4	2	3130	0	3130
245	584	13	0	0	0	2	3130	50	3180
246	583.5	13	0	0	0	2	3130	0	3130
247	584	13	0	0	0	2	3130	50	3180
248	584.5	13	0	0	0	2	3130	100	3230
249	584	13	0	0	0	2	3130	50	3180
250	584.5	13	0	0	0	2	3130	100	3230
251	584.25	13	0	0	0	2	3130	75	3205
252	584.5	13	0	0	0	2	3130	100	3230
253	584	13	0	0	0	2	3130	50	3180

254	584.5	13	0	0	0	2	3130	100	3230
255	585	13	-2	-4	-5	-3	3215	0	3215
256	584.5	13	0	0	0	-3	3215	75	3290
257	585	13	0	0	0	-3	3215	0	3215
258	584.5	13	0	0	0	-3	3215	75	3290
259	584.25	13	0	0	0	-3	3215	112.5	3327.5
260	584.5	13	0	0	0	-3	3215	75	3290
261	584.25	13	0	0	0	-3	3215	112.5	3327.5
262	584.5	13	0	0	0	-3	3215	75	3290
263	584	13	0	0	0	-3	3215	150	3365
264	583.5	13	2	5	6	3	3362	0	3362
265	584	13	0	0	0	3	3362	75	3437
266	584.25	13	-2	-6	-6	-3	3396.5	0	3396.5
267	584	13	0	0	0	-3	3396.5	37.5	3434
268	584.25	13	0	0	0	-3	3396.5	0	3396.5
269	584	13	0	0	0	-3	3396.5	37.5	3434
270	584.25	13	0	0	0	-3	3396.5	0	3396.5
271	584	13	0	0	0	-3	3396.5	37.5	3434
272	583.75	13	0	0	0	-3	3396.5	75	3471.5
273	583.5	13	2	6	6	3	3431	0	3431
274	583.75	13	0	0	0	3	3431	37.5	3468.5
275	584	13	0	0	0	3	3431	75	3506
276	584.25	13	-2	-6	-6	-3	3465.5	0	3465.5
277	584	13	0	0	0	-3	3465.5	37.5	3503
278	583.75	13	0	0	0	-3	3465.5	75	3540.5
279	583.5	13	2	6	6	3	3500	0	3500
280	583.75	13	0	0	0	3	3500	37.5	3537.5
281	584	13	0	0	0	3	3500	75	3575
282	583.75	13	0	0	0	3	3500	37.5	3537.5
283	584	13	0	0	0	3	3500	75	3575
284	583.75	13	0	0	0	3	3500	37.5	3537.5
285	584	13	0	0	0	3	3500	75	3575
286	584.25	13	0	0	0	3	3500	112.5	3612.5
287	584.5	13	0	0	0	3	3500	150	3650
288	584.25	13	0	0	0	3	3500	112.5	3612.5
289	584.5	13	0	0	0	3	3500	150	3650
290	585	13	0	0	0	3	3500	225	3725
291	584.5	13	0	0	0	3	3500	150	3650
292	585	13	0	0	0	3	3500	225	3725
293	585.5	13	-2	-6	-6	-3	3722	0	3722
294	585.25	13	0	0	0	-3	3722	37.5	3759.5
295	585.5	13	0	0	0	-3	3722	0	3722
296	585.25	13	0	0	0	-3	3722	37.5	3759.5
297	585	13	0	0	0	-3	3722	75	3797
298	584.5	13	0	0	0	-3	3722	150	3872

299	585	13	0	0	0	-3	3722	75	3797
300	584.75	13	0	0	0	-3	3722	112.5	3834.5
301	584.5	13	0	0	0	-3	3722	150	3872
302	584.25	13	2	6	6	3	3831.5	0	3831.5
303	584.5	13	0	0	0	3	3831.5	37.5	3869
304	584.75	13	0	0	0	3	3831.5	75	3906.5
305	585	13	0	0	0	3	3831.5	112.5	3944
306	584.75	13	0	0	0	3	3831.5	75	3906.5
307	585	13	0	0	0	3	3831.5	112.5	3944
308	584.5	13	0	0	0	3	3831.5	37.5	3869
309	585	13	0	0	0	3	3831.5	112.5	3944
310	585.25	13	-2	-6	-6	-3	3903.5	0	3903.5
311	585	13	0	0	0	-3	3903.5	37.5	3941
312	584.5	13	0	0	0	-3	3903.5	112.5	4016
313	584.75	13	0	0	0	-3	3903.5	75	3978.5
314	584.5	13	0	0	0	-3	3903.5	112.5	4016
315	584.75	13	0	0	0	-3	3903.5	75	3978.5
316	584.5	13	0	0	0	-3	3903.5	112.5	4016
317	584.75	13	0	0	0	-3	3903.5	75	3978.5
318	584.5	13	0	0	0	-3	3903.5	112.5	4016
319	584.25	13	0	0	0	-3	3903.5	150	4053.5
320	584.5	13	0	0	0	-3	3903.5	112.5	4016
321	584.75	13	0	0	0	-3	3903.5	75	3978.5
322	584.5	13	0	0	0	-3	3903.5	112.5	4016
323	584.25	13	0	0	0	-3	3903.5	150	4053.5
324	584.5	13	0	0	0	-3	3903.5	112.5	4016
325	584	13	2	6	6	3	4013	0	4013
326	584.25	13	0	0	0	3	4013	37.5	4050.5
327	584.5	13	0	0	0	3	4013	75	4088
328	584.25	13	0	0	0	3	4013	37.5	4050.5
329	584.5	13	0	0	0	3	4013	75	4088
330	584.25	13	0	0	0	3	4013	37.5	4050.5
331	584.5	13	0	0	0	3	4013	75	4088
332	584.25	13	0	0	0	3	4013	37.5	4050.5
333	584.5	13	0	0	0	3	4013	75	4088
334	584.75	13	0	0	0	3	4013	112.5	4125.5
335	585	13	-2	-6	-6	-3	4085	0	4085
336	584.5	13	0	0	0	-3	4085	75	4160
337	584.25	13	2	6	6	3	4119.5	0	4119.5
338	584.5	13	0	0	0	3	4119.5	37.5	4157
339	584.75	13	0	0	0	3	4119.5	75	4194.5
340	585	13	0	0	0	3	4119.5	112.5	4232
341	584.75	13	0	0	0	3	4119.5	75	4194.5
342	584.5	13	0	0	0	3	4119.5	37.5	4157
343	585	13	0	0	0	3	4119.5	112.5	4232

344	584.75	13	0	0	0	3	4119.5	75	4194.5
345	584.5	13	0	0	0	3	4119.5	37.5	4157
346	584.75	13	0	0	0	3	4119.5	75	4194.5
347	585	13	0	0	0	3	4119.5	112.5	4232
348	584.75	13	0	0	0	3	4119.5	75	4194.5
349	584.5	13	0	0	0	3	4119.5	37.5	4157
350	585	13	0	0	0	3	4119.5	112.5	4232
351	584.75	13	0	0	0	3	4119.5	75	4194.5
352	585	13	0	0	0	3	4119.5	112.5	4232
353	585.5	13	0	0	0	3	4119.5	187.5	4307
354	585.25	13	0	0	0	3	4119.5	150	4269.5
355	585	13	0	0	0	3	4119.5	112.5	4232
356	585.5	13	0	0	0	3	4119.5	187.5	4307
357	585.75	13	-2	-6	-6	-3	4266.5	0	4266.5
358	585.5	13	0	0	0	-3	4266.5	37.5	4304
359	585.25	13	0	0	0	-3	4266.5	75	4341.5
360	585.5	13	0	0	0	-3	4266.5	37.5	4304
361	585.25	13	0	0	0	-3	4266.5	75	4341.5
362	585	13	0	0	0	-3	4266.5	112.5	4379
363	585.25	13	0	0	0	-3	4266.5	75	4341.5
364	585	13	0	0	0	-3	4266.5	112.5	4379
365	584.75	13	2	6	7	4	4325.5	0	4325.5
366	585	13	0	0	0	4	4325.5	50	4375.5
367	585.25	13	0	0	0	4	4325.5	100	4425.5
368	585	13	0	0	0	4	4325.5	50	4375.5
369	585.5	13	0	0	0	4	4325.5	150	4475.5
370	585.25	13	0	0	0	4	4325.5	100	4425.5
371	585	13	0	0	0	4	4325.5	50	4375.5
372	585.5	13	0	0	0	4	4325.5	150	4475.5
373	585	13	0	0	0	4	4325.5	50	4375.5
374	585.5	13	0	0	0	4	4325.5	150	4475.5
375	585	13	0	0	0	4	4325.5	50	4375.5
376	585.25	13	0	0	0	4	4325.5	100	4425.5
377	585.5	13	0	0	0	4	4325.5	150	4475.5
378	585.75	13	0	0	0	4	4325.5	200	4525.5
379	586	13	-2	-7	-8	-4	4471.5	0	4471.5
380	585.75	13	0	0	0	-4	4471.5	50	4521.5
381	585.5	13	0	0	0	-4	4471.5	100	4571.5
382	586	13	0	0	0	-4	4471.5	0	4471.5
383	585.5	13	0	0	0	-4	4471.5	100	4571.5
384	585.75	13	0	0	0	-4	4471.5	50	4521.5
385	586	13	0	0	0	-4	4471.5	0	4471.5
386	585.75	13	0	0	0	-4	4471.5	50	4521.5
387	585.5	13	0	0	0	-4	4471.5	100	4571.5
388	585.5	13	0	0	0	-4	4471.5	100	4571.5

389	585.75	13	0	0	0	-4	4471.5	50	4521.5
390	585.5	13	0	0	0	-4	4471.5	100	4571.5
391	585.75	13	0	0	0	-4	4471.5	50	4521.5
392	585.5	13	0	0	0	-4	4471.5	100	4571.5
393	585.75	13	0	0	0	-4	4471.5	50	4521.5
394	586	13	0	0	0	-4	4471.5	0	4471.5
395	585.75	13	0	0	0	-4	4471.5	50	4521.5
396	586	13	0	0	0	-4	4471.5	0	4471.5
397	585.75	13	0	0	0	-4	4471.5	50	4521.5
398	585.5	13	0	0	0	-4	4471.5	100	4571.5
399	585.25	13	0	0	0	-4	4471.5	150	4621.5
400	585.5	13	0	0	0	-4	4471.5	100	4571.5
401	585	13	0	0	0	-4	4471.5	200	4671.5
402	585.25	13	0	0	0	-4	4471.5	150	4621.5
403	585.5	13	0	0	0	-4	4471.5	100	4571.5
404	585	13	0	0	0	-4	4471.5	200	4671.5
405	585.25	13	0	0	0	-4	4471.5	150	4621.5
406	585	13	0	0	0	-4	4471.5	200	4671.5
407	585.25	13	0	0	0	-4	4471.5	150	4621.5
408	585	13	0	0	0	-4	4471.5	200	4671.5
409	585.25	13	0	0	0	-4	4471.5	150	4621.5
410	585.5	13	0	0	0	-4	4471.5	100	4571.5
411	585.25	13	0	0	0	-4	4471.5	150	4621.5
412	585	13	0	0	0	-4	4471.5	200	4671.5
413	585.25	13	0	0	0	-4	4471.5	150	4621.5
414	585	13	0	0	0	-4	4471.5	200	4671.5
415	585.25	13	0	0	0	-4	4471.5	150	4621.5
416	585	13	0	0	0	-4	4471.5	200	4671.5
417	585.25	13	0	0	0	-4	4471.5	150	4621.5
418	585	13	0	0	0	-4	4471.5	200	4671.5
419	585.25	13	0	0	0	-4	4471.5	150	4621.5
420	585	13	0	0	0	-4	4471.5	200	4671.5
421	584.75	13	0	0	0	-4	4471.5	250	4721.5
422	584.5	13	2	8	8	4	4667.5	0	4667.5
423	584.75	13	0	0	0	4	4667.5	50	4717.5
424	585	13	0	0	0	4	4667.5	100	4767.5
425	584.75	13	0	0	0	4	4667.5	50	4717.5
426	585	13	0	0	0	4	4667.5	100	4767.5
427	585.25	13	-2	-8	-8	-4	4713.5	0	4713.5
428	585	13	0	0	0	-4	4713.5	50	4763.5
429	584.75	13	0	0	0	-4	4713.5	100	4813.5
430	585	13	0	0	0	-4	4713.5	50	4763.5
431	584.75	13	0	0	0	-4	4713.5	100	4813.5
432	585	13	0	0	0	-4	4713.5	50	4763.5
433	584.75	13	0	0	0	-4	4713.5	100	4813.5

434	584.5	13	0	0	0	-4	4713.5	150	4863.5
435	584.75	13	0	0	0	-4	4713.5	100	4813.5
436	584.5	13	0	0	0	-4	4713.5	150	4863.5
437	584.75	13	0	0	0	-4	4713.5	100	4813.5
438	584.5	13	0	0	0	-4	4713.5	150	4863.5
439	584.25	13	0	0	0	-4	4713.5	200	4913.5
440	584.5	13	0	0	0	-4	4713.5	150	4863.5
441	584.25	13	0	0	0	-4	4713.5	200	4913.5
442	584.5	13	0	0	0	-4	4713.5	150	4863.5
443	584.25	13	0	0	0	-4	4713.5	200	4913.5
444	584	13	0	0	0	-4	4713.5	250	4963.5
445	584.25	13	0	0	0	-4	4713.5	200	4913.5
446	584.5	13	0	0	0	-4	4713.5	150	4863.5
447	584.25	13	0	0	0	-4	4713.5	200	4913.5
448	584.5	13	0	0	0	-4	4713.5	150	4863.5
449	584.25	13	0	0	0	-4	4713.5	200	4913.5
450	584.5	13	0	0	0	-4	4713.5	150	4863.5
451	584	13	0	0	0	-4	4713.5	250	4963.5
452	583.75	13	2	8	8	4	4909.5	0	4909.5
453	584	13	0	0	0	4	4909.5	50	4959.5
454	584.25	13	0	0	0	4	4909.5	100	5009.5
455	584	13	0	0	0	4	4909.5	50	4959.5
456	584.25	13	0	0	0	4	4909.5	100	5009.5
457	584	13	0	0	0	4	4909.5	50	4959.5
458	584.25	13	0	0	0	4	4909.5	100	5009.5
459	584	13	0	0	0	4	4909.5	50	4959.5
460	584.25	13	0	0	0	4	4909.5	100	5009.5
461	584.5	13	-2	-8	-8	-4	4955.5	0	4955.5
462	584.25	13	0	0	0	-4	4955.5	50	5005.5
463	584	13	0	0	0	-4	4955.5	100	5055.5
464	584.25	13	0	0	0	-4	4955.5	50	5005.5
465	584	13	0	0	0	-4	4955.5	100	5055.5
466	583.75	13	2	8	8	4	5001.5	0	5001.5
467	584	13	0	0	0	4	5001.5	50	5051.5
468	583.75	13	0	0	0	4	5001.5	0	5001.5
469	584	13	0	0	0	4	5001.5	50	5051.5
470	584.25	13	0	0	0	4	5001.5	100	5101.5
471	584	13	0	0	0	4	5001.5	50	5051.5
472	584.25	13	0	0	0	4	5001.5	100	5101.5
473	584	13	0	0	0	4	5001.5	50	5051.5
474	584.25	13	0	0	0	4	5001.5	100	5101.5
475	584	13	0	0	0	4	5001.5	50	5051.5
476	584.25	13	0	0	0	4	5001.5	100	5101.5
477	584.5	13	0	0	0	4	5001.5	150	5151.5
478	584.75	13	-2	-8	-8	-4	5097.5	0	5097.5

479	584.5	13	0	0	0	-4	5097.5	50	5147.5
480	584.25	13	0	0	0	-4	5097.5	100	5197.5
481	584	13	0	0	0	-4	5097.5	150	5247.5
482	583.75	13	0	0	0	-4	5097.5	200	5297.5
483	583.5	13	0	0	0	-4	5097.5	250	5347.5
484	583.25	13	0	0	0	-4	5097.5	300	5397.5
485	583	13	2	8	8	4	5343.5	0	5343.5
486	584	13	0	0	0	4	5343.5	200	5543.5
487	583.5	13	0	0	1	5	5330.5	100	5430.5
488	583.75	13	0	0	0	5	5330.5	162.5	5493
489	584	13	0	0	0	5	5330.5	225	5555.5
490	584.25	13	0	0	0	5	5330.5	287.5	5618
491	584	13	0	0	0	5	5330.5	225	5555.5
492	584.25	13	0	0	0	5	5330.5	287.5	5618
493	584	13	0	0	0	5	5330.5	225	5555.5
494	583.75	13	0	0	0	5	5330.5	162.5	5493
495	584	13	0	0	0	5	5330.5	225	5555.5
496	584.25	13	0	0	0	5	5330.5	287.5	5618
497	584	13	0	0	0	5	5330.5	225	5555.5
498	584.25	13	0	0	0	5	5330.5	287.5	5618
499	584	13	0	0	0	5	5330.5	225	5555.5
500	584.5	13	0	0	0	5	5330.5	350	5680.5
501	584.25	13	0	0	0	5	5330.5	287.5	5618
502	584	13	0	0	0	5	5330.5	225	5555.5
503	584.25	13	0	0	0	5	5330.5	287.5	5618
504	584.5	13	0	0	0	5	5330.5	350	5680.5
505	584.25	13	0	0	0	5	5330.5	287.5	5618
506	584.5	13	0	0	0	5	5330.5	350	5680.5
507	584.25	13	0	0	0	5	5330.5	287.5	5618
508	584.5	13	0	0	0	5	5330.5	350	5680.5
509	584.25	13	0	0	0	5	5330.5	287.5	5618
510	584.5	13	0	0	0	5	5330.5	350	5680.5
511	584.25	13	0	0	0	5	5330.5	287.5	5618
512	584.5	13	0	0	0	5	5330.5	350	5680.5
513	584.75	13	0	0	0	5	5330.5	412.5	5743
514	585	13	-2	-9	-10	-5	5675.5	0	5675.5
515	584.75	13	0	0	0	-5	5675.5	62.5	5738
516	584.5	13	0	0	0	-5	5675.5	125	5800.5
517	585	13	0	0	0	-5	5675.5	0	5675.5
518	584.5	13	0	0	0	-5	5675.5	125	5800.5
519	585	13	0	0	0	-5	5675.5	0	5675.5
520	584.5	13	0	0	0	-5	5675.5	125	5800.5
521	584.75	13	0	0	0	-5	5675.5	62.5	5738
522	585	13	0	0	0	-5	5675.5	0	5675.5
523	584.5	13	0	0	0	-5	5675.5	125	5800.5

524	585	13	0	0	0	-5	5675.5	0	5675.5
525	584.5	13	0	0	0	-5	5675.5	125	5800.5
526	584.75	13	0	0	0	-5	5675.5	62.5	5738
527	584.5	13	0	0	0	-5	5675.5	125	5800.5
528	585	13	0	0	0	-5	5675.5	0	5675.5
529	584.5	13	0	0	0	-5	5675.5	125	5800.5
530	584.75	13	0	0	0	-5	5675.5	62.5	5738
531	584.5	13	0	0	0	-5	5675.5	125	5800.5
532	584.75	13	0	0	0	-5	5675.5	62.5	5738
533	584.5	13	0	0	0	-5	5675.5	125	5800.5
534	584.75	13	0	0	0	-5	5675.5	62.5	5738
535	585	13	0	0	0	-5	5675.5	0	5675.5
536	584.75	13	0	0	0	-5	5675.5	62.5	5738
537	584.5	13	0	0	0	-5	5675.5	125	5800.5
538	584.75	13	0	0	0	-5	5675.5	62.5	5738
539	584.5	13	0	0	0	-5	5675.5	125	5800.5
540	584.75	13	0	0	0	-5	5675.5	62.5	5738
541	584.5	13	0	0	0	-5	5675.5	125	5800.5
542	584	13	2	10	10	5	5795.5	0	5795.5
543	584.5	13	0	0	0	5	5795.5	125	5920.5
544	585	13	-2	-10	-10	-5	5915.5	0	5915.5
545	584.5	13	0	0	0	-5	5915.5	125	6040.5
546	585	13	0	0	0	-5	5915.5	0	5915.5
547	584	13	2	10	10	5	6035.5	0	6035.5
548	584.75	13	-2	-10	-10	-5	6093	0	6093
549	584.5	13	0	0	0	-5	6093	62.5	6155.5
550	584.75	13	0	0	0	-5	6093	0	6093
551	584.5	13	0	0	0	-5	6093	62.5	6155.5
552	584.25	13	0	0	0	-5	6093	125	6218
553	584.5	13	0	0	0	-5	6093	62.5	6155.5
554	584.75	13	0	0	0	-5	6093	0	6093
555	584.5	13	0	0	0	-5	6093	62.5	6155.5
556	584.75	13	0	0	0	-5	6093	0	6093
557	584.5	13	0	0	0	-5	6093	62.5	6155.5
558	584.25	13	0	0	0	-5	6093	125	6218
559	584.5	13	0	0	0	-5	6093	62.5	6155.5
560	584.25	13	0	0	0	-5	6093	125	6218
561	584	13	2	10	10	5	6150.5	0	6150.5
562	584.25	13	0	0	0	5	6150.5	62.5	6213
563	584.5	13	0	0	0	5	6150.5	125	6275.5
564	584	13	0	0	0	5	6150.5	0	6150.5
565	584.5	13	0	0	0	5	6150.5	125	6275.5
566	584	13	0	0	0	5	6150.5	0	6150.5
567	584.75	13	-1	-5	-5	0	6273	0	6273
568	584.5	13	0	0	0	0	6273	0	6273

```
A0 = 1080 P&L = 2447.5 P&L1 = 5009.5 P&L2 = 5193 IM = 1080 MM = 800
```

The transaction cost used in the program is $13, which means that a round-turn (a complete trade) is $26. This is typical of the transaction fee for a discount brokerage firm but does not include any slippage. The second profit-and-loss (P&L) reserve strategy is completely shown for each price change and time, including the position, cash balance, open position equity, and total equity. For the other two strategies, only the actions and final P&L are given. It is important to know that adding five ticks (each tick equal to 0.25—two-eighths of 1 cent) for slippage is equal to 5 × $12.50 = $62.50 and brings the total transaction cost to $75.50 per contract. This results in:

```
#        S  Cost  PPS   PPS1   PPS2   Pos2    Cash2  Equity2   Total2
0      589  75.5    0      0      0      0     1080        0     1080
1      590  75.5    0      0      0      0     1080        0     1080
2    589.5  75.5    0      0      0      0     1080        0     1080
3   589.75  75.5    0      0      0      0     1080        0     1080
4      590  75.5    0      0      0      0     1080        0     1080
5    589.5  75.5    0      0      0      0     1080        0     1080
6      590  75.5    0      0      0      0     1080        0     1080
7    590.5  75.5    0      0      0      0     1080        0     1080
8      591  75.5   -1     -1     -1     -1   1004.5        0   1004.5
9    590.5  75.5    0      0      0     -1   1004.5       25   1029.5
...
568  584.5  75.5    0      0      0      0     1329        0     1329
A0 = 1080 P&L = 249 P&L1 = 249 P&L2 = 249 IM = 1080 MM = 800
```

Because the soybean price range and fluctuations were relatively low on this day, raising the cost to $151 per trade prevented the two reserve strategies from increasing their positions and reinvesting profits. With this high cost and price data, the two strategies are the same as the potential profit strategy. The higher level of transaction cost caused many of the transactions to be filtered out.

This program will also return Pardo's potential profit if the costs are set to zero. The result is:

```
...
A0 = 1080 P&L = 10275 P&L1 = 7.1307e+006 P&L2 = 7.55455e+006 IM = 1080
MM = 800
```

Pardo's profit corresponds to the P&L of the potential profit strategy without money management. It is equal to $10,275. We cannot, however, neglect the commission portion of transaction costs.

Application to Daily Price Data

The most available and frequently used price data are those markets published every business day in the *Wall Street Journal* or available from many other electronic or printed sources.

Daily data contain open, high, low, and settlement prices and total volume. For futures markets, open interest is also available. But we know that the same high or low price can be reached several times during a trading session, and there are several other potentially profitable price fluctuations that may happen. A potential profit strategy could effectively exploit this lost information but many analysts would like to apply the potential profit strategy to daily data because it is far more convenient than intraday data. The only thing that can be said with confidence is that the opening price comes before the settlement or closing prices. Another thing is that both high and low prices, if they do not coincide with open and/or closing price, come between opening and closing prices. When analyzing daily prices, we do not know whether the high or the low price happens first. How should we proceed?

The algorithms can be applied to any price flow. However, when applying them only to settlement prices, one needs to keep in mind that the result will miss many opportunities that can be seen using only intraday data, and therefore it will generate less profit. One can put the four daily prices in a row—open-high-low-close—however, this also would not catch all the opportunities and the order of high and low prices may incorrectly influence the result. The following example shows the use of daily price data (Data source: XPRESSTRADE, www.xpresstrade.com) for the soybean contract SK05 (May 2005) for the calendar months January, February, and March 2005. The close prices are arranged in the file `CBOT_2005JFM_SK05_C_DATA.txt` in the format suitable for `maxprof3`:

```
S 1 2700 2500 76
 541.25
 530.00
 531.00
...
```

The initial and maintenance margins are set to $2,700 and $2,500, respectively. Such big numbers may reflect higher soybean prices and greater volatility in this period. This higher initial investment requirement may put additional stress on the strategy and reduce the result. Also, the cost per contract per transaction is set at $76. This higher amount allows us to bundle the commission cost and some intraday slippage into one value. One can argue that soybean slippage can be significantly greater than 10 ticks per trade. This is true. A gap opening that spans a few points or even few dozen points is not an extraordinary event for this market. However, we are not studying the slippage patterns of soybeans, but simply using these estimates to illustrate some results from the program. In many situations, one can apply the true range or an average true range—techniques that will be discussed in the next chapter—to get reasonable values. The following is the run `maxprof3 < CBOT_2005JFM_SK05_C_DATA.txt`:

```
#        S  Cost  PPS   PPS1   PPS2   Pos2    Cash2  Equity2   Total2
0   541.25    76   -1     -1     -1     -1     2624        0     2624
1      530    76    2      2      2      1   3034.5        0   3034.5
2      531    76    0      0      0      1   3034.5       50   3084.5
3   536.25    76    0      0      0      1   3034.5    312.5     3347
4    546.5    76    0      0      0      1   3034.5      825   3859.5
5      551    76   -2     -2     -2     -1   3932.5        0   3932.5
6    546.5    76    0      0      0     -1   3932.5      225   4157.5
```

7	536.25	76	0	0	0	-1	3932.5	737.5	4670
8	539	76	0	0	0	-1	3932.5	600	4532.5
9	522.75	76	0	0	0	-1	3932.5	1412.5	5345
10	516.25	76	2	3	3	2	5442	0	5442
11	518.75	76	0	0	0	2	5442	250	5692
12	521	76	-2	-4	-4	-2	5613	0	5613
13	516	76	2	4	4	2	5809	0	5809
14	520.25	76	0	0	0	2	5809	425	6234
15	524	76	-2	-4	-4	-2	6305	0	6305
16	521.25	76	0	0	0	-2	6305	275	6580
17	514	76	0	0	0	-2	6305	1000	7305
18	513	76	0	0	0	-2	6305	1100	7405
19	512.5	76	0	0	0	-2	6305	1150	7455
20	507	76	0	0	0	-2	6305	1700	8005
21	506.25	76	0	0	0	-2	6305	1775	8080
22	504.25	76	0	0	0	-2	6305	1975	8280
23	502.25	76	2	5	5	3	8100	0	8100
24	505	76	0	0	0	3	8100	412.5	8512.5
25	506.5	76	0	0	0	3	8100	637.5	8737.5
26	511.25	76	0	0	0	3	8100	1350	9450
27	515.25	76	0	0	0	3	8100	1950	10050
28	526.5	76	0	0	1	4	8024	3637.5	11661.5
29	536.25	76	0	0	1	5	7948	5587.5	13535.5
30	535.5	76	0	0	0	5	7948	5400	13348
31	534.75	76	0	0	0	5	7948	5212.5	13160.5
32	553	76	0	0	1	6	7872	9775	17647
33	555.75	76	0	0	0	6	7872	10600	18472
34	583	76	0	0	0	6	7872	18775	26647
35	582.5	76	0	0	3	9	7644	18625	26269
36	587	76	0	0	1	10	7568	20650	28218
37	604.5	76	0	0	3	13	7340	29400	36740
38	622	76	-2	-12	-30	-17	45835	0	45835
39	613.25	76	2	19	36	19	50536.5	0	50536.5
40	627.25	76	0	0	0	19	50536.5	13300	63836.5
41	627.25	76	0	0	0	19	50536.5	13300	63836.5
42	629.75	76	-2	-23	-42	-23	63019.5	0	63019.5
43	616	76	2	28	51	28	74956	0	74956
44	625.5	76	0	0	4	32	74652	13300	87952
45	629.5	76	0	0	2	34	74500	19700	94200
46	639.25	76	0	0	7	41	73968	36275	110243
47	662.5	76	-2	-42	-98	-57	150457.5	0	150457.5
48	656	76	2	56	117	60	160090.5	0	160090.5
49	681	76	-2	-70	-145	-85	224070.5	0	224070.5
50	673.5	76	0	0	-9	-94	223386.5	31875	255261.5
51	671.5	76	0	0	-4	-98	223082.5	41275	264357.5

```
 52      649   76   0     0    -40   -138 220042.5   151525 371567.5
 53    626.5   76   0     0      0   -138 220042.5   306775 526817.5
 54   627.25   76   0     0    -55   -193 215862.5   301600 517462.5
 55   623.25   76   2   123    393    200 526194.5        0 526194.5
 56   628.75   76  -2  -168   -409   -209 550110.5        0 550110.5
 57   625.75   76   0     0      0   -209 550110.5    31350 581460.5
 58      624   76   2   175    425    216   567448        0   567448
 59      641   76  -2  -201   -488   -272   713960        0   713960
 60    627.5   76   1   112    272      0   876888        0   876888
A0 = 2700 P&L = 19199.5 P&L1 = 358796 P&L2 = 874188 IM = 2700 MM = 2500
```

These results give the answer to the question formulated at the beginning of Chapter 1: "If one says that he made a 100 percent return on margin trading soybean futures in the first quarter of 2005..., should we conclude that this is a good return?" The 100 percent in this case is equivalent to the initial margin of $2,700. This is 100 percent × $2,700/$19,199.50 ~ 14 percent of the potential profit without the application of any money management. The result is also 100 percent × $2,700/$874,188 ~ 0.3 percent of the result of the second P&L reserve strategy. Do not forget that the potential profits from using intraday data are missing from these results. Literally, starting with a single contract, the third strategy made almost a million dollars in three months. This was what the market offered a trader for an investment of $2,700 in January 2005. Nobody knew that the market would offer this opportunity in January 2005. However, by studying the results in Williams's book (2005), you would see that during January and February 2005 there was a *bullish market setup* for soybeans. This was especially visible in the first days of February. Taking into account the seasonality of the grain markets and selecting a reasonable *oversold condition entry indicator*, and after probably several attempts, which lost money, one could finally establish a sustainable long position in soybeans. This would yield about 100 to 120 points per contract by sometime in the middle of March of the same year, where each point has a value of $50.

This is an appropriate moment to remember one of the important government disclaimers:

Warning: Futures trading, stock trading, currency trading, options trading, etc., involve high risk and you can lose a lot of money.

WAR AND PEACE

The efforts in the previous sections try to create a bridge that can unite the positions of two opposing worlds—that of technical analysis and others that produce sophisticated models describing price behavior. There are a number of possible outcomes from this conflict. Two of the positive possibilities are that the elements of technical analysis will naturally evolve from the stochastic models or they could help introduce corrections in the models. With either approach, the resolution has a peaceful character. Will this help reduce the percentage of losing traders to below 90 percent?

There are several reasons why the high ratio of losers to winners will continue at a high level. One is the psychological aspect, illustrated by a price definition given by Alexander Elder (1993):

Price is what the greater fool is ready to pay.

Another is the source of money (Elder 1993):

The only reason there is money in the markets is that other traders put it there. The money you want to make belongs to other people who have no intention of giving it to you. . . . Trading means trying to rob other people while they are trying to rob you. It is a hard business.

Part of the total flow of funds must go to the brokers and floor traders as commissions and slippage. The "big money," as we demonstrated in the Chapter 4, has a better chance of protecting the initial investment and surviving longer sequences of loses. When viewed in greater detail, the operation of the market participants is similar to military battles. Warlords distribute their armies and small troops in different fields of the battle in the same way that portions of the margin account are allocated to different markets and trades. Many of them die. A role of the financial commander is to distribute his money resources. He must know how much money he is going to make and how much he can afford to lose. He must have a system and know why he is entering a trade.

If we consider a market as a system, then it should possess an ability to minimize the influence of factors acting on it and potentially damaging it. A natural reflection of this relationship between a system and an external factor is formulated by the principle of Le Shatel'e applied in thermodynamics. Another concept that comes to mind is *homeostasis*, a property of an open system to regulate its internal conditions and maintain stable existence. This also can be viewed as a boundary or a region of critical values of parameters that a system must not exceed in order not to be destroyed. A system always attempts to go into the center of the region far from the dangerous conditions that may cease its existence. This concept has been actively used for solving *mathematical optimization problems* by *system analysis* (Moiseev 1982). What is dangerous for the market? The market is nothing more than people trading something. The absence of trades is a death for this organism by definition. Flat prices may also lead to a loss of public interest. An attempt to distribute a successful trading system among all market participants is controversial because everybody cannot win. After all, if everybody follows the same system and the system says "buy," where can you find a counterparty for the transaction? The market will resist such factors. The market with flat prices must explode one day. The successful system distributed among too many traders will stop bringing profits. Somebody must lose in order that others can win. Their gains will attract others who did not yet lose. Those who lost should become more careful. Developing new and faster techniques will change the market but not the ratio.

However, what if all trading properties have no repetitive nature? Even if this concept is proved, it does not invalidate the setup of the following task: what is a reasonable behavior of a trader or trading system under these nonrepetitive conditions? The ability to build a potential profit strategy would hint that some reasonable behavior was always possible. The battle will continue.

CONCLUSIONS

- It has been suggested that software able to parse and recognize human messaging, especially on the Internet, should be applied to the evaluation of bullish and bearish market sentiment.
- Instead of arguing about the applicability of technical methods of analysis and creating a contest between the world of traders and that of academicians, it would be more constructive to build bridges between the worlds and find how traditional elements of technical analysis, such as patterns, trend lines, and indicators, follow from the price distribution assumptions already accepted in pricing derivatives.
- The algorithms of potential profit and the first and second P&L reserve strategies have been applied to intraday and daily market data for a soybean contract traded on the CBOT. Applying these methods to intraday data is best way of evaluating the maximum profit.
- The potential profit and corresponding strategies are fundamental market properties.

CHAPTER 8

Indicators Based on Potential Profit

Potential profit and its corresponding strategies combine profitable price moves and efficient money management. They depend on prices, transaction costs, and account maintenance rules determined by the futures industry. This makes them rich concepts that transform market information into the form that allows us to achieve our final goal. Let us consider various applications and their relationship to other trading concepts.

PERFORMANCE MEASURES AND INDICATORS

Profit Performance of a System

As suggested by Robert Pardo (1993), performance of a model (trading system) or a trader can be measured by the ratio of the achieved profit and loss (P&L) to the potential market profit:

$$\text{Profit performance} = \text{P\&L} / \text{Potential profit} \tag{8.1}$$

Because transaction costs cannot be excluded from actual trading, it is important to include their effect. This leads to two results: not all trades suggested by Pardo's algorithm can be profitable, and the profit obtained from the rest of trades is reduced by transaction costs. To evaluate the ratio, one needs to use the same time interval for both the actual P&L and the potential profits. It is also important to use the same initial number of contracts. The three principal algorithms proposed in this book apply an initial number of contracts as a parameter. If trading is done in such a manner that at any moment an open position has the same absolute number of contracts, then the denominator must be obtained by `potential_profit_ralg` or `potential_profit_lalg`. If a trader applies money management resulting in positions of different sizes or complex positions where contracts are bought or sold at different prices, then it makes sense to divide the P&L by values returned by `second_pl_reserve_prime_alg` or `second_pl_reserve_alg`.

Performance of a System Defined as Return on Capital

While the best strategy does not lose money, it still requires a certain amount of capital to start trading. The minimum initial capital A_0 is computed by `potential_profit_min_account_alg`. This algorithm depends on the initial number of contracts to be traded. For all three profit algorithms it is important that the same A_0 is used. We will call the ratio of the potential profit to the minimum initial capital the *optimal return on capital:*

$$\begin{aligned}\text{Optimal return on capital} &= \text{Potential profit} / \text{Minimal initial capital} \\ &= \text{Potential profit} / A_0 \end{aligned} \qquad (8.2)$$

This value is relative to a certain time interval and can be annualized using standard conventions.

The initial capital needed for real trading, which will experience losses and sustained drawdowns, must be bigger than A_0. It must provide the account with sufficient survival properties (see Chapter 4). The ratio of the achieved P&L to the initial capital is the *return on capital:*

$$\text{Return on capital} = \text{P\&L} / \text{Initial capital} \qquad (8.3)$$

This value can also be annualized. The ratio of the return on capital to the optimal return on capital is the *return on capital performance* measure:

$$\begin{aligned}\text{Return on capital performance} &= \text{Return on capital} / \text{Optimal return on capital} \\ &= \text{P\&L} \times A_0 / (\text{Potential profit} \times \text{Initial capital}) \end{aligned} \qquad (8.4)$$

In order to annualize values given by Equation (8.4), it is necessary to annualize the values given by the Equations (8.2) and (8.3).

Comparing Single-Market Performance

Instead of comparing trading systems applied to the same historical interval, one can investigate *market performance* over different time intervals. A way to compare performance over different time intervals of the same length is to compare the potential profit strategies from each interval. In this case, Equations (8.1) through (8.4) can be applied to the results of the two intervals. Clearly, under such conditions, the ratios can sometimes be > 1.0. This means that market performance in the numerator is greater than that of the denominator. The difference in the performance of individual markets observed over different time intervals is an important characteristic of dynamic market properties.

Comparing Markets

Alternatively, the same time interval can be selected for different markets. Application of the potential profit strategy to one time interval on different markets is another way to compare markets. Because of the differences in margins and contract specifications, the initial cash balance A_0 required for trading the same number of contracts can be different. However, markets can be compared using corresponding optimal returns on capital.

Moving Versions of Strategies

All three potential profit strategies can be applied to moving, or rolling, time intervals. In a manner similar to a moving average, one can shift a window of the same length and compute the distribution of transactions and potential profit within the time window. In this manner, we come to the concept of a *moving potential profit*. Corresponding curves of moving potential profit calculated for time windows of different lengths can be drawn on the same price charts after scaling them, in the same way as other moving indicators. These applications use the fact that potential profit obtained on the interval ending at a specific date and time can be charted as one point at that date and time. Once potential profits have been calculated as a continuous series of rolling values, we can produce *moving averages of potential profits*. In this case, the window for the moving average may have the same or different length as the length of the interval in which the profit was originally evaluated.

These moving potential profits and average potential profit indicators observed in time windows corresponding to different time scales (intraday trading, daily trading, weekly trading) reflect changes in what the market has to offer. Comparing today's moving potential profit for the last n days with maximum and minimum historical values or maximum and minimum values of the potential profit over the last n days reflects the changing trend and volatility properties of the market's offering.

Relationship to Trend and Volatility

The potential profit value and its corresponding strategy can serve as a characteristic of trend and volatility. In order to see this better, consider the following two price sequences $\boldsymbol{P1} = \boldsymbol{P1}(420, 430, 440)$:

```
echo GC 1 1350 1000 20 420 430 440 | maxprof3
   #        GC  Cost  PPS   PPS1   PPS2   Pos2    Cash2  Equity2   Total2
   0       420    20    1      1      1      1     1330        0     1330
   1       430    20    0      0      0      1     1330     1000     2330
   2       440    20   -1     -1     -1      0     3310        0     3310
A0 = 1350 P&L = 1960 P&L1 = 1960 P&L2 = 1960 IM = 1350 MM = 1000
```

and P2 = P2(420, 430.2, 420)

```
echo GC 1 1350 1000 20 420 430.2 420 | maxprof3
   #        GC  Cost  PPS   PPS1   PPS2   Pos2    Cash2  Equity2   Total2
   0       420    20    1      1      1      1     1330        0     1330
   1     430.2    20   -2     -2     -2     -1     2310        0     2310
```

```
   2        420    20    1       1       1       0       3310         0      3310
A0 = 1350 P&L = 1960 P&L1 = 1960 P&L2 = 1960 IM = 1350 MM = 1000
```

This example intentionally simulated sequences of prices that gave the same profit values. The profit value alone cannot distinguish between these two cases. In the first case, there is a linear increase in prices. In the second case, there is a price swing or price range. The first case represents a trending market. The second case is associated with a volatile market trading in a sideways range. The profit value together with the number and type of transactions is able to serve as a characteristic of trend and volatility. In a trending market, the same profit is achieved with fewer transactions. In a volatile market, the number of transactions can be significantly greater. This means that the average potential profit per transaction is less in a volatile market than in a trending market if total potential profits are the same in both markets. It is interesting to use moving averages of potential profit together with moving potential profits, where the averaging is done on a per-trade basis.

Reversal Points and Events Filter

The algorithms `potential_profit_ralg` and `potential_profit_lalg` identify *profitable reversal price points*. The vector of transaction costs serves as a mechanism to filter out nonprofitable trades. Increasing the costs reduces the number of *reversal points* and leaves only the most significant of them. Once a vector of the strategy is obtained, the reversal points can be mapped onto other price patterns and market events known during that time period. This can help to evaluate those events that are statistically meaningful.

When profitable reversal points are determined, it makes sense to apply different transaction costs. Because the element of transaction fees cannot be eliminated, it should be used as minimal cost. Under these conditions, the potential profit reaches its maximum and at the same time shows the largest number of transactions. However, a gradual cost increase will change the distribution of transactions and profit values. One can use a half of initial margin or a half of some average true range as a cost per transaction per contract. This filter will exclude all trades where the price differences and consequently the trading profit do not offset the initial margin or average true range.

It is interesting to plot a chart of the potential profit strategy under its corresponding price chart. The potential profit strategy can be graphed so that it shows the strategy actions (number of contracts per transaction) versus the time of the transaction (see Figure 8.1).

Figure 8.1 looks the same as an atomic linear spectrum! If we begin to vary the transaction costs, then for a while the spectrum does not change. However, after certain increases or decreases in the transaction costs, several lines are eliminated or added, resulting in a new spectrum. The discrete transaction costs that trigger changes remind us of energy levels in a quantum system. We can also draw a parallel of this image, which characterizes current market conditions, with that of a fingerprint.

The graph in Figure 8.1 was created using the chart object available in software packages such as Microsoft Office. The daily settlement prices were used as an input to the program `maxprof` (see Chapter 3). The dates were applied as simple text markers to the chart and were not used by the computing program. The transaction cost of $600 means that price differences are profitable only if they are > $1,200.

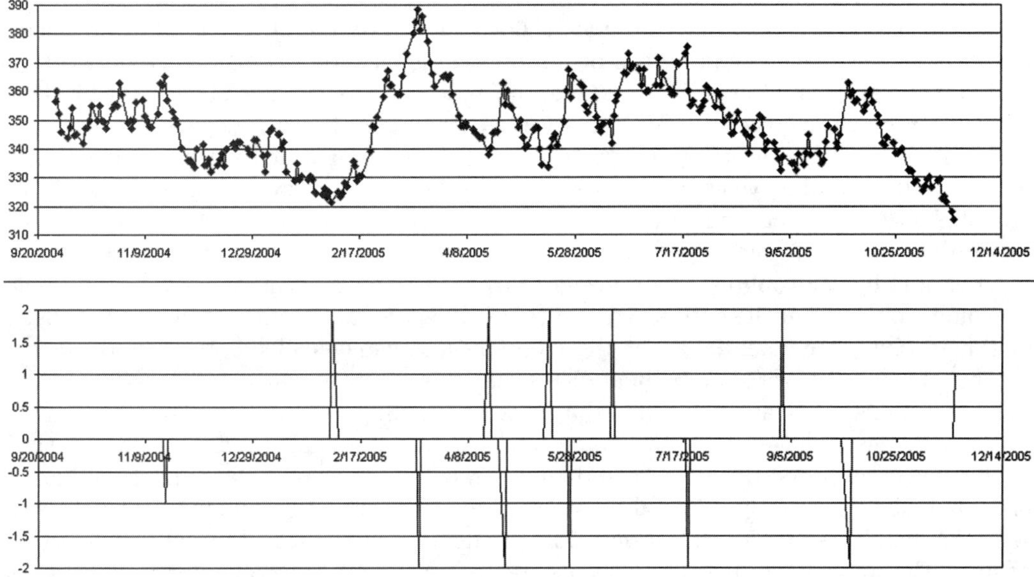

FIGURE 8.1 Settlement prices for March 2006 wheat (WH06) traded on the Chicago Board of Trade (CBOT) during selected months in 2004 and 2005 together with trading signals obtained by *r*-algorithm and with transaction cost set to $600.
Data courtesy of XPRESSTRADE, www.xpresstrade.com.

While the time intervals between transactions vary, we don't find either very short or very long intervals in this particular chart. For instance, there are no positions that must be offset or reversed on the next day following an entry. Also, within this period of slightly more than a year, the market provided several good opportunities. There seems to be a well-defined distribution of the time intervals corresponding to entry and exit points. This hints that knowing this distribution would allow us estimate how long to hold a position with a certain probability for a given market. Of course, this first requires some preliminary research using tools described earlier in this book as well as other sources. Also, the implementation of such decisions depends on money and the risk management considerations discussed in Chapter 4.

Increasing Position Points

The algorithm `second_pl_reserve_alg` and `second_pl_reserve_prime_alg` return strategies established points where positions can be increased. This marks the second layer of important points. A long sequence of such points between two reversal points is an indication of a trend and the result of increasing account equity.

Options on Potential Profit

Consider an ordinary European call or put option. At the expiration date, its payoff depends on the difference between the current spot price of an underlying asset and the option strike price. The payoff does not depend on the price path observed prior to expiration. Some types of options are designed so that their payoff does depend on the price path. For instance, a payoff of an Asian average price call or put option depends on the difference between the option strike price and the average value of the underlying asset calculated over a predetermined averaging period (Hull 1997). Clearly, the potential profit value depends on the prices and costs from a certain time interval. They also depend on which price frequency (tick, daily, weekly, monthly, yearly) is selected. Using the terminology of options payoffs, the potential profit is a price- and cost path–dependent property. Hence, similar to Asian options, we can introduce different types of path-dependent call and put *options on the potential profit*. Naturally, such options can be designed with a European or American style of exercise. Depending on whether the options are written on the potential profit or any return transformation involving the potential profit, these options also can be called options on the market potential profit or return offer. Without further analysis of any practical or theoretical aspects of these options, these are mentioned simply as a possibility.

An interesting and essential part of the application of potential profit deals with the study of the statistical properties of corresponding strategies, especially the extreme values. In order to make this as easy as possible, we need an algorithm that evaluates a strategy and a class that handles statistics operations. Both are developed in the sections at the end of this chapter. The statistical properties of trades are described in the next chapter.

STRATEGY EVALUATION

In order to study statistical properties of a strategy and particularly the potential profit strategies, we need an algorithm that evaluates the overall strategy as well as subdivides the strategies' transactions into individual trades from their entry point to where they are offset. Such an algorithm should input prices, costs, strategy, initial and maintenance margin, and initial account value. The reason why the margin and cash balance (account value) are input is so that the program becomes generic. It then works with arbitrary strategies, not only a potential profit strategy, and guarantees that margin and trading rules are obeyed. With this information the program can diagnose when a margin call occurs and where trading should be terminated because of the self-financing restriction.

The Evaluation Algorithm

The following `evaluate_strategy_alg` is the function algorithm for strategy evaluation from the header file `EvaluateStrategyAlg.h`:

```
#ifndef __EvaluateStrategyAlg_h__
#define __EvaluateStrategyAlg_h__

#include <vector>
#include <sstream>
#include <stdexcept>
```

```
using namespace std;

#include "Trade.h"
#include "Position.h"
#include "Prices.h"
#include "Strategy.h"
#include "Cost.h"
#include "SpecCost.h"

namespace PPBOOK {

    // Given prices, costs, strategy, initial account balance,
    // and initial and maintenence margins returns P&L and fills
    // trades, and vectors of equity and cash. If position at the
    // end remains open, then it is "artificially" offset using the
    // last price and cost. Corresponding offsetting trade is added
    // to trades. Throws exception, if input is inconsistent or if
    // trading impossible because of financial account restrictions.
    inline  double
    evaluate_strategy_alg(const Prices& prices, const
        vector<Cost<SpecAbsoluteCost> >& costs, const Strategy& strategy,
        double a0, double imargin, double mmargin, Trades& trades,
        vector<double>& openEquity, vector<double>& cashBalance)
    {
        // Checks input
        if(prices.size() != costs.size() || prices.size()
            != strategy.size()) {
            ostringstream   s;
            s   << "evaluate_strategy_alg: vectors prices["
                << (unsigned int)prices.size() << "], costs["
                << (unsigned int)costs.size() << "], and strategy["
                << (unsigned int)strategy.size()
                << "] must be of one size.";
            throw   invalid_argument(s.str());
        }
        if(imargin <= 0.0) {
            ostringstream   s;
            s   << "evaluate_strategy_alg: initial margin "
                << imargin << " must be positive";
            throw   invalid_argument(s.str());
        }
        if(mmargin <= 0.0) {
            ostringstream   s;
            s   << "evaluate_strategy_alg: maintenance margin "
                << mmargin << " must be positive";
```

```
        throw   invalid_argument(s.str());
    }
    if(mmargin > imargin) {
        ostringstream   s;
        s   << "evaluate_strategy_alg: maintenance margin "
            << mmargin << " must be less than or equal to initial "
            << "margin " << imargin;
        throw   invalid_argument(s.str());
    }
    if(a0 < imargin) {
        ostringstream   s;
        s   << "evaluate_strategy_alg: initial balance a0 " << a0
            << " must be greater than or equal to initial "
            << " margin " << imargin;
        throw   invalid_argument(s.str());
    }
    // Prepares external collectors of information
    trades.clear();
    openEquity.clear();
    cashBalance.clear();
    if(!strategy.size())
        return  0.0;
    // Creates postion object
    Position    p;
    double      cash = a0;
    double      k = prices.tickValue() / prices.tick();
    // Iterates transactions.
    for(Strategy::size_type j = 0; j < strategy.size(); j++) {
        // Determines if requested transaction is possible.
        if(strategy[j] != 0) {
            double  eq = p.openEquity(prices[j], k);
            double  total = cash + eq;
            int     curPos = p.contracts();
            int     newPos = curPos + strategy[j];
            int     sgnCurPos = !curPos ? 0 : (curPos > 0 ? 1 : -1);
            int     sgnNewPos = !newPos ? 0 : (newPos > 0 ? 1 : -1);
            double  tmargin = imargin * (sgnCurPos == sgnNewPos ?
                    abs(newPos - curPos) : abs(newPos));
            if(total < tmargin) {
                ostringstream   s;
                s   << "evaluate_strategy_alg: Trading power ("
                    << (total - imargin * abs(curPos))
                    << ") = cash (" << cash << ") + open equity ("
                    << eq << ") - total initial margin ("
```

```
                    << (imargin * abs(curPos)) << ") is not enough "
                    << "for transaction strategy["
                    << (unsigned int)j << "] = " << strategy[j]
                    << ". Use a0 greater than " << a0;
                throw   invalid_argument(s.str());
            } // if(total < tmargin)
        } // if(strategy[j] != 0)
        // Adjusts cash balance and open equity.
        cash -= abs(strategy[j]) * costs[j].cost();
        cash += p.change(prices[j], costs[j].cost(), strategy[j],
                    j, k, trades);
        openEquity.push_back(p.openEquity(prices[j], k));
        cashBalance.push_back(cash);
        // Checks for margin call.
        if(cashBalance[j] + openEquity[j] < mmargin *
            abs(p.contracts())) {
            ostringstream   s;
            s   << "evaluate_strategy_alg: margin call! Total "
                << "equity (" << (cashBalance[j] + openEquity[j])
                << ") = cash (" << cashBalance[j]
                << ") + open equity (" << openEquity[j]
                << ") is less than total maintenance margin "
                << mmargin * abs(p.contracts()) << " = "
                << mmargin << " * abs(" << p.contracts() << ") for "
                << "index = " << (unsigned int)j
                << ". Use a0 greater than " << a0;
            throw   invalid_argument(s.str());
        }
    }
    if(p.isOpen()) {
        cash -= abs(p.contracts()) * costs[costs.size() - 1].cost();
        cash += p.change(prices[prices.size() - 1],
                    costs[costs.size() - 1].cost(), -p.contracts(),
                    costs.size() - 1, k, trades);
    }
    return  cash - a0;
}

} // PPBOOK

#endif /* __EvaluateStrategyAlg_h__ */
```

After checking the initial inputs for consistency and preparing collectors for gathering information about trades, current cash balance, and open position equity, the algorithm iterates the strategy actions. Adjusting the cash balance and open position equity is straightforward and greatly simplified by the class `Position`, which handles simple as well as complex positions. The first `if`-statement inside the `for`-loop before the account adjustment checks the ability to make a new transaction. The second `if`-statement after the account adjustment verifies the margin call condition. This function is suitable for the three "best" strategies developed in the previous chapters as well as for ordinary strategies. Because a typical strategy can lose money, it is important that the function throw diagnostics exceptions.

Example Test8.cpp

The following program `test8.cpp` illustrates the function `evaluate_strategy_alg()`:

```
#include <iostream>
#include <iomanip>
#include <vector>
using namespace std;

#include "EvaluateStrategyAlg.h"
using namespace PPBOOK;

int main(int, char*[])
{
    try {
        Prices          p("GC");
        p.append(429);
        p.append(428);
        p.append(443);
        p.append(455);
        p.append(449);
        p.append(430);

        vector<Cost<SpecAbsoluteCost> > c(p.size(), 50.0);
        Strategy        s(p.size(), 0);
        s[0] = -1;
        s[2] = 2;
        s[4] = -2;

        const double    a0 = 5000;       // initial balance
        const double    imargin = 1350; // initial margin
        const double    mmargin = 1000; // maintenance margin

        Trades          ts;
        vector<double>  eq;
        vector<double>  ch;
```

```
        double  pl = evaluate_strategy_alg(p, c, s, a0, imargin,
                        mmargin, ts, eq, ch);
        cout    << setw(4) << "#" << " "
                << setw(8) << "Price" << " "
                << setw(5) << "Cost" << " "
                << setw(5) << "Trans" << " "
                << setw(8) << "Cash" << " "
                << setw(8) << "Equity" << " "
                << setw(8) << "Total"
                << endl;

        for(Strategy::size_type j = 0; j < s.size(); j++) {
            cout    << setw(4) << (unsigned int)j << " "
                    << setw(8) << p[j] << " "
                    << setw(5) << c[j].cost() << " "
                    << setw(5) << s[j] << " "
                    << setw(8) << ch[j] << " "
                    << setw(8) << eq[j] << " "
                    << setw(8) << (ch[j] + eq[j])
                    << endl;
        }
        cout    << "A0 = " << a0 << " P&L = " << pl
                << " Final = " << a0 + pl
                << " IMargin = " << imargin
                << " MMargin = " << mmargin
                << endl;
        for(Trades::size_type i = 0; i < ts.size(); i++) {
            cout    << (unsigned int)i
                    << " (" << (unsigned int)ts[i].entryIndex() << ","
                    << (unsigned int)ts[i].exitIndex() << ")"
                    << " P&L=" << setw(5) << ts[i].pl()
                    << " E=" << setw(5) << ts[i].equityChange()
                    << " C=" << setw(3) << ts[i].totalCost()
                    << " P&L/S=" << setw(5) << ts[i].plPerUnit()
                    << " S=" << setw(2) << ts[i].entrySize()
                    << endl;
        }
    }
    catch(const exception& e) {
        cerr    << e.what() << endl;
    }
    catch(...) {
        cerr    << "Unknown exception" << endl;
    }
```

```
    return  0;
}
The output from this program example is
    #     Price  Cost Trans      Cash   Equity     Total
    0       429    50    -1      4950        0      4950
    1       428    50     0      4950      100      5050
    2       443    50     2      3450        0      3450
    3       455    50     0      3450     1200      4650
    4       449    50    -2      3950        0      3950
    5       430    50     0      3950     1900      5850
A0 = 5000 P&L = 800 Final = 5800 IMargin = 1350 MMargin = 1000
0 (0,2) P&L=-1500 E=-1400 C=100 P&L/S=-1500 S=-1
1 (2,4) P&L=  500 E=  600 C=100 P&L/S=  500 S= 1
2 (4,5) P&L= 1800 E= 1900 C=100 P&L/S= 1800 S=-1
```

As we see at the end (index 5 of the output), the selected strategy does leave an open short position ($-1 + 2 - 2 = -1$). The program adds an artificial offsetting trade by marking the last position to the market at the last data point. The corresponding profit or loss is added to the total P&L. The class `Trades` provides information suitable for collecting trade statistics.

Class Distribution

We now need a simple class for applying statistical operations to a sample of values of the built-in type `double`. In addition to the traditional computation of the mean, variance, standard deviation, maximum, and minimum values, it also should return frequencies for building distribution histograms that will be used to plot frequencies versus values. The mean of a sample of size N is defined as:

$$\text{Mean} = (\Sigma^N_{i=1} x_i)/N \tag{8.5}$$

The calculation of variance is done by computing the sum of squares of the deviations from the mean:

$$\text{Sum of squares of the deviations from mean} = S = \Sigma^N_{i=1} (x_i - \text{Mean})^2 \tag{8.6}$$

Depending on the application, the sample variance is then defined as S/N or $S/(N - 1)$. The well-known theoretically equivalent formula for S,

$$S = \Sigma^N_{i=1} x_i^2 - (\Sigma^N_{i=1} x_i)^2/N \tag{8.7}$$

is convenient but not particularly suitable for practical computations, especially if the samples are big and the variances are small. A good analysis of accumulated rounding errors for several algorithms is described in Chan (1983). For our purposes of computing mean and variance we will apply the Youngs and Cramer (Youngs 1971) updating formulas

$$T_{1,j} = T_{1,j-1} + x_j \tag{8.8}$$

$$S_{1,j} = S_{1,j-1} + (j \times x_j - T_{1,j})^2/(j \times (j-1)) \tag{8.9}$$

where $T_{1,1} = x_1$ and $S_{1,1} = 0$. In formulas (8.5) through (8.9), we use the notations from Chan et al. (1983). The formula (8.9) accumulates only non-negative numbers and is more stable than formula (8.7). While pairwise two-path algorithms (Chan et al. 1983) can stabilize the formulas (8.8) and (8.9) even further, we apply these formulas directly because it is much simpler implementation. Then combining two samples also becomes simple:

$$T_{1,m+n} = \mathrm{T}_{1,m} + T_{1,n} \tag{8.10}$$

$$S_{1,m+n} = S_{1,m} + S_{1,n} + m \times (n \times T_{1,m}/m - T_{1,n})^2/(n \times (m+n)) \tag{8.11}$$

The following is the class `Distribution` from the header file `Distribution.h`:

```
#ifndef __Distribution_h__
#define __Distribution_h__

#include <cmath>
#include <sstream>
#include <stdexcept>
#include <vector>
#include <algorithm>
#include <functional>
#include <numeric>
using namespace std;

namespace PPBOOK {

    // Predicate class suitable for count_if. The operator() returns
    // true if a value is greater than left boundary and less or equal
    // than right boundary of an interval.
    class ValueInRange {
        double  l_, r_;
    public:
        ValueInRange(double left, double right) : l_(left), r_(right){}
        bool     operator()(double v) const {return l_ < v && v <= r_;}
    };
```

```
// The class distribution collects samples represented by values of
// built-in type double and makes simple statistics operations on
// them. See a reference to Chan 1983 for more stable algorithms of
// variance computation.
class Distribution {
public:
    Distribution() : t_(0.0), s_(0.0), max_(0.0), min_(0.0){}
    size_t  size() const {return data_.size();}
    const vector<double>&   values() const {return data_;}
    double  maxValue() const
            {
                if(!size()) throw invalid_argument(
                    "Distribution::maxValue: empty object");
                return  max_;
            }
    double  minValue() const
            {
                if(!size()) throw invalid_argument(
                    "Distribution::minValue: empty object");
                return  min_;
            }
    // Returns sample mean.
    double  mean() const
            {
                if(!size()) throw invalid_argument(
                    "Distribution::mean: empty object");
                return  t_ / size();
            }
    // Returns the sum of squares of the deviations from the mean
    // divided by size() - 1.
    double  variance() const
            {
                if(!size()) throw invalid_argument(
                    "Distribution::variance: empty object");
                return size() == 1 ? 0.0 : s_ / (size() - 1);
            }
    // Returns square root of variance.
    double  standardDeviation() const
            {
                if(!size()) throw invalid_argument(
                    "Distribution::standardDeviation: empty object");
                return  sqrt(variance());
            }
```

```
void    frequencies(double width, vector<size_t>& f,
            double& left, double& right) const
        {
            if(!size()) throw invalid_argument(
                "Distribution::frequencies: empty object");
            if(width <= 0.0) {
                ostringstream   s;
                s   << "Distribution::distribution: width ("
                    << width << ") must be positive.";
                throw   invalid_argument(s.str());
            }
            f.clear();
            int begInd = (int)floor(min_ / width);
            if(begInd * width == minValue())
                begInd-;
            int endInd = (int)ceil(max_ / width);
            left = width * begInd;
            right = width * endInd;
            for(int j = begInd; j < endInd; j++) {
                size_t  c = count_if(data_.begin(),
                    data_.end(), ValueInRange(j * width,
                    (j + 1) * width));
                f.push_back(c);
            }
        }
// Uses Young and Cramer updating formulas for sum of values
// and sum of squares of the deviations from mean.
void    add(double v)
        {
            data_.push_back(v);
            size_t  sz = size();
            if(sz == 1) {
                t_ = max_ = min_ = v;
                s_ = 0.0;
            }
            else {
                if(v > max_)
                    max_ = v;
                if(v < min_)
                    min_ = v;
                t_ += v;
                double  tmpQ = (sz * v - t_);
                s_ += tmpQ * tmpQ / (sz * (sz - 1));
```

```
            }
        }
    // Makes object empty and ready for new updates.
    void    clear()
        {
            data_.clear();
            t_ = s_ = max_ = min_ = 0.0;
        }
    // Appends two distribution objects. Assigns result to self.
    // Throws exception on attempt to append self to self.
    void    append(const Distribution& d)
        {
            if(this == &d)
                throw invalid_argument("Distribution::append: "
                    "cannot append self to self.");
            if(!d.size())
                return;
            size_t  sz = size();
            size_t  szD = d.size();
            data_.insert(data_.end(), d.data_.begin(),
                d.data_.end());
            t_ += d.t_;
            double  tmpQ = sz * t_ / szD - d.t_;
            s_ += d.s_ + szD * tmpQ * tmpQ / (sz * (szD + sz));
        }

  private:
    vector<double>  data_;
    double          t_;
    double          s_;
    double          max_;
    double          min_;
  };

} // PPBOOK

#endif /* __Distribution_h__ */
```

An object of this class accumulates values. If it is not empty, then at any moment it is ready for reporting the basic properties such as sample size, mean, variance, standard deviation, and maximum and minimum values and frequencies. The program `distrib.cpp` that follows is more than a test. It can handle data from a standard input.

```
#include <iostream>
#include <iomanip>
```

```
#include <vector>
using namespace std;

#include "Distribution.h"
using namespace PPBOOK;

void
outputDistribution(ostream& o, const Distribution& d, double width)
{
    if(o) {
        if(d.size() == 0) {
            o   << "Distribution is empty" << endl;
            return;
        }
        o   << "Mean            = " << d.mean() << endl
            << "Sample size     = " << (unsigned int)d.size() << endl
            << "Variance        = " << d.variance() << endl
            << "Std. deviation  = " << d.standardDeviation() << endl
            << "Maximum value   = " << d.maxValue() << endl
            << "Minimum value   = " << d.minValue()
            << endl;
        const vector<double>&   v = d.values();
        o   << "All values [";
        for(vector<double>::size_type j = 0; j < v.size(); j++) {
            o   << v[j];
            if(j + 1 != v.size())
                o   << ", ";
        }
        o   << "]" << endl;
        vector<size_t>  freq;
        double          left, right;
        d.frequencies(width, freq, left, right);
        o << "Width           = " << width << endl;
        for(vector<size_t>::size_type f = 0; f < freq.size(); f++) {
            o   << (unsigned int)f << " ("
                << (width * f + left) << ", "
                << (width * (f + 1) + left) << "] "
                << (unsigned int)freq[f]
                << endl;
        }
    }
}

int main(int argc, char *argv[])
{
```

```
    try {
        if(argc < 2) {
            cout    << "Usage: " << argv[0] << " width" << endl;
            return  0;
        }
        double  width = atof(argv[1]);
        Distribution    d;
        double  v;
        while(cin >> v)
            d.add(v);
        outputDistribution(cout, d, width);
    }
    catch(const exception& e) {
        cerr    << e.what() << endl;
    }
    catch(...) {
        cerr    << "Unknown exception" << endl;
    }
    return  0;
}
```

The following is a running example:

```
echo -3 1 2 2 -2 3 2 3 | distrib 2
Mean           = 1
Sample size    = 8
Variance       = 5.14286
Std. deviation = 2.26779
Maximum value  = 3
Minimum value  = -3
All values [-3, 1, 2, 2, -2, 3, 2, 3]
Width          = 2
0 (-4, -2] 2
1 (-2, 0] 0
2 (0, 2] 4
3 (2, 4] 2
```

Given the sample values (integers were used for simplicity of visual testing) and width of an interval bucket, the program automatically divides the entire range into four (in this case) subintervals and, along with traditional statistical information, outputs how frequently values are observed within a particular subinterval. The notation (–4, –2] means that the value –4 itself is not included into the interval (opened from the left) but the value –2 is included (closed from the right).

CONCLUSIONS

- It was shown how potential profits obtained by the three algorithms can form trading and market performance characteristics, serving as a common base of comparison.
- The combination of potential profit values and strategy signals is sensitive to the trending and volatility conditions of a market.
- Transaction cost works as a filter for selecting the most profitable trades and leads to further investigation of meaningful events.
- Options on potential profits or returns can be designed in a manner similar to other path-dependent options.
- The function `evaluate_strategy_alg()` is provided for breaking down transactions into complete trades.
- The class `Distribution` and the program `distrib.cpp` are developed for building empirical distributions.

CHAPTER 9

Statistics of Trades and Potential Profit

The importance of having complete distributions of profitable and losing trades was first mentioned in Chapter 4. A potential profit strategy by definition cannot lose. In addition, it has no breakeven trades (profit and loss [P&L] = 0). However, winning trades are normally different; therefore, the maximum winning trade, average winning trade, and in general the distribution of profitable trades is also important for potential profit strategies. These statistics are market characteristics. It is also interesting to know the absolute maximum of the winning trades observed in historic testing. All this information helps to better understand the potential profit and its statistical properties.

STATISTICAL PROPERTIES OF TRADES

Selection

An object of the class `Trades` contains information about each individual trade produced by a strategy. Additionally, information about the current cash balance and open position equity is used to produce the total equity fluctuations. The operations of the class `Trade` (an element of `Trades`) `Trade::entryIndex()` and `Trade::exitIndex()` provide access to the entries in the vectors of prices, costs, strategy, and the vectors of cash balance and open position equity. All together, this is sufficient to get a comprehensive understanding of the characteristics of a strategy and to evaluate many interesting properties.

All transactions in the strategy are split and combined into a set of trades collected by an object of the class `Trades`. Each trade may have a different number (size) of contracts or shares collectively named *units*. Within one trade, each unit is bought or sold at the same price regardless the size. It is important that a complex position, where units can be bought and sold at different prices, can always be split, based on the position offsetting rules, into a set of trades where each one has a single entry and exit price. If the position is not closed at the end of the strategy vector, then an artificial extra trade must be added to the object of class `Trades` in order to calculate the final profit or loss.

For some properties, such as the number of winning trades, it is not important that the size of each trade may be different. For other properties, such as the gross profit, it is more interesting to calculate both the gross profit and the gross profit per unit. The first value is obtained by summing the profits for all trades and the second value by summing profits per unit for all trades. Clearly, if each trade has the same size, 1 (long) or –1 (short), then the gross profits and per-unit profits have the same value. It is also useful to get the average per-trade values of these properties. The following naming convention is applied to statistical properties in the next sections. A property of a trade is named *property*. The property value divided by size of a trade is referred to as *property per unit*. If these properties are averaged over a set of trades, then the names are *property per trade* and *property per unit per trade*, respectively. If a summation of values of properties is done for all trades, then names are *total property* or *gross property* and *total property per unit* or *gross property per unit*, respectively.

For selecting interesting statistical properties, the sources Babcock (1989), Jones (1999), Pardo (1992), and Williams (2000) were used. These statistics are:

1. Total P&L
2. Total P&L per unit
3. Gross profit
4. Gross profit per unit
5. Gross loss
6. Gross loss per unit
7. Total number of trades
8. Number of winning trades
9. Number of losing trades
10. Average profit per trade
11. Average profit per unit per trade
12. Average loss per trade
13. Average loss per unit per trade
14. Largest winning trade (largest profit)
15. Largest winning trade per unit (largest profit per unit)
16. Largest losing trade (largest loss)
17. Largest losing trade per unit (largest loss per unit)
18. Maximum number of consecutive winning trades
19. Maximum number of consecutive losing trades

20. Maximum consecutive profit
21. Maximum consecutive profit per unit
22. Maximum consecutive loss
23. Maximum consecutive loss per unit
24. Distribution of trades versus P&L (typically not reported)
25. Distribution of trades versus P&L per unit scale (typically not reported)

These 25 properties, including per-unit variations, can be evaluated solely from an object of the class `Trades`. Additional information can be obtained by combining the input and output of the function `evaluate_strategy_alg()`:

26. Return on account
27. Maximum account value (typically not reported)
28. Minimum account value (typically not reported)

Interesting notes about drawdown can be found in Jones (1999):

There have been disputes over the definition of a drawdown. This is the correct definition: the distance between a high point in equity followed by a lowest point in equity until a new high is made.

If we follow this definition, then the total equity, Total (see the `test8.cpp` from the previous section), which is equal to sum of the cash balance (Cash) and open position equity (Equity), is suitable for the evaluation of drawdowns. For instance, the first local maximum corresponds to the initial cash balance A_0 = \$5,000. This value drops at index 0, where the first transaction reduces the total equity to \$4,950 because of the \$50 transaction costs. At the next point 1, the total equity grows to \$5,050—the second local maximum—and becomes higher than the previous value \$5,000. We can conclude that the first drawdown is equal to \$50 because it has been completed at the point where there is a new high in equity. This can be written as –\$50 instead, assuming that a positive drawdown value represents a loss. The third total equity that is higher is \$5,850, observed at index 5. The minimum \$3,450 found between the second and third local maximum corresponds to index 2. This means that the second drawdown will be calculated as \$5,050 – \$3,450 = \$1,600 or as –\$1,600. If a strategy produces more cases similar to these two (let's say that the total equity continues to drop below the value \$5,850 after index 5), then we have additional drawdowns. One of these will be the:

29. Largest drawdown

In the previous example, the largest (from the two \$50 and \$1,600) drawdown was equal to \$1,600. Ryan Jones (1999) also suggests averaging the drawdowns and introduces the:

30. Average drawdown

In the example, the average drawdown is equal to ($50 + $1,600) / 2 = $825. It is useful to complete the list of statistics with:

31. Distribution of drawdowns (typically not reported)

In order to compute these 31 properties, algorithms available in the C++ Standard Template Library (Stroustrup 2000; Musser 1996; International Standard ISO/IEC 14882 2003) and the class `Distribution` have been applied.

Implementing One by One

The following is the entire header file `TradeStatisticsAlg.h`. The comments embedded in this file are intended to clarify the contents of this section and have not been repeated as separate text.

```
#ifndef __TradeStatisticsAlg_h__
#define __TradeStatisticsAlg_h__

#include <cmath>
#include <sstream>
#include <stdexcept>
#include <algorithm>
#include <functional>
#include <numeric>
using namespace std;

#include "Trade.h"
#include "Distribution.h"
using namespace PPBOOK;

namespace PPBOOK {

    // 1) Total P&L is returned by total_pl_alg.
    // An object of the class Trades is filled by the algorithms
    // evaluate_strategy_alg, first_pl_reserve_prime_alg,
    // first_pl_reserve_alg, second_pl_reserve_prime_alg,
    // second_pl_reserve_alg. Each of them returns corresponding total
    // P&L. However, a similar object can be filled by the operation
    // Position::change() not returning P&L. There is also a need to
    // modify the object and/or analyze it independently. In such cases
    // it is required to get total P&L directly from the object.
    inline  double  add_trade_pl(double v, const Trade& t)
        {return v + t.pl();}

    inline  double  total_pl_alg(const Trades& t)
```

```
{
    double  v = 0.0;
    return  accumulate(t.begin(), t.end(), v, add_trade_pl);
}

// 2) Total P&L per unit is returned by total_pl_unit_alg.
// Each trade may have a different unit size. It is possible to
// compute P&L per unit (contract) for each trade and then get the
// total P&L from such per unit values.
inline  double  add_trade_pl_unit(double v, const Trade& t)
    {return v + t.plPerUnit();}

inline  double  total_pl_unit_alg(const Trades& t)
{
    double  v = 0.0;
    return  accumulate(t.begin(), t.end(), v, add_trade_pl_unit);
}

// 3) Gross profit is returned by calling gross_profit_alg.
inline  double  add_trade_profit(double v, const Trade& t)
    {return t.pl() > 0.0 ? v + t.pl() : v;}

inline  double  gross_profit_alg(const Trades& t)
{
    double  v = 0.0;
    return  accumulate(t.begin(), t.end(), v, add_trade_profit);
}

// 4) Gross profit per unit is returned by gross_profit_unit_alg.
inline  double  add_trade_profit_unit(double v, const Trade& t)
    {return t.plPerUnit() > 0.0 ? v + t.plPerUnit() : v;}

inline  double  gross_profit_unit_alg(const Trades& t)
{
    double  v = 0.0;
    return  accumulate(t.begin(), t.end(), v, add_trade_profit_unit);
}

// 5) Gross loss is returned by gross_loss_alg.
inline  double  add_trade_loss(double v, const Trade& t)
    {return t.pl() < 0.0 ? v + t.pl() : v;}

inline  double  gross_loss_alg(const Trades& t)
{
    double  v = 0.0;
```

```
    return  accumulate(t.begin(), t.end(), v, add_trade_loss);
}

// 6) Gross loss per unit is returned by gross_loss_unit_alg.
inline  double  add_trade_loss_unit(double v, const Trade& t)
            {return t.plPerUnit() < 0.0 ? v + t.plPerUnit() : v;}

inline  double  gross_loss_unit_alg(const Trades& t)
{
    double  v = 0.0;
    return  accumulate(t.begin(), t.end(), v, add_trade_loss_unit);
}

// 7) Total number of trades is not represented by an algorithm;
// it is returned by Trades::size().

// 8) Number of winning trades is returned by
// number_winning_trades_alg.
inline  size_t  add_number_winning_trades(size_t v, const Trade& t)
    {return t.pl() > 0.0 ? v + 1 : v;}

Trades::size_type   number_winning_trades_alg(const Trades& t)
{
    Trades::size_type   v = 0;
    return  accumulate(t.begin(), t.end(), v,
                add_number_winning_trades);
}

// 9) Number of losing trades is returned by
// number_losing_trades_alg and includes breakeven trades.
inline  size_t  add_number_losing_trades(size_t v, const Trade& t)
    {return t.pl() <= 0.0 ? v + 1 : v;}

inline  Trades::size_type   number_losing_trades_alg(const Trades& t)
{
    Trades::size_type   v = 0;
    return  accumulate(t.begin(), t.end(), v,
            add_number_losing_trades);
}

// 10) Average profit per trade is returned by average_profit_alg.
inline  double  average_profit_alg(const Trades& t)
{
    size_t  n = number_winning_trades_alg(t);
    return n == 0 ? 0.0 : gross_profit_alg(t) / n;
```

```
}

// 11) Average profit per unit per trade is returned by
// average_profit_unit_alg.
inline  double  average_profit_unit_alg(const Trades& t)
{
    size_t  n = number_winning_trades_alg(t);
    return n == 0 ? 0.0 : gross_profit_unit_alg(t) / n;
}

// 12) Average loss per trade is returned by average_loss_alg and
// includes breakeven trades.
inline  double  average_loss_alg(const Trades& t)
{
    size_t  n = number_losing_trades_alg(t);
    return n == 0 ? 0.0 : gross_loss_alg(t) / n;
}

// 13) Average loss per unit per trade is returned by
// average_loss_unit_alg and includes breakeven trades.
inline  double  average_loss_unit_alg(const Trades& t)
{
    size_t  n = number_losing_trades_alg(t);
    return n == 0 ? 0.0 : gross_loss_unit_alg(t) / n;
}

// 14) Largest winning trade is returned by
// largest_winning_trade_alg. If no profitable trade is found,
// then t.end() is returned.
inline  bool    cmp_trades_pl(const Trade& a, const Trade& b)
    {return a.pl() < b.pl();}

inline  Trades::const_iterator
largest_winning_trade_alg(const Trades& t)
{
    Trades::const_iterator  p = max_element(t.begin(), t.end(),
                                    cmp_trades_pl);
    if(p == t.end()) return p;
    return  (*p).pl() > 0.0 ? p : t.end();
}

// 15) Largest winning trade per unit is returned by
// largest_winning_trade_unit_alg. If no profitable trade is found,
// then t.end() is returned.
inline  bool    cmp_trades_pl_unit(const Trade& a, const Trade& b)
```

```
    {return a.plPerUnit() < b.plPerUnit();}

inline  Trades::const_iterator  largest_winning_trade_unit_alg(
    const Trades& t)
{
    Trades::const_iterator  p = max_element(t.begin(), t.end(),
                                    cmp_trades_pl_unit);
    if(p == t.end()) return p;
    return  (*p).plPerUnit() > 0.0 ? p : t.end();
}

// 16) Largest losing trade is returned by
// largest_losing_trade_alg. If no losing or breakeven trade
// is found, then t.end() is returned.
inline  Trades::const_iterator
largest_losing_trade_alg(const Trades& t)
{
    Trades::const_iterator  p = min_element(t.begin(), t.end(),
                                    cmp_trades_pl);
    if(p == t.end()) return p;
    return  (*p).pl() <= 0.0 ? p : t.end();
}

// 17) Largest losing trade per unit is returned by
// largest_losing_trade_unit_alg.  If no losing or breakeven trade
// is found, then t.end() is returned.
inline  Trades::const_iterator
largest_losing_trade_unit_alg(const Trades& t)
{
    Trades::const_iterator  p = min_element(t.begin(), t.end(),
                                    cmp_trades_pl_unit);
    if(p == t.end()) return p;
    return  (*p).plPerUnit() <= 0.0 ? p : t.end();
}

// 18) Maximum number of consecutive winning trades is returned by
// max_number_consecutive_winning_trades_alg.
inline  Trades::size_type
max_number_consecutive_winning_trades_alg(const Trades& t)
{
    Trades::size_type   v = 0, c = 0;
    for(Trades::const_iterator i = t.begin(); i != t.end(); ++i) {
        if((*i).pl() > 0.0)
            c++;
        else {
```

```
            if(c > v) v = c;
            c = 0;
        }
    }
    return  c > v ? c : v;
}

// 19) Maximum number of consecutive losing trades is returned by
// max_number_consecutive_losing_trades_alg. It also includes
// consecutive breakeven trades.
inline  Trades::size_type
max_number_consecutive_losing_trades_alg(const Trades& t)
{
    Trades::size_type   v = 0, c = 0;
    for(Trades::const_iterator i = t.begin(); i != t.end(); ++i) {
        if((*i).pl() <= 0.0)
            c++;
        else {
            if(c > v)
                v = c;
            c = 0;
        }
    }
    return  c > v ? c : v;
}

// 20) Maximum consecutive profit is returned by
// max_consecutive_profit_alg.
inline  double  max_consecutive_profit_alg(const Trades& t)
{
    double  v = 0.0, s = 0.0;
    for(Trades::const_iterator i = t.begin(); i != t.end(); ++i) {
        double  pl = (*i).pl();
        if(pl > 0.0)
            s += pl;
        else {
            if(s > v) v = s;
            s = 0.0;
        }
    }
    return  s > v ? s : v;
}

// 21) Maximum consecutive profit per unit is returned by
// max_consecutive_profit_unit_alg.
```

```
inline  double  max_consecutive_profit_unit_alg(const Trades& t)
{
    double  v = 0.0, s = 0.0;
    for(Trades::const_iterator i = t.begin(); i != t.end(); ++i) {
        double  pl = (*i).plPerUnit();
        if(pl > 0.0)
            s += pl;
        else {
            if(s > v) v = s;
            s = 0.0;
        }
    }
    return  s > v ? s : v;
}

// 22) Maximum consecutive loss is returned by
// max_consecutive_loss_alg.
inline  double  max_consecutive_loss_alg(const Trades& t)
{
    double  v = 0.0, s = 0.0;
    for(Trades::const_iterator i = t.begin(); i != t.end(); ++i) {
        double  pl = (*i).pl();
        if(pl <= 0.0)
            s += pl;
        else {
            if(s < v) v = s;
            s = 0.0;
        }
    }
    return  s < v ? s : v;
}

// 23) Maximum consecutive loss per unit is returned by
// max_consecutive_loss_unit_alg.
inline  double  max_consecutive_loss_unit_alg(const Trades& t)
{
    double  v = 0.0, s = 0.0;
    for(Trades::const_iterator i = t.begin(); i != t.end(); ++i) {
        double  pl = (*i).plPerUnit();
        if(pl <= 0.0)
            s += pl;
        else {
            if(s < v) v = s;
            s = 0.0;
        }
```

```
    }
    return  s < v ? s : v;
}

// 24) Distribution P&L is returned by distribution_pl_alg.
inline  void
distribution_pl_alg(const Trades& t, Distribution& d)
{
    d.clear();
    for(Trades::size_type j = 0; j < t.size(); j++)
        d.add(t[j].pl());
}

// 25) Distribution P&L per unit is returned by
// distribution_pl_unit_alg.
inline  void
distribution_pl_unit_alg(const Trades& t, Distribution& d)
{
    for(Trades::size_type j = 0; j < t.size(); j++)
        d.add(t[j].plPerUnit());
}

// 26) Return on account does not require a special algorithm.
// This value is obtained as a ratio of P&L returned by
// evaluate_strategy_alg to the initial account size a0 used by
// this algorithm. If total_pl_alg is applied instead of
// evaluate_strategy_alg, then make sure that a0 corresponds to
// Trades object given to total_pl_alg.

// 27) Maximum account value is returned by
// max_min_account_value_alg as maxAccount parameter.

// 28) Minimum account value is returned by
// max_min_account_value_alg as minAccount parameter.
inline  void
max_min_account_value_alg(double a0, const vector<double>&
            openEquity, const vector<double>& cashBalance,
            double& maxAccount, double& minAccount)
{
    if(openEquity.size() != cashBalance.size()) {
        ostringstream   s;
        s   << "max_min_account_value_alg: vectors openEquity["
            << (unsigned int)openEquity.size()
            << "] and cashBalance["
            << (unsigned int)cashBalance.size()
```

```
            << "] must be of one size.";
        throw   invalid_argument(s.str());
    }
    maxAccount = minAccount = a0;
    for(vector<double>::size_type j = 0; j < openEquity.size();
        j++) {
        double  total = openEquity[j] + cashBalance[j];
        if(total > maxAccount)
            maxAccount = total;
        if(total < minAccount)
            minAccount = total;
    }
}

// 29) Largest drawdown can be obtained from a Distribution
// object returned by distribution_drawdown_alg. For this
// purpose use Distribution::minValue(), because values are
// negative.

// 30) Average drawdown can be obtained from a Distribution
// object returned by distribution_drawdown_alg. For this
// purpose use Distribution::mean().

// 31) Distribution drawdown is filled by
// distribution_drawdown_alg.
inline  void
distribution_drawdown_alg(double a0, const vector<double>&
            openEquity, const vector<double>& cashBalance,
            Distribution& d)
{
    if(openEquity.size() != cashBalance.size()) {
        ostringstream   s;
        s   << "distribution_drawdown_alg: vectors openEquity["
            << (unsigned int)openEquity.size()
            << "] and cashBalance["
            << (unsigned int)cashBalance.size()
            << "] must be of one size.";
        throw   invalid_argument(s.str());
    }
    d.clear();
    double  lastMax = a0;
    double  drop = 0.0;
    double  drawdown = 0.0;
    for(vector<double>::size_type j = 0; j < openEquity.size();
        j++) {
```

```
            double  total = openEquity[j] + cashBalance[j];
            if(total < lastMax) {
                drop = total - lastMax;
                if(drop < drawdown)
                    drawdown = drop;
                if(j + 1 == openEquity.size())
                    d.add(drawdown);
            }
            else {
                lastMax = total;
                d.add(drawdown);
                drawdown = drop = 0.0;
            }
        }
    }

} // PPBOOK

#endif /* __TradeStatisticsAlg_h__ */
```

PROGRAM EVALUATING STRATEGY AND TRADES

The program that evaluates statistics is a filter. It takes the standard input, evaluates the strategy, and computes statistical properties, then sends the results to the standard output.

Input Format

The input includes the type of contract specifications, initial and maintenance margins, initial account cash balance, widths of buckets for building P&L and P&L per-unit distributions, prices, costs, and strategy.

```
SYMBOL IM MM A0 PLWIDTH PLUNITWIDTH price0 cost0 action0 …
```

There are several ways to create the input file or stream either manually, semi-automatically, or fully automatically. First, we will see how the stream can be generated using `maxprof3` described in Chapter 6. The program `maxprof3` requires input files similar to `CBOT_2005JFM_SK05_C_DATA.txt`. There are three types of lines distinguished by the contents of tokens in the output of this program.

```
maxprof3 < CBOT_2005JFM_SK05_C_DATA.txt
   #         S  Cost  PPS    PPS1    PPS2    Pos2     Cash2  Equity2    Total2
   0    541.25    76   -1      -1      -1      -1      2624        0      2624
...
```

```
A0 = 2700 P&L = 19795.5 P&L1 = 569343 P&L2 = 995209 IM = 2700 MM = 2500
```

The first token or field in the first line is always "#". The second field in the first line contains the contract symbol. This line is followed by lines containing 10 fields each, where the first field is not "#". The fields that need to be extracted are field 2—price, field 3—cost, and either fields 4 or 5 or 6, depending on the type of strategy to be evaluated. Finally, we get to the last line containing 18 fields. All fields are separated by spaces. The fields containing an "=" are also counted because there are spaces on both sides of the fields. From this last line, we need to extract and print field 15—initial margin, field 18—maintenance margin, and field 3—initial cash balance (in this specific order). This task can be routinely solved with a one-line command after piping (|) the output from `maxprof3` to the input of `awk` (Aho et al. 1988).

```
maxprof3 < CBOT_2005JFM_SK05_C_DATA.txt | awk '{if(NR==1)n=$2;if(NF==10 &&
NR>1){p[NR]=$2;c[NR]=$3;s[NR]=$6;}if(NF==18){a0=$3;im=$15;mm=$18}}END
{printf("%s %f %f %f 20000 1500\n",n,im,mm,a0);for(i=2; i<NR;i++)
printf("%f %f %d\n",p[i],c[i],s[i]);}'
```

When actually running the program, the previous code must be one line. For the convenience of reading, it has been broken into several lines. The width values 20000 and 1500 are hard-coded within the command. One can change the strategy field marked as $6 to $4 (potential profit strategy) or $5 (the first P&L reserve strategy). Because this line does not require compilation, changing these values is easy. You might notice that the statements of the AWK language are similar to the C language. The following are just two initial lines and the last line from the output:

```
S 2700.000000 2500.000000 2700.000000 20000 1500
541.250000 76.000000 -1
...
627.500000 76.000000 309
```

This is exactly what we need. It is not important whether the fields in the last output are on one line or split between several lines. The only relevant conditions are the sequence of fields and the separation of fields by an arbitrary combination of the white space characters (spaces, tabulations, and new line characters).

The Program Evaluate.cpp

The main effort in writing this program is designing the related classes and algorithms. This task has been accomplished in the previous chapters. In the following program, they are simply reused. The code takes care when reading the input and formatting the output. Below is the program from the file `evaluate.cpp`:

```
#include <iostream>
#include <iomanip>
```

```
#include <vector>
using namespace std;

#include "EvaluateStrategyAlg.h"
#include "TradeStatisticsAlg.h"
#include "Distribution.h"
using namespace PPBOOK;

void
reportDistribution(ostream& o, const Distribution& d, double width);

int main(int, char*[])
{
    try {
        // Collects input
        string      contract;
        double      imargin, mmargin, a0, wPl, wPlUnit;
        cin >> contract >> imargin >> mmargin >> a0 >> wPl >> wPlUnit;
        Prices      p(contract);
        vector<Cost<SpecAbsoluteCost> > c;
        Strategy    s;
        double      price, cost;
        int         action;
        while(cin >> price >> cost >> action) {
            p.append(price);
            c.push_back(cost);
            s.push_back(action);
        }
        // Evaluates strategy and reports results
        Trades          ts;
        vector<double>  eq, ch;
        double  pl = evaluate_strategy_alg(p, c, s, a0, imargin,
                        mmargin, ts, eq, ch);
        cout    << "STRATEGY EVALUATION" << endl;
        cout    << setw(4) << "#" << " "
                << setw(9) << p.name() << " "
                << setw(5) << "Cost" << " "
                << setw(5) << "Trans" << " "
                << setw(8) << "Cash" << " "
                << setw(8) << "Equity" << " "
                << setw(8) << "Total"
                << endl;

        for(Strategy::size_type j = 0; j < s.size(); j++) {
```

```
    cout    << setw(4) << (unsigned int)j << " "
            << setw(9) << setprecision(9) << p[j] << " "
            << setw(5) << c[j].cost() << " "
            << setw(5) << s[j] << " "
            << setw(8) << ch[j] << " "
            << setw(8) << eq[j] << " "
            << setw(8) << (ch[j] + eq[j])
            << endl;
}
cout    << "A0 = " << a0 << " P&L = " << pl
        << " Final = " << a0 + pl
        << " IM = " << imargin
        << " MM = " << mmargin
        << endl;
// Reports individual trades
cout    << "INDIVIDUAL TRADES" << endl;
for(Trades::size_type i = 0; i < ts.size(); i++) {
    cout    << (unsigned int)i
            << " (" << (unsigned int)ts[i].entryIndex() << ","
            << (unsigned int)ts[i].exitIndex() << ")"
            << " P&L=" << ts[i].pl()
            << " SIZE=" << ts[i].entrySize()
            << " P&L/SIZE=" << ts[i].plPerUnit()
            << " EQ=" << ts[i].equityChange()
            << " COST=" << ts[i].totalCost()
            << endl;
}
// Reports statistics of trades
cout    << "STATISTICS OF TRADES" << endl;
cout    << "Total P&L                           = "
        << total_pl_alg(ts) << endl;
cout    << "Total P&L/unit                      = "
        << total_pl_unit_alg(ts) << endl;
cout    << "Gross profit                        = "
        << gross_profit_alg(ts) << endl;
cout    << "Gross profit/unit                   = "
        << gross_profit_unit_alg(ts) << endl;
cout    << "Gross loss                          = "
        << gross_loss_alg(ts) << endl;
cout    << "Gross loss/unit                     = "
        << gross_loss_unit_alg(ts) << endl;
cout    << "Total number of trades              = "
        << (unsigned int)ts.size() << endl;
cout    << "Number of winning trades            = "
```

```
        << (unsigned int)number_winning_trades_alg(ts)
        << endl;
cout    << "Number of losing trades          = "
        << (unsigned int)number_losing_trades_alg(ts)
        << endl;
cout    << "Average profit                   = "
        << average_profit_alg(ts) << endl;
cout    << "Average profit/unit              = "
        << average_profit_unit_alg(ts) << endl;
cout    << "Average loss                     = "
        << average_loss_alg(ts) << endl;
cout    << "Average loss/unit                = "
        << average_loss_unit_alg(ts) << endl;

Trades::const_iterator  wTrade = largest_winning_trade_alg(ts);
cout    << "Largest winning trade            = "
        << (wTrade != ts.end() ? (*wTrade).pl() : 0.0)
        << endl;
Trades::const_iterator  wTradeU =
    largest_winning_trade_unit_alg(ts);
cout    << "Largest winning trade/unit       = "
        << (wTradeU != ts.end() ? (*wTradeU).plPerUnit() : 0.0)
        << endl;
Trades::const_iterator  lTrade = largest_losing_trade_alg(ts);
cout    << "Largest losing trade             = "
        << (lTrade != ts.end() ? (*lTrade).pl() : 0.0)
        << endl;
Trades::const_iterator  lTradeU =
    largest_losing_trade_unit_alg(ts);
cout    << "Largest losing trade/unit        = "
        << (lTradeU != ts.end() ? (*lTradeU).plPerUnit() : 0.0)
        << endl;

cout    << "Max number of consecutive wins   = "
        << (unsigned int)
           max_number_consecutive_winning_trades_alg(ts) << endl;
cout    << "Max number of consecutive losses = "
        << (unsigned int)
           max_number_consecutive_losing_trades_alg(ts) << endl;
cout    << "Maximum consecutive profit       = "
        << max_consecutive_profit_alg(ts) << endl;
cout    << "Maximum consecutive profit/unit  = "
        << max_consecutive_profit_unit_alg(ts) << endl;
cout    << "Maximum consecutive loss         = "
```

```
                << max_consecutive_loss_alg(ts) << endl;
        cout    << "Maximum consecutive loss/unit    = "
                << max_consecutive_loss_unit_alg(ts) << endl;

        Distribution    dPl;
        distribution_pl_alg(ts, dPl);
        cout    << "PL distribution" << endl;
        reportDistribution(cout, dPl, wPl);

        Distribution    dPlUnit;
        distribution_pl_unit_alg(ts, dPlUnit);
        cout    << "PL/unit distribution" << endl;
        reportDistribution(cout, dPlUnit, wPlUnit);

        double  maxAccount, minAccount;
        max_min_account_value_alg(a0, eq, ch, maxAccount, minAccount);
        cout    << "Maximum account value            = "
                << maxAccount << endl;
        cout    << "Minimum account value            = "
                << minAccount << endl;

        Distribution    ddDistr;
        distribution_drawdown_alg(a0, eq, ch, ddDistr);
        cout    << "Largest drawdown                 = "
                << ddDistr.minValue() << endl;
        cout    << "Average drawdown                 = "
                << ddDistr.mean() << endl;
    }
    catch(const exception& e) {
        cerr    << e.what() << endl;
    }
    catch(...) {
        cerr    << "Unknown exception" << endl;
    }
    return  0;
}

void
reportDistribution(ostream& o, const Distribution& d, double width)
{
    vector<size_t>  freq;
    double          left, right;
    d.frequencies(width, freq, left, right);
    for(vector<size_t>::size_type j = 0; j < freq.size(); j++) {
```

```
        cout    << (unsigned int)j << " ("
                << (width * j + left) << ", "
                << (width * (j + 1) + left) << "] "
                << (unsigned int)freq[j]
                << endl;
    }
}
```

Application of Evaluate.cpp to SK05

The pipes (|) combine the filter programs with compatible or easily adjustable inputs and outputs:

```
maxprof3 < CBOT_2005JFM_SK05_C_DATA.txt | awk '{if(NR==1)n=$2; if(NF==10&&
NR>1){p[NR]=$2;c[NR]=$3;s[NR]=$6;}if(NF==18){a0=$3;im=$15;mm=$18}}END
{printf("%s %f %f %f 20000 1500\n",n,im,mm,a0);for(i=2; i<NR;i++)
printf("%f %f %d\n",p[i],c[i],s[i]);}' | evaluate
```

Again, the previous statement must be one line when issued as a command. This produces the following output:

```
STRATEGY EVALUATION
  #       S  Cost Trans    Cash  Equity    Total
  0  541.25    76    -1    2624       0     2624
  1     530    76     2  3034.5       0   3034.5
  2     531    76     0  3034.5      50   3084.5
  3  536.25    76     0  3034.5   312.5     3347
  4   546.5    76     0  3034.5     825   3859.5
  5     551    76    -2  3932.5       0   3932.5
  6   546.5    76     0  3932.5     225   4157.5
  7  536.25    76     0  3932.5   737.5     4670
  8     539    76     0  3932.5     600   4532.5
  9  522.75    76     0  3932.5  1412.5     5345
 10  516.25    76     3    5442       0     5442
 11  518.75    76     0    5442     250     5692
 12     521    76    -4    5613       0     5613
 13     516    76     4    5809       0     5809
 14  520.25    76     0    5809     425     6234
 15     524    76    -4    6305       0     6305
 16  521.25    76     0    6305     275     6580
 17     514    76     0    6305    1000     7305
 18     513    76     0    6305    1100     7405
 19   512.5    76     0    6305    1150     7455
 20     507    76     0    6305    1700     8005
```

```
  21    506.25    76     0      6305      1775      8080
  22    504.25    76     0      6305      1975      8280
  23    502.25    76     5      8100         0      8100
  24       505    76     0      8100     412.5    8512.5
  25     506.5    76     0      8100     637.5    8737.5
  26    511.25    76     0      8100      1350      9450
  27    515.25    76     0      8100      1950     10050
  28     526.5    76     1      8024    3637.5   11661.5
  29    536.25    76     1      7948    5587.5   13535.5
  30     535.5    76     0      7948      5400     13348
  31    534.75    76     0      7948    5212.5   13160.5
  32       553    76     1      7872      9775     17647
  33    555.75    76     0      7872     10600     18472
  34       583    76     0      7872     18775     26647
  35     582.5    76     3      7644     18625     26269
  36       587    76     1      7568     20650     28218
  37     604.5    76     3      7340     29400     36740
  38       622    76   -30     45835         0     45835
  39    613.25    76    36   50536.5         0   50536.5
  40    627.25    76     0   50536.5     13300   63836.5
  41    627.25    76     0   50536.5     13300   63836.5
  42    629.75    76   -42   63019.5         0   63019.5
  43       616    76    51     74956         0     74956
  44     625.5    76     4     74652     13300     87952
  45     629.5    76     2     74500     19700     94200
  46    639.25    76     7     73968     36275    110243
  47     662.5    76   -98  150457.5         0  150457.5
  48       656    76   117  160090.5         0  160090.5
  49       681    76  -145  224070.5         0  224070.5
  50     673.5    76    -9  223386.5     31875  255261.5
  51     671.5    76    -4  223082.5     41275  264357.5
  52       649    76   -40  220042.5    151525  371567.5
  53     626.5    76     0  220042.5    306775  526817.5
  54    627.25    76   -55  215862.5    301600  517462.5
  55    623.25    76   393  526194.5         0  526194.5
  56    628.75    76  -409  550110.5         0  550110.5
  57    625.75    76     0  550110.5     31350  581460.5
  58       624    76   425    567448         0    567448
  59       641    76  -488    713960         0    713960
  60     627.5    76   272    876888         0    876888
A0 = 2700 P&L = 874188 Final = 876888 IM = 2700 MM = 2500
INDIVIDUAL TRADES
0 (0,1) P&L=410.5 SIZE=-1 P&L/SIZE=410.5 EQ=562.5 COST=152
1 (1,5) P&L=898 SIZE=1 P&L/SIZE=898 EQ=1050 COST=152
```

```
2 (5,10) P&L=1585.5 SIZE=-1 P&L/SIZE=1585.5 EQ=1737.5 COST=152
3 (10,12) P&L=171 SIZE=2 P&L/SIZE=85.5 EQ=475 COST=304
4 (12,13) P&L=196 SIZE=-2 P&L/SIZE=98 EQ=500 COST=304
5 (13,15) P&L=496 SIZE=2 P&L/SIZE=248 EQ=800 COST=304
6 (15,23) P&L=1871 SIZE=-2 P&L/SIZE=935.5 EQ=2175 COST=304
7 (23,38) P&L=17506.5 SIZE=3 P&L/SIZE=5835.5 EQ=17962.5 COST=456
8 (28,38) P&L=4623 SIZE=1 P&L/SIZE=4623 EQ=4775 COST=152
9 (29,38) P&L=4135.5 SIZE=1 P&L/SIZE=4135.5 EQ=4287.5 COST=152
10 (32,38) P&L=3298 SIZE=1 P&L/SIZE=3298 EQ=3450 COST=152
11 (35,38) P&L=5469 SIZE=3 P&L/SIZE=1823 EQ=5925 COST=456
12 (36,38) P&L=1598 SIZE=1 P&L/SIZE=1598 EQ=1750 COST=152
13 (37,38) P&L=2169 SIZE=3 P&L/SIZE=723 EQ=2625 COST=456
14 (38,39) P&L=4853.5 SIZE=-17 P&L/SIZE=285.5 EQ=7437.5 COST=2584
15 (39,42) P&L=12787 SIZE=19 P&L/SIZE=673 EQ=15675 COST=2888
16 (42,43) P&L=12316.5 SIZE=-23 P&L/SIZE=535.5 EQ=15812.5 COST=3496
17 (43,47) P&L=60844 SIZE=28 P&L/SIZE=2173 EQ=65100 COST=4256
18 (44,47) P&L=6792 SIZE=4 P&L/SIZE=1698 EQ=7400 COST=608
19 (45,47) P&L=2996 SIZE=2 P&L/SIZE=1498 EQ=3300 COST=304
20 (46,47) P&L=7073.5 SIZE=7 P&L/SIZE=1010.5 EQ=8137.5 COST=1064
21 (47,48) P&L=9861 SIZE=-57 P&L/SIZE=173 EQ=18525 COST=8664
22 (48,49) P&L=65880 SIZE=60 P&L/SIZE=1098 EQ=75000 COST=9120
23 (49,55) P&L=232517.5 SIZE=-85 P&L/SIZE=2735.5 EQ=245437.5 COST=12920
24 (50,55) P&L=21244.5 SIZE=-9 P&L/SIZE=2360.5 EQ=22612.5 COST=1368
25 (51,55) P&L=9042 SIZE=-4 P&L/SIZE=2260.5 EQ=9650 COST=608
26 (52,55) P&L=45420 SIZE=-40 P&L/SIZE=1135.5 EQ=51500 COST=6080
27 (54,55) P&L=2640 SIZE=-55 P&L/SIZE=48 EQ=11000 COST=8360
28 (55,56) P&L=24600 SIZE=200 P&L/SIZE=123 EQ=55000 COST=30400
29 (56,58) P&L=17869.5 SIZE=-209 P&L/SIZE=85.5 EQ=49637.5 COST=31768
30 (58,59) P&L=150768 SIZE=216 P&L/SIZE=698 EQ=183600 COST=32832
31 (59,60) P&L=142256 SIZE=-272 P&L/SIZE=523 EQ=183600 COST=41344
STATISTICS OF TRADES
Total P&L                       = 874188
Total P&L/unit                  = 45411
Gross profit                    = 874188
Gross profit/unit               = 45411
Gross loss                      = 0
Gross loss/unit                 = 0
Total number of trades          = 32
Number of winning trades        = 32
Number of losing trades         = 0
Average profit                  = 27318.375
Average profit/unit             = 1419.09375
Average loss                    = 0
Average loss/unit               = 0
```

```
Largest winning trade              = 232517.5
Largest winning trade/unit         = 5835.5
Largest losing trade               = 0
Largest losing trade/unit          = 0
Max number of consecutive wins     = 32
Max number of consecutive losses = 0
Maximum consecutive profit         = 874188
Maximum consecutive profit/unit   = 45411
Maximum consecutive loss           = 0
Maximum consecutive loss/unit      = 0
PL distribution
0 (0, 20000] 24
1 (20000, 40000] 2
2 (40000, 60000] 1
3 (60000, 80000] 2
4 (80000, 100000] 0
5 (100000, 120000] 0
6 (120000, 140000] 0
7 (140000, 160000] 2
8 (160000, 180000] 0
9 (180000, 200000] 0
10 (200000, 220000] 0
11 (220000, 240000] 1
PL/unit distribution
0 (0, 1500] 20
1 (1500, 3000] 8
2 (3000, 4500] 2
3 (4500, 6000] 2
Maximum account value              = 876888
Minimum account value              = 2624
Largest drawdown                   = -14012.5
Average drawdown                   = -508.2
```

The second P&L reserve strategy does not contain losing or breakeven trades. However, it does experience a drop in equity at the moment of a transaction due to transaction costs. This program can be applied not only to potential profit strategies but to other strategies that include losing and breakeven trades.

We have already seen that the second P&L reserve strategy increases the size of transactions only when it is permitted by the account equity and when that action is profitable. As a result, the size of the trades have grown by the end of the strategy's application. It is questionable whether a distribution should be built for trades of different size, which is why the program also reports the P&L per-unit distribution. We see that 20 of 32 trades generate a profit per unit < $1,500 each. At the same time, 28 of 32 trades generate P&L per unit < $3,000 each.

When studying these results, remember that only the close/settlement prices for the contract SK05 were selected. This ignores the potential profit of intraday trading.

CONCLUSIONS

- The 31 statistical properties that characterize trading strategies are implemented.
- The filter-program `evaluate.cpp` is written. It takes as input the type of contract specifications, initial and maintenance margins, initial account cash balance, prices, costs, and strategy, then evaluates the strategy, computes statistical properties of trades, and reports results to the standard output.
- The program `evaluate.cpp` is applied to the settlement prices of the soybean contract SK05 traded on CBOT during the calendar months January, February, and March 2005.

CHAPTER 10

Comparing Markets

Contract specifications, margin requirements, trends, the volatility of prices, and liquidity differ with each market. It is interesting to have some idea of the size of the potential profits that can be expected for different markets. This chapter will create those results.

TIME FRAME AND PRICES

In the following comparison, only one week of daily open, high, low, and settlement prices are used. This means that we cannot take advantage of intraday tick opportunities. The prices for the five business days December 19 through 23, all in 2005, were accurately retyped into text files from futures market tables in the daily issues of the *Wall Street Journal*. All prices are used as they are presented in the *Wall Street Journal* except for Treasury bonds. Bonds are quoted in thirty-seconds of a point. This means that the quote 113-09 must be translated into the decimal number $113 + 9 / 32 = 113.28125$.

SELECTED CONTRACTS

In order to operate with a longer list of contracts and get a diversified test, the number of contract specification classes and the function `Prices::create()` were expanded (see Chapter 1). The contracts where `maxprof3` and `evaluate` have been applied include: CH06—March 2006 corn, SH06—March 2006 soybeans, WH06—March 2006 wheat, LCG06—February 2006 live cattle, GCG06—February 2006 gold, HGH06—March 2006 copper, CCH06—March 2006 cocoa, KCH06—March 2006 coffee, SBH06—March 2006 #11 sugar, CTH06—March 2006 cotton, LBH06—March 2006 lumber, CLH06—March 2006 crude oil, USH06—March 2006 30-year Treasury bonds, SPH06—March 2006 Standard and Poor's (S&P) 500.

DATA FILE FORMAT

A file for each contract contains the symbol, initial number of contracts, initial and maintenance margins, transaction cost, and 20 prices—four for each day. The transaction cost is set to one half of the commissions per trade per contract. The commissions $13 ($26 per trade) was considered realistic. The following is an example of the first contract, CH06:

```
C 1 340 250 13
207.00 209.75 206.50 208.75
208.50 212.00 208.25 209.75
209.25 210.25 207.75 210.00
209.50 213.00 209.50 212.75
212.75 214.25 212.25 214.00
```

Each file is named using the contract ticker symbol and dates: `CH06_20051219_20051223.txt`. Because the values found in the files are also present in the output results, there is no reason to show all of the initial data files.

RESULTS OF APPLICATION OF MAXPROF3 AND EVALUATE

The following is the output for the contract CH06 using the program maxprof3. Getting results for this contract is described in detail. Other contracts are treated similarly.

CH06

```
maxprof3 < CH06_20051219_20051223.txt
```

#	C	Cost	PPS	PPS1	PPS2	Pos2	Cash2	Equity2	Total2
0	207	13	1	1	1	1	327	0	327
1	209.75	13	-2	-2	-2	-1	438.5	0	438.5
2	206.5	13	2	2	2	1	575	0	575
3	208.75	13	0	0	1	2	562	112.5	674.5
4	208.5	13	0	0	0	2	562	87.5	649.5
5	212	13	-2	-3	-4	-2	947.5	0	947.5
6	208.25	13	2	5	5	3	1257.5	0	1257.5
7	209.75	13	0	0	0	3	1257.5	225	1482.5
8	209.25	13	0	0	1	4	1244.5	150	1394.5

```
  9   210.25   13  -2     -7     -8     -4  1490.5        0  1490.5
 10   207.75   13   2      9      9      5  1873.5        0  1873.5
 11      210   13   0      0      0      5  1873.5    562.5    2436
 12    209.5   13   0      0      1      6  1860.5    437.5    2298
 13      213   13  -2    -13    -15     -9    3153        0    3153
 14    209.5   13   2     20     22     13    4442        0    4442
 15   212.75   13   0      0      6     19    4364   2112.5  6476.5
 16   212.75   13   0      0      0     19    4364   2112.5  6476.5
 17   214.25   13  -2    -31    -41    -22  7368.5        0  7368.5
 18   212.25   13   2     42     49     27  8931.5        0  8931.5
 19      214   13  -1    -23    -27      0   10943        0   10943
A0 = 340 P&L = 1564 P&L1 = 9171 P&L2 = 10603 IM = 340 MM = 250
```

In the second command, this output is piped to awk, which adjusts and makes it friendly for the program evaluate.cpp. After the adjustment, the new output is redirected to the program evaluate.cpp (see also Chapter 9). This last program reports the statistics of trades and their profit-and-loss (P&L) distributions. However, it also repeats the prices, costs, strategy, cash, open position equity, and total equity for the selected strategy. In order to save space, only the lines beginning from the section "Individual Trades" are printed below:

```
maxprof3 < CH06_20051219_20051223.txt | awk '{if(NR==1)n=$2;if(NF==10&&
NR>1){p[NR]=$2;c[NR]=$3;s[NR]=$6;}if(NF==18){a0=$3;im=$15;mm=$18}}END{
printf("%s %f %f %f 1000 100\n",n,im,mm,a0);for(i=2;i<NR;i++)
printf("%f %f %d\n",p[i],c[i],s[i]);}' | evaluate | awk
'{if($1=="INDIVIDUAL"){y=1;}if(y==1)print $0}'
```

This command line (it must be one continuous line when issued as a command) is the same for all contracts except that the data file and width of the P&L distributions are different. The widths can be found in the output where the first distribution interval is reported. For example:

```
...
PL distribution
0 (0, 1000] 10
...
```

In the output above, the value 1000 is the width for building the P&L distribution for the corn trades. All evaluation reports corresponding to the second P&L reserve strategy come from maxprof3. The following is the one for CH06:

```
INDIVIDUAL TRADES
0 (0,1) P&L=111.5 SIZE=1 P&L/SIZE=111.5 EQ=137.5 COST=26
1 (1,2) P&L=136.5 SIZE=-1 P&L/SIZE=136.5 EQ=162.5 COST=26
2 (2,5) P&L=249 SIZE=1 P&L/SIZE=249 EQ=275 COST=26
```

```
3 (3,5) P&L=136.5 SIZE=1 P&L/SIZE=136.5 EQ=162.5 COST=26
4 (5,6) P&L=323 SIZE=-2 P&L/SIZE=161.5 EQ=375 COST=52
5 (6,9) P&L=222 SIZE=3 P&L/SIZE=74 EQ=300 COST=78
6 (8,9) P&L=24 SIZE=1 P&L/SIZE=24 EQ=50 COST=26
7 (9,10) P&L=396 SIZE=-4 P&L/SIZE=99 EQ=500 COST=104
8 (10,13) P&L=1182.5 SIZE=5 P&L/SIZE=236.5 EQ=1312.5 COST=130
9 (12,13) P&L=149 SIZE=1 P&L/SIZE=149 EQ=175 COST=26
10 (13,14) P&L=1341 SIZE=-9 P&L/SIZE=149 EQ=1575 COST=234
11 (14,17) P&L=2749.5 SIZE=13 P&L/SIZE=211.5 EQ=3087.5 COST=338
12 (15,17) P&L=294 SIZE=6 P&L/SIZE=49 EQ=450 COST=156
13 (17,18) P&L=1628 SIZE=-22 P&L/SIZE=74 EQ=2200 COST=572
14 (18,19) P&L=1660.5 SIZE=27 P&L/SIZE=61.5 EQ=2362.5 COST=702
STATISTICS OF TRADES
Total P&L                          = 10603
Total P&L/unit                     = 1922.5
Gross profit                       = 10603
Gross profit/unit                  = 1922.5
Gross loss                         = 0
Gross loss/unit                    = 0
Total number of trades             = 15
Number of winning trades           = 15
Number of losing trades            = 0
Average profit                     = 706.866667
Average profit/unit                = 128.166667
Average loss                       = 0
Average loss/unit                  = 0
Largest winning trade              = 2749.5
Largest winning trade/unit         = 249
Largest losing trade               = 0
Largest losing trade/unit          = 0
Max number of consecutive wins     = 15
Max number of consecutive losses = 0
Maximum consecutive profit         = 10603
Maximum consecutive profit/unit    = 1922.5
Maximum consecutive loss           = 0
Maximum consecutive loss/unit      = 0
PL distribution
0 (0, 1000] 10
1 (1000, 2000] 4
2 (2000, 3000] 1
PL/unit distribution
0 (0, 100] 6
1 (100, 200] 6
2 (200, 300] 3
```

```
Maximum account value            = 10943
Minimum account value            = 327
Largest drawdown                 = -138
Average drawdown                 = -16.5
```

The following printout shows output pairs from `maxprof3` and `evaluate`. Instead of typing and running each command separately, all of them have been placed in a shell script. The commodity being referenced (only one expiration month is selected as shown in the list of contracts in the section above) can be found in the second field of the first line (and, of course, in the section heading).

SH06

```
 #        S  Cost  PPS   PPS1   PPS2   Pos2     Cash2  Equity2    Total2
 0      603    13    1      1      1      1      1087        0      1087
 1      622    13   -2     -2     -2     -1      2011        0      2011
 2    602.5    13    2      3      3      2      2947        0      2947
 3      620    13   -2     -6     -6     -4      4619        0      4619
 4   619.25    13    2      8      8      4      4665        0      4665
 5    627.5    13   -2     -9     -9     -5      6198        0      6198
 6    615.5    13    2     13     13      8      9029        0      9029
 7    616.5    13   -2    -16    -16     -8      9221        0      9221
 8    613.5    13    2     17     17      9     10200        0     10200
 9      620    13   -2    -20    -20    -11     12865        0     12865
10   608.25    13    2     28     28     17   18963.5        0   18963.5
11      619    13   -2    -42    -42    -25     27555        0     27555
12   618.25    13    2     50     50     25   27842.5        0   27842.5
13      629    13   -2    -62    -62    -37     40474        0     40474
14   618.25    13    2     91     91     54   59178.5        0   59178.5
15   625.25    13   -2   -124   -124    -70   76466.5        0   76466.5
16    621.5    13    2    150    150     80   87641.5        0   87641.5
17      626    13   -2   -175   -175    -95  103366.5        0  103366.5
18    620.5    13    2    211    211    116  126748.5        0  126748.5
19      625    13   -1   -116   -116      0  151340.5        0  151340.5
A0 = 1100 P&L = 7381 P&L1 = 150240.5 P&L2 = 150240.5 IM = 1100 MM = 750
INDIVIDUAL TRADES
0 (0,1) P&L=924 SIZE=1 P&L/SIZE=924 EQ=950 COST=26
1 (1,2) P&L=949 SIZE=-1 P&L/SIZE=949 EQ=975 COST=26
2 (2,3) P&L=1698 SIZE=2 P&L/SIZE=849 EQ=1750 COST=52
3 (3,4) P&L=46 SIZE=-4 P&L/SIZE=11.5 EQ=150 COST=104
4 (4,5) P&L=1546 SIZE=4 P&L/SIZE=386.5 EQ=1650 COST=104
5 (5,6) P&L=2870 SIZE=-5 P&L/SIZE=574 EQ=3000 COST=130
6 (6,7) P&L=192 SIZE=8 P&L/SIZE=24 EQ=400 COST=208
7 (7,8) P&L=992 SIZE=-8 P&L/SIZE=124 EQ=1200 COST=208
```

```
8 (8,9) P&L=2691 SIZE=9 P&L/SIZE=299 EQ=2925 COST=234
9 (9,10) P&L=6176.5 SIZE=-11 P&L/SIZE=561.5 EQ=6462.5 COST=286
10 (10,11) P&L=8695.5 SIZE=17 P&L/SIZE=511.5 EQ=9137.5 COST=442
11 (11,12) P&L=287.5 SIZE=-25 P&L/SIZE=11.5 EQ=937.5 COST=650
12 (12,13) P&L=12787.5 SIZE=25 P&L/SIZE=511.5 EQ=13437.5 COST=650
13 (13,14) P&L=18925.5 SIZE=-37 P&L/SIZE=511.5 EQ=19887.5 COST=962
14 (14,15) P&L=17496 SIZE=54 P&L/SIZE=324 EQ=18900 COST=1404
15 (15,16) P&L=11305 SIZE=-70 P&L/SIZE=161.5 EQ=13125 COST=1820
16 (16,17) P&L=15920 SIZE=80 P&L/SIZE=199 EQ=18000 COST=2080
17 (17,18) P&L=23655 SIZE=-95 P&L/SIZE=249 EQ=26125 COST=2470
18 (18,19) P&L=23084 SIZE=116 P&L/SIZE=199 EQ=26100 COST=3016
STATISTICS OF TRADES
Total P&L                        = 150240.5
Total P&L/unit                   = 7381
Gross profit                     = 150240.5
Gross profit/unit                = 7381
Gross loss                       = 0
Gross loss/unit                  = 0
Total number of trades           = 19
Number of winning trades         = 19
Number of losing trades          = 0
Average profit                   = 7907.39474
Average profit/unit              = 388.473684
Average loss                     = 0
Average loss/unit                = 0
Largest winning trade            = 23655
Largest winning trade/unit       = 949
Largest losing trade             = 0
Largest losing trade/unit        = 0
Max number of consecutive wins   = 19
Max number of consecutive losses = 0
Maximum consecutive profit       = 150240.5
Maximum consecutive profit/unit  = 7381
Maximum consecutive loss         = 0
Maximum consecutive loss/unit    = 0
PL distribution
0 (0, 5000] 10
1 (5000, 10000] 2
2 (10000, 15000] 2
3 (15000, 20000] 3
4 (20000, 25000] 2
PL/unit distribution
0 (0, 500] 11
1 (500, 1000] 8
Maximum account value            = 151340.5
```

```
Minimum account value          = 1087
Largest drawdown               = -13
Average drawdown               = -0.684210526
```

WH06

#	W	Cost	PPS	PPS1	PPS2	Pos2	Cash2	Equity2	Total2
0	320.5	13	1	1	1	1	497	0	497
1	323.5	13	-2	-2	-2	-1	621	0	621
2	318.5	13	2	2	2	1	845	0	845
3	323.25	13	0	0	1	2	832	237.5	1069.5
4	323.25	13	0	0	0	2	832	237.5	1069.5
5	329	13	-2	-3	-5	-3	1579.5	0	1579.5
6	323.25	13	2	5	7	4	2351	0	2351
7	328	13	-2	-7	-10	-6	3171	0	3171
8	327.25	13	2	9	12	6	3240	0	3240
9	328.5	13	-2	-10	-12	-6	3459	0	3459
10	324.75	13	2	11	14	8	4402	0	4402
11	327.5	13	0	0	2	10	4376	1100	5476
12	328	13	0	0	1	11	4363	1350	5713
13	331.25	13	-2	-16	-25	-14	7175.5	0	7175.5
14	327.5	13	2	23	32	18	9384.5	0	9384.5
15	330.75	13	0	0	6	24	9306.5	2925	12231.5
16	332	13	0	0	2	26	9280.5	4425	13705.5
17	336	13	-2	-36	-62	-36	18099.5	0	18099.5
18	331	13	2	56	88	52	25955.5	0	25955.5
19	334.5	13	-1	-33	-52	0	34379.5	0	34379.5

```
A0 = 510 P&L = 2762 P&L1 = 21705.5 P&L2 = 33869.5 IM = 510 MM = 375
INDIVIDUAL TRADES
0 (0,1) P&L=124 SIZE=1 P&L/SIZE=124 EQ=150 COST=26
1 (1,2) P&L=224 SIZE=-1 P&L/SIZE=224 EQ=250 COST=26
2 (2,5) P&L=499 SIZE=1 P&L/SIZE=499 EQ=525 COST=26
3 (3,5) P&L=261.5 SIZE=1 P&L/SIZE=261.5 EQ=287.5 COST=26
4 (5,6) P&L=784.5 SIZE=-3 P&L/SIZE=261.5 EQ=862.5 COST=78
5 (6,7) P&L=846 SIZE=4 P&L/SIZE=211.5 EQ=950 COST=104
6 (7,8) P&L=69 SIZE=-6 P&L/SIZE=11.5 EQ=225 COST=156
7 (8,9) P&L=219 SIZE=6 P&L/SIZE=36.5 EQ=375 COST=156
8 (9,10) P&L=969 SIZE=-6 P&L/SIZE=161.5 EQ=1125 COST=156
9 (10,13) P&L=2392 SIZE=8 P&L/SIZE=299 EQ=2600 COST=208
10 (11,13) P&L=323 SIZE=2 P&L/SIZE=161.5 EQ=375 COST=52
11 (12,13) P&L=136.5 SIZE=1 P&L/SIZE=136.5 EQ=162.5 COST=26
12 (13,14) P&L=2261 SIZE=-14 P&L/SIZE=161.5 EQ=2625 COST=364
13 (14,17) P&L=7182 SIZE=18 P&L/SIZE=399 EQ=7650 COST=468
14 (15,17) P&L=1419 SIZE=6 P&L/SIZE=236.5 EQ=1575 COST=156
15 (16,17) P&L=348 SIZE=2 P&L/SIZE=174 EQ=400 COST=52
```

```
16 (17,18) P&L=8064 SIZE=-36 P&L/SIZE=224 EQ=9000 COST=936
17 (18,19) P&L=7748 SIZE=52 P&L/SIZE=149 EQ=9100 COST=1352
STATISTICS OF TRADES
Total P&L                         = 33869.5
Total P&L/unit                    = 3732
Gross profit                      = 33869.5
Gross profit/unit                 = 3732
Gross loss                        = 0
Gross loss/unit                   = 0
Total number of trades            = 18
Number of winning trades          = 18
Number of losing trades           = 0
Average profit                    = 1881.63889
Average profit/unit               = 207.333333
Average loss                      = 0
Average loss/unit                 = 0
Largest winning trade             = 8064
Largest winning trade/unit        = 499
Largest losing trade              = 0
Largest losing trade/unit         = 0
Max number of consecutive wins    = 18
Max number of consecutive losses = 0
Maximum consecutive profit        = 33869.5
Maximum consecutive profit/unit  = 3732
Maximum consecutive loss          = 0
Maximum consecutive loss/unit    = 0
PL distribution
0 (0, 3000] 15
1 (3000, 6000] 0
2 (6000, 9000] 3
PL/unit distribution
0 (0, 300] 16
1 (300, 600] 2
Maximum account value             = 34379.5
Minimum account value             = 497
Largest drawdown                  = -13
Average drawdown                  = -0.684210526
```

LCG06

#	LC	Cost	PPS	PPS1	PPS2	Pos2	Cash2	Equity2	Total2
0	96.9	13	1	1	1	1	1087	0	1087
1	97.275	13	-2	-2	-2	-1	1211	0	1211
2	96.7	13	2	2	2	1	1415	0	1415
3	96.8	13	0	0	0	1	1415	40	1455

```
  4   96.75   13   0    0    0    1   1415   20   1435
  5    97.4   13  -2   -2   -2   -1   1669    0   1669
  6   96.75   13   2    2    2    1   1903    0   1903
  7  97.275   13  -2   -2   -2   -1   2087    0   2087
  8    97.2   13   2    2    2    1   2091    0   2091
  9    97.4   13  -2   -2   -2   -1   2145    0   2145
 10   95.85   13   2    3    3    2   2726    0   2726
 11  96.175   13  -2   -4   -4   -2   2934    0   2934
 12    95.8   13   2    4    4    2   3182    0   3182
 13  95.875   13  -2   -4   -4   -2   3190    0   3190
 14    95.3   13   2    5    5    3   3585    0   3585
 15   95.55   13   0    0    0    3   3585  300   3885
 16    95.5   13   0    0    0    3   3585  240   3825
 17   95.95   13  -2   -6   -6   -3   4287    0   4287
 18    95.4   13   2    7    7    4   4856    0   4856
 19  95.725   13  -1   -4   -4    0   5324    0   5324
A0 = 1100 P&L = 2620 P&L1 = 4224 P&L2 = 4224 IM = 1100 MM = 805
INDIVIDUAL TRADES
0 (0,1) P&L=124 SIZE=1 P&L/SIZE=124 EQ=150 COST=26
1 (1,2) P&L=204 SIZE=-1 P&L/SIZE=204 EQ=230 COST=26
2 (2,5) P&L=254 SIZE=1 P&L/SIZE=254 EQ=280 COST=26
3 (5,6) P&L=234 SIZE=-1 P&L/SIZE=234 EQ=260 COST=26
4 (6,7) P&L=184 SIZE=1 P&L/SIZE=184 EQ=210 COST=26
5 (7,8) P&L=4 SIZE=-1 P&L/SIZE=4 EQ=30 COST=26
6 (8,9) P&L=54 SIZE=1 P&L/SIZE=54 EQ=80 COST=26
7 (9,10) P&L=594 SIZE=-1 P&L/SIZE=594 EQ=620 COST=26
8 (10,11) P&L=208 SIZE=2 P&L/SIZE=104 EQ=260 COST=52
9 (11,12) P&L=248 SIZE=-2 P&L/SIZE=124 EQ=300 COST=52
10 (12,13) P&L=8 SIZE=2 P&L/SIZE=4 EQ=60 COST=52
11 (13,14) P&L=408 SIZE=-2 P&L/SIZE=204 EQ=460 COST=52
12 (14,17) P&L=702 SIZE=3 P&L/SIZE=234 EQ=780 COST=78
13 (17,18) P&L=582 SIZE=-3 P&L/SIZE=194 EQ=660 COST=78
14 (18,19) P&L=416 SIZE=4 P&L/SIZE=104 EQ=520 COST=104
STATISTICS OF TRADES
Total P&L                       = 4224
Total P&L/unit                  = 2620
Gross profit                    = 4224
Gross profit/unit               = 2620
Gross loss                      = 0
Gross loss/unit                 = 0
Total number of trades          = 15
Number of winning trades        = 15
Number of losing trades         = 0
Average profit                  = 281.6
Average profit/unit             = 174.666667
```

```
Average loss                      = 0
Average loss/unit                 = 0
Largest winning trade             = 702
Largest winning trade/unit        = 594
Largest losing trade              = 0
Largest losing trade/unit         = 0
Max number of consecutive wins    = 15
Max number of consecutive losses = 0
Maximum consecutive profit        = 4224
Maximum consecutive profit/unit   = 2620
Maximum consecutive loss          = 0
Maximum consecutive loss/unit     = 0
PL distribution
0 (0, 500] 12
1 (500, 1000] 3
PL/unit distribution
0 (0, 250] 13
1 (250, 500] 1
2 (500, 750] 1
Maximum account value             = 5324
Minimum account value             = 1087
Largest drawdown                  = -60
Average drawdown                  = -5.47058824
```

GCG06

#	GC	Cost	PPS	PPS1	PPS2	Pos2	Cash2	Equity2	Total2
0	505.7	13	1	1	1	1	2087	0	2087
1	512.1	13	-2	-2	-2	-1	2701	0	2701
2	503.6	13	2	2	2	1	3525	0	3525
3	506.1	13	0	0	0	1	3525	250	3775
4	506.9	13	0	0	0	1	3525	330	3855
5	511.4	13	-2	-3	-3	-2	4266	0	4266
6	496.6	13	2	5	5	3	7161	0	7161
7	497	13	0	0	0	3	7161	120	7281
8	497.5	13	0	0	0	3	7161	270	7431
9	497.7	13	-2	-6	-6	-3	7413	0	7413
10	492.3	13	2	7	7	4	8942	0	8942
11	495.3	13	0	0	0	4	8942	1200	10142
12	497.5	13	0	0	1	5	8929	2080	11009
13	507.3	13	-2	-11	-12	-7	15753	0	15753
14	492.3	13	2	19	19	12	26006	0	26006
15	505	13	-2	-31	-31	-19	40843	0	40843
16	504.6	13	2	38	38	19	41109	0	41109
17	508.8	13	-2	-41	-42	-23	48543	0	48543

```
  18     502.2    13    2     51     53     30    63034       0    63034
  19     505.2    13   -1    -29    -30      0    71644       0    71644
A0 = 2100 P&L = 9752 P&L1 = 67682 P&L2 = 69544 IM = 2100 MM = 1500
INDIVIDUAL TRADES
0 (0,1) P&L=614 SIZE=1 P&L/SIZE=614 EQ=640 COST=26
1 (1,2) P&L=824 SIZE=-1 P&L/SIZE=824 EQ=850 COST=26
2 (2,5) P&L=754 SIZE=1 P&L/SIZE=754 EQ=780 COST=26
3 (5,6) P&L=2908 SIZE=-2 P&L/SIZE=1454 EQ=2960 COST=52
4 (6,9) P&L=252 SIZE=3 P&L/SIZE=84 EQ=330 COST=78
5 (9,10) P&L=1542 SIZE=-3 P&L/SIZE=514 EQ=1620 COST=78
6 (10,13) P&L=5896 SIZE=4 P&L/SIZE=1474 EQ=6000 COST=104
7 (12,13) P&L=954 SIZE=1 P&L/SIZE=954 EQ=980 COST=26
8 (13,14) P&L=10318 SIZE=-7 P&L/SIZE=1474 EQ=10500 COST=182
9 (14,15) P&L=14928 SIZE=12 P&L/SIZE=1244 EQ=15240 COST=312
10 (15,16) P&L=266 SIZE=-19 P&L/SIZE=14 EQ=760 COST=494
11 (16,17) P&L=7486 SIZE=19 P&L/SIZE=394 EQ=7980 COST=494
12 (17,18) P&L=14582 SIZE=-23 P&L/SIZE=634 EQ=15180 COST=598
13 (18,19) P&L=8220 SIZE=30 P&L/SIZE=274 EQ=9000 COST=780
STATISTICS OF TRADES
Total P&L                         = 69544
Total P&L/unit                    = 10706
Gross profit                      = 69544
Gross profit/unit                 = 10706
Gross loss                        = 0
Gross loss/unit                   = 0
Total number of trades            = 14
Number of winning trades          = 14
Number of losing trades           = 0
Average profit                    = 4967.42857
Average profit/unit               = 764.714286
Average loss                      = 0
Average loss/unit                 = 0
Largest winning trade             = 14928
Largest winning trade/unit        = 1474
Largest losing trade              = 0
Largest losing trade/unit         = 0
Max number of consecutive wins    = 14
Max number of consecutive losses = 0
Maximum consecutive profit        = 69544
Maximum consecutive profit/unit   = 10706
Maximum consecutive loss          = 0
Maximum consecutive loss/unit     = 0
PL distribution
0 (0, 5000] 8
1 (5000, 10000] 3
```

```
2 (10000, 15000] 3
PL/unit distribution
0 (0, 500] 4
1 (500, 1000] 6
2 (1000, 1500] 4
Maximum account value          = 71644
Minimum account value          = 2087
Largest drawdown               = -18
Average drawdown               = -1.72222222
```

HGH06

#	HG	Cost	PPS	PPS1	PPS2	Pos2	Cash2	Equity2	Total2
0	202.9	13	1	1	1	1	3737	0	3737
1	203.2	13	-2	-2	-2	-1	3786	0	3786
2	201.1	13	2	2	2	1	4285	0	4285
3	201.3	13	0	0	0	1	4285	50	4335
4	201.3	13	0	0	0	1	4285	50	4335
5	202.6	13	-2	-2	-2	-1	4634	0	4634
6	200.45	13	2	2	2	1	5145.5	0	5145.5
7	202	13	0	0	0	1	5145.5	387.5	5533
8	202	13	0	0	0	1	5145.5	387.5	5533
9	202.4	13	-2	-2	-2	-1	5607	0	5607
10	199.3	13	2	2	2	1	6356	0	6356
11	201.75	13	0	0	0	1	6356	612.5	6968.5
12	202	13	0	0	0	1	6356	675	7031
13	203.35	13	-2	-2	-2	-1	7342.5	0	7342.5
14	199.3	13	2	3	3	2	8316	0	8316
15	202.55	13	0	0	0	2	8316	1625	9941
16	203.4	13	0	0	0	2	8316	2050	10366
17	204.1	13	-2	-4	-4	-2	10664	0	10664
18	203	13	2	4	4	2	11162	0	11162
19	203.95	13	-1	-2	-2	0	11611	0	11611

```
A0 = 3750 P&L = 6226.5 P&L1 = 7861 P&L2 = 7861 IM = 3750 MM = 2750
INDIVIDUAL TRADES
0 (0,1) P&L=49 SIZE=1 P&L/SIZE=49 EQ=75 COST=26
1 (1,2) P&L=499 SIZE=-1 P&L/SIZE=499 EQ=525 COST=26
2 (2,5) P&L=349 SIZE=1 P&L/SIZE=349 EQ=375 COST=26
3 (5,6) P&L=511.5 SIZE=-1 P&L/SIZE=511.5 EQ=537.5 COST=26
4 (6,9) P&L=461.5 SIZE=1 P&L/SIZE=461.5 EQ=487.5 COST=26
5 (9,10) P&L=749 SIZE=-1 P&L/SIZE=749 EQ=775 COST=26
6 (10,13) P&L=986.5 SIZE=1 P&L/SIZE=986.5 EQ=1012.5 COST=26
7 (13,14) P&L=986.5 SIZE=-1 P&L/SIZE=986.5 EQ=1012.5 COST=26
8 (14,17) P&L=2348 SIZE=2 P&L/SIZE=1174 EQ=2400 COST=52
9 (17,18) P&L=498 SIZE=-2 P&L/SIZE=249 EQ=550 COST=52
```

```
10 (18,19) P&L=423 SIZE=2 P&L/SIZE=211.5 EQ=475 COST=52
STATISTICS OF TRADES
Total P&L                          = 7861
Total P&L/unit                     = 6226.5
Gross profit                       = 7861
Gross profit/unit                  = 6226.5
Gross loss                         = 0
Gross loss/unit                    = 0
Total number of trades             = 11
Number of winning trades           = 11
Number of losing trades            = 0
Average profit                     = 714.636364
Average profit/unit                = 566.045455
Average loss                       = 0
Average loss/unit                  = 0
Largest winning trade              = 2348
Largest winning trade/unit         = 1174
Largest losing trade               = 0
Largest losing trade/unit          = 0
Max number of consecutive wins     = 11
Max number of consecutive losses = 0
Maximum consecutive profit         = 7861
Maximum consecutive profit/unit    = 6226.5
Maximum consecutive loss           = 0
Maximum consecutive loss/unit      = 0
PL distribution
0 (0, 1000] 10
1 (1000, 2000] 0
2 (2000, 3000] 1
PL/unit distribution
0 (0, 500] 6
1 (500, 1000] 4
2 (1000, 1500] 1
Maximum account value              = 11611
Minimum account value              = 3737
Largest drawdown                   = -13
Average drawdown                   = -0.684210526
```

CCH06

#	CC	Cost	PPS	PPS1	PPS2	Pos2	Cash2	Equity2	Total2
0	1147	13	1	1	1	1	967	0	967
1	1451	13	-2	-5	-5	-4	3942	0	3942
2	1436	13	2	8	8	4	4438	0	4438
3	1439	13	-2	-8	-8	-4	4454	0	4454

```
  4      1140   13    2    20    20    16   16154       0   16154
  5      1454   13   -2   -83   -83   -67   65315       0   65315
  6      1427   13    2   151   151    84   81442       0   81442
  7      1448   13    0     0    17   101   81221   17640   98861
  8      1450   13    0     0     1   102   81208   19660  100868
  9      1460   13   -2  -194  -213  -111  108299       0  108299
 10      1442   13    2   237   240   129  125159       0  125159
 11      1450   13    0     0     9   138  125042   10320  135362
 12      1462   13    0     0    17   155  124821   26880  151701
 13      1482   13   -2  -303  -339  -184  178294       0  178294
 14      1455   13    2   395   414   230  222592       0  222592
 15      1478   13   -2  -484  -508  -278  268888       0  268888
 16      1475   13    0     0    -4  -282  268836    8340  277176
 17      1475   13    0     0     0  -282  268836    8340  277176
 18      1459   13    2   574   607   325  314405       0  314405
 19      1463   13   -1  -309  -325     0  323180       0  323180
A0 = 980 P&L = 10922 P&L1 = 306934 P&L2 = 322200 IM = 980 MM = 700
INDIVIDUAL TRADES
0 (0,1) P&L=3014 SIZE=1 P&L/SIZE=3014 EQ=3040 COST=26
1 (1,2) P&L=496 SIZE=-4 P&L/SIZE=124 EQ=600 COST=104
2 (2,3) P&L=16 SIZE=4 P&L/SIZE=4 EQ=120 COST=104
3 (3,4) P&L=11856 SIZE=-4 P&L/SIZE=2964 EQ=11960 COST=104
4 (4,5) P&L=49824 SIZE=16 P&L/SIZE=3114 EQ=50240 COST=416
5 (5,6) P&L=16348 SIZE=-67 P&L/SIZE=244 EQ=18090 COST=1742
6 (6,9) P&L=25536 SIZE=84 P&L/SIZE=304 EQ=27720 COST=2184
7 (7,9) P&L=1598 SIZE=17 P&L/SIZE=94 EQ=2040 COST=442
8 (8,9) P&L=74 SIZE=1 P&L/SIZE=74 EQ=100 COST=26
9 (9,10) P&L=17094 SIZE=-111 P&L/SIZE=154 EQ=19980 COST=2886
10 (10,13) P&L=48246 SIZE=129 P&L/SIZE=374 EQ=51600 COST=3354
11 (11,13) P&L=2646 SIZE=9 P&L/SIZE=294 EQ=2880 COST=234
12 (12,13) P&L=2958 SIZE=17 P&L/SIZE=174 EQ=3400 COST=442
13 (13,14) P&L=44896 SIZE=-184 P&L/SIZE=244 EQ=49680 COST=4784
14 (14,15) P&L=46920 SIZE=230 P&L/SIZE=204 EQ=52900 COST=5980
15 (15,18) P&L=45592 SIZE=-278 P&L/SIZE=164 EQ=52820 COST=7228
16 (16,18) P&L=536 SIZE=-4 P&L/SIZE=134 EQ=640 COST=104
17 (18,19) P&L=4550 SIZE=325 P&L/SIZE=14 EQ=13000 COST=8450
STATISTICS OF TRADES
Total P&L                        = 322200
Total P&L/unit                   = 11692
Gross profit                     = 322200
Gross profit/unit                = 11692
Gross loss                       = 0
Gross loss/unit                  = 0
Total number of trades           = 18
Number of winning trades         = 18
```

```
Number of losing trades          = 0
Average profit                   = 17900
Average profit/unit              = 649.555556
Average loss                     = 0
Average loss/unit                = 0
Largest winning trade            = 49824
Largest winning trade/unit       = 3114
Largest losing trade             = 0
Largest losing trade/unit        = 0
Max number of consecutive wins   = 18
Max number of consecutive losses = 0
Maximum consecutive profit       = 322200
Maximum consecutive profit/unit  = 11692
Maximum consecutive loss         = 0
Maximum consecutive loss/unit    = 0
PL distribution
0 (0, 10000] 9
1 (10000, 20000] 3
2 (20000, 30000] 1
3 (30000, 40000] 0
4 (40000, 50000] 5
PL/unit distribution
0 (0, 1000] 15
1 (1000, 2000] 0
2 (2000, 3000] 1
3 (3000, 4000] 2
Maximum account value            = 323180
Minimum account value            = 967
Largest drawdown                 = -13
Average drawdown                 = -0.684210526
```

KCH06

#	KC	Cost	PPS	PPS1	PPS2	Pos2	Cash2	Equity2	Total2
0	98.3	13	1	1	1	1	3287	0	3287
1	101.7	13	-2	-2	-2	-1	4536	0	4536
2	97.7	13	2	2	2	1	6010	0	6010
3	101.35	13	-2	-3	-3	-2	7339.75	0	7339.75
4	100.8	13	2	4	4	2	7700.25	0	7700.25
5	103.6	13	-2	-4	-4	-2	9748.25	0	9748.25
6	100.7	13	2	5	5	3	11858.25	0	11858.25
7	102.4	13	-2	-7	-7	-4	13679.75	0	13679.75
8	100.25	13	2	9	9	5	16787.75	0	16787.75
9	101.9	13	-2	-11	-11	-6	19738.5	0	19738.5
10	100.25	13	2	13	13	7	23282	0	23282

```
  11      101.2    13   -2    -14    -14     -7 25593.75        0 25593.75
  12      100.2    13    2     15     15      8 28023.75        0 28023.75
  13      103.1    13   -2    -19    -19    -11 36476.75        0 36476.75
  14       99.7    13    2     26     26     15 50163.75        0 50163.75
  15      102.8    13   -2    -35    -35    -20 67146.25        0 67146.25
  16      102.7    13    2     40     40     20 67376.25        0 67376.25
  17     103.75    13   -2    -42    -42    -22 74705.25        0 74705.25
  18     102.25    13    2     48     48     26 86456.25        0 86456.25
  19      102.6    13   -1    -26    -26      0 89530.75        0 89530.75
A0 = 3300 P&L = 14056 P&L1 = 86230.75 P&L2 = 86230.75 IM = 3300 MM = 2300
INDIVIDUAL TRADES
0 (0,1) P&L=1249 SIZE=1 P&L/SIZE=1249 EQ=1275 COST=26
1 (1,2) P&L=1474 SIZE=-1 P&L/SIZE=1474 EQ=1500 COST=26
2 (2,3) P&L=1342.75 SIZE=1 P&L/SIZE=1342.75 EQ=1368.75 COST=26
3 (3,4) P&L=360.5 SIZE=-2 P&L/SIZE=180.25 EQ=412.5 COST=52
4 (4,5) P&L=2048 SIZE=2 P&L/SIZE=1024 EQ=2100 COST=52
5 (5,6) P&L=2123 SIZE=-2 P&L/SIZE=1061.5 EQ=2175 COST=52
6 (6,7) P&L=1834.5 SIZE=3 P&L/SIZE=611.5 EQ=1912.5 COST=78
7 (7,8) P&L=3121 SIZE=-4 P&L/SIZE=780.25 EQ=3225 COST=104
8 (8,9) P&L=2963.75 SIZE=5 P&L/SIZE=592.75 EQ=3093.75 COST=130
9 (9,10) P&L=3556.5 SIZE=-6 P&L/SIZE=592.75 EQ=3712.5 COST=156
10 (10,11) P&L=2311.75 SIZE=7 P&L/SIZE=330.25 EQ=2493.75 COST=182
11 (11,12) P&L=2443 SIZE=-7 P&L/SIZE=349 EQ=2625 COST=182
12 (12,13) P&L=8492 SIZE=8 P&L/SIZE=1061.5 EQ=8700 COST=208
13 (13,14) P&L=13739 SIZE=-11 P&L/SIZE=1249 EQ=14025 COST=286
14 (14,15) P&L=17047.5 SIZE=15 P&L/SIZE=1136.5 EQ=17437.5 COST=390
15 (15,16) P&L=230 SIZE=-20 P&L/SIZE=11.5 EQ=750 COST=520
16 (16,17) P&L=7355 SIZE=20 P&L/SIZE=367.75 EQ=7875 COST=520
17 (17,18) P&L=11803 SIZE=-22 P&L/SIZE=536.5 EQ=12375 COST=572
18 (18,19) P&L=2736.5 SIZE=26 P&L/SIZE=105.25 EQ=3412.5 COST=676
STATISTICS OF TRADES
Total P&L                         = 86230.75
Total P&L/unit                    = 14056
Gross profit                      = 86230.75
Gross profit/unit                 = 14056
Gross loss                        = 0
Gross loss/unit                   = 0
Total number of trades            = 19
Number of winning trades          = 19
Number of losing trades           = 0
Average profit                    = 4538.46053
Average profit/unit               = 739.789474
Average loss                      = 0
Average loss/unit                 = 0
Largest winning trade             = 17047.5
```

```
Largest winning trade/unit      = 1474
Largest losing trade            = 0
Largest losing trade/unit       = 0
Max number of consecutive wins  = 19
Max number of consecutive losses = 0
Maximum consecutive profit      = 86230.75
Maximum consecutive profit/unit = 14056
Maximum consecutive loss        = 0
Maximum consecutive loss/unit   = 0
PL distribution
0 (0, 5000] 14
1 (5000, 10000] 2
2 (10000, 15000] 2
3 (15000, 20000] 1
PL/unit distribution
0 (0, 500] 6
1 (500, 1000] 5
2 (1000, 1500] 8
Maximum account value           = 89530.75
Minimum account value           = 3287
Largest drawdown                = -13
Average drawdown                = -0.684210526
```

SBH06

#	SB	Cost	PPS	PPS1	PPS2	Pos2	Cash2	Equity2	Total2
0	14.25	13	1	1	1	1	787	0	787
1	14.43	13	-2	-2	-2	-1	962.6	0	962.6
2	14.25	13	2	2	2	1	1138.2	0	1138.2
3	14.33	13	0	0	0	1	1138.2	89.6	1227.8
4	14.39	13	0	0	0	1	1138.2	156.8	1295
5	14.42	13	-2	-2	-2	-1	1302.6	0	1302.6
6	14.15	13	2	2	2	1	1579	0	1579
7	14.21	13	0	0	0	1	1579	67.2	1646.2
8	14.21	13	0	0	0	1	1579	67.2	1646.2
9	14.23	13	-2	-3	-3	-2	1629.6	0	1629.6
10	14.09	13	0	0	0	-2	1629.6	313.6	1943.2
11	14.1	13	0	0	0	-2	1629.6	291.2	1920.8
12	14.06	13	2	4	4	2	1958.4	0	1958.4
13	14.53	13	-2	-5	-5	-3	2946.2	0	2946.2
14	14.06	13	2	8	8	5	4421.4	0	4421.4
15	14.5	13	0	0	3	8	4382.4	2464	6846.4
16	14.85	13	0	0	4	12	4330.4	5600	9930.4
17	14.89	13	-2	-16	-24	-12	10156	0	10156
18	14.62	13	1	11	12	0	13628.8	0	13628.8

```
  19     14.63    13    0      0      0      0  13628.8         0  13628.8
A0 = 800 P&L = 3200.8 P&L1 = 11244.8 P&L2 = 12828.8 IM = 800 MM = 600
INDIVIDUAL TRADES
0 (0,1) P&L=175.6 SIZE=1 P&L/SIZE=175.6 EQ=201.6 COST=26
1 (1,2) P&L=175.6 SIZE=-1 P&L/SIZE=175.6 EQ=201.6 COST=26
2 (2,5) P&L=164.4 SIZE=1 P&L/SIZE=164.4 EQ=190.4 COST=26
3 (5,6) P&L=276.4 SIZE=-1 P&L/SIZE=276.4 EQ=302.4 COST=26
4 (6,9) P&L=63.6 SIZE=1 P&L/SIZE=63.6 EQ=89.6 COST=26
5 (9,12) P&L=328.8 SIZE=-2 P&L/SIZE=164.4 EQ=380.8 COST=52
6 (12,13) P&L=1000.8 SIZE=2 P&L/SIZE=500.4 EQ=1052.8 COST=52
7 (13,14) P&L=1501.2 SIZE=-3 P&L/SIZE=500.4 EQ=1579.2 COST=78
8 (14,17) P&L=4518 SIZE=5 P&L/SIZE=903.6 EQ=4648 COST=130
9 (15,17) P&L=1232.4 SIZE=3 P&L/SIZE=410.8 EQ=1310.4 COST=78
10 (16,17) P&L=75.2 SIZE=4 P&L/SIZE=18.8 EQ=179.2 COST=104
11 (17,18) P&L=3316.8 SIZE=-12 P&L/SIZE=276.4 EQ=3628.8 COST=312
STATISTICS OF TRADES
Total P&L                          = 12828.8
Total P&L/unit                     = 3630.4
Gross profit                       = 12828.8
Gross profit/unit                  = 3630.4
Gross loss                         = 0
Gross loss/unit                    = 0
Total number of trades             = 12
Number of winning trades           = 12
Number of losing trades            = 0
Average profit                     = 1069.06667
Average profit/unit                = 302.533333
Average loss                       = 0
Average loss/unit                  = 0
Largest winning trade              = 4518
Largest winning trade/unit         = 903.6
Largest losing trade               = 0
Largest losing trade/unit          = 0
Max number of consecutive wins     = 12
Max number of consecutive losses = 0
Maximum consecutive profit         = 12828.8
Maximum consecutive profit/unit    = 3630.4
Maximum consecutive loss           = 0
Maximum consecutive loss/unit      = 0
PL distribution
0 (0, 3000] 10
1 (3000, 6000] 2
PL/unit distribution
0 (0, 300] 8
1 (300, 600] 3
```

```
2 (600, 900] 0
3 (900, 1200] 1
Maximum account value           = 13628.8
Minimum account value           = 787
Largest drawdown                = -22.4
Average drawdown                = -3.05882353
```

CTH06

#	CT	Cost	PPS	PPS1	PPS2	Pos2	Cash2	Equity2	Total2
0	53.5	13	1	1	1	1	1537	0	1537
1	53.65	13	-2	-2	-2	-1	1586	0	1586
2	53.39	13	2	2	2	1	1690	0	1690
3	53.63	13	-2	-2	-2	-1	1784	0	1784
4	53.35	13	2	2	2	1	1898	0	1898
5	53.5	13	-2	-2	-2	-1	1947	0	1947
6	53.1	13	2	2	2	1	2121	0	2121
7	53.22	13	0	0	0	1	2121	60	2181
8	53.3	13	0	0	0	1	2121	100	2221
9	53.45	13	-2	-2	-2	-1	2270	0	2270
10	52.71	13	2	2	2	1	2614	0	2614
11	52.85	13	0	0	0	1	2614	70	2684
12	53.15	13	0	0	0	1	2614	220	2834
13	54.25	13	-2	-3	-3	-2	3345	0	3345
14	53.05	13	2	4	4	2	4493	0	4493
15	54.14	13	0	0	0	2	4493	1090	5583
16	54.15	13	0	0	0	2	4493	1100	5593
17	54.19	13	-2	-5	-5	-3	5568	0	5568
18	53.22	13	2	7	7	4	6932	0	6932
19	53.54	13	-1	-4	-4	0	7520	0	7520

```
A0 = 1550 P&L = 3532 P&L1 = 5970 P&L2 = 5970 IM = 1550 MM = 1100
INDIVIDUAL TRADES
0 (0,1) P&L=49 SIZE=1 P&L/SIZE=49 EQ=75 COST=26
1 (1,2) P&L=104 SIZE=-1 P&L/SIZE=104 EQ=130 COST=26
2 (2,3) P&L=94 SIZE=1 P&L/SIZE=94 EQ=120 COST=26
3 (3,4) P&L=114 SIZE=-1 P&L/SIZE=114 EQ=140 COST=26
4 (4,5) P&L=49 SIZE=1 P&L/SIZE=49 EQ=75 COST=26
5 (5,6) P&L=174 SIZE=-1 P&L/SIZE=174 EQ=200 COST=26
6 (6,9) P&L=149 SIZE=1 P&L/SIZE=149 EQ=175 COST=26
7 (9,10) P&L=344 SIZE=-1 P&L/SIZE=344 EQ=370 COST=26
8 (10,13) P&L=744 SIZE=1 P&L/SIZE=744 EQ=770 COST=26
9 (13,14) P&L=1148 SIZE=-2 P&L/SIZE=574 EQ=1200 COST=52
10 (14,17) P&L=1088 SIZE=2 P&L/SIZE=544 EQ=1140 COST=52
11 (17,18) P&L=1377 SIZE=-3 P&L/SIZE=459 EQ=1455 COST=78
12 (18,19) P&L=536 SIZE=4 P&L/SIZE=134 EQ=640 COST=104
```

```
STATISTICS OF TRADES
Total P&L                         = 5970
Total P&L/unit                    = 3532
Gross profit                      = 5970
Gross profit/unit                 = 3532
Gross loss                        = 0
Gross loss/unit                   = 0
Total number of trades            = 13
Number of winning trades          = 13
Number of losing trades           = 0
Average profit                    = 459.230769
Average profit/unit               = 271.692308
Average loss                      = 0
Average loss/unit                 = 0
Largest winning trade             = 1377
Largest winning trade/unit        = 744
Largest losing trade              = 0
Largest losing trade/unit         = 0
Max number of consecutive wins    = 13
Max number of consecutive losses = 0
Maximum consecutive profit        = 5970
Maximum consecutive profit/unit   = 3532
Maximum consecutive loss          = 0
Maximum consecutive loss/unit     = 0
PL distribution
0 (0, 1000] 10
1 (1000, 2000] 3
PL/unit distribution
0 (0, 500] 10
1 (500, 1000] 3
Maximum account value             = 7520
Minimum account value             = 1537
Largest drawdown                  = -25
Average drawdown                  = -2.11111111
```

LBH06

#	LB	Cost	PPS	PPS1	PPS2	Pos2	Cash2	Equity2	Total2
0	351.7	13	1	1	1	1	1887	0	1887
1	354.5	13	-2	-2	-2	-1	2169	0	2169
2	349.3	13	2	2	2	1	2715	0	2715
3	349.8	13	-2	-2	-2	-1	2744	0	2744
4	349.2	13	2	2	2	1	2784	0	2784
5	353.1	13	-2	-2	-2	-1	3187	0	3187
6	348	13	2	2	2	1	3722	0	3722

```
 7      353    13   0    0    1    2    3709   550   4259
 8      363    13  -2   -3   -5   -3    6394     0   6394
 9      363    13   0    0    0   -3    6394     0   6394
10    361.5    13   2    4    6    3    6811     0   6811
11      363    13   0    0    0    3    6811   495   7306
12      366    13   0    0    1    4    6798  1485   8283
13    370.7    13  -2   -6   -9   -5   10234     0  10234
14    365.6    13   2    9   11    6   12896     0  12896
15    368.2    13  -2  -10  -13   -7   14443     0  14443
16      367    13   0    0   -1   -8   14430   924  15354
17      367    13   0    0    0   -8   14430   924  15354
18    361.7    13   2   12   18   10   19784     0  19784
19    363.1    13  -1   -7  -10    0   21194     0  21194
A0 = 1900 P&L = 6196 P&L1 = 13490 P&L2 = 19294 IM = 1900 MM = 1300
INDIVIDUAL TRADES
0 (0,1) P&L=282 SIZE=1 P&L/SIZE=282 EQ=308 COST=26
1 (1,2) P&L=546 SIZE=-1 P&L/SIZE=546 EQ=572 COST=26
2 (2,3) P&L=29 SIZE=1 P&L/SIZE=29 EQ=55 COST=26
3 (3,4) P&L=40 SIZE=-1 P&L/SIZE=40 EQ=66 COST=26
4 (4,5) P&L=403 SIZE=1 P&L/SIZE=403 EQ=429 COST=26
5 (5,6) P&L=535 SIZE=-1 P&L/SIZE=535 EQ=561 COST=26
6 (6,8) P&L=1624 SIZE=1 P&L/SIZE=1624 EQ=1650 COST=26
7 (7,8) P&L=1074 SIZE=1 P&L/SIZE=1074 EQ=1100 COST=26
8 (8,10) P&L=417 SIZE=-3 P&L/SIZE=139 EQ=495 COST=78
9 (10,13) P&L=2958 SIZE=3 P&L/SIZE=986 EQ=3036 COST=78
10 (12,13) P&L=491 SIZE=1 P&L/SIZE=491 EQ=517 COST=26
11 (13,14) P&L=2675 SIZE=-5 P&L/SIZE=535 EQ=2805 COST=130
12 (14,15) P&L=1560 SIZE=6 P&L/SIZE=260 EQ=1716 COST=156
13 (15,18) P&L=4823 SIZE=-7 P&L/SIZE=689 EQ=5005 COST=182
14 (16,18) P&L=557 SIZE=-1 P&L/SIZE=557 EQ=583 COST=26
15 (18,19) P&L=1280 SIZE=10 P&L/SIZE=128 EQ=1540 COST=260
STATISTICS OF TRADES
Total P&L                        = 19294
Total P&L/unit                   = 8318
Gross profit                     = 19294
Gross profit/unit                = 8318
Gross loss                       = 0
Gross loss/unit                  = 0
Total number of trades           = 16
Number of winning trades         = 16
Number of losing trades          = 0
Average profit                   = 1205.875
Average profit/unit              = 519.875
Average loss                     = 0
Average loss/unit                = 0
```

```
Largest winning trade             = 4823
Largest winning trade/unit        = 1624
Largest losing trade              = 0
Largest losing trade/unit         = 0
Max number of consecutive wins    = 16
Max number of consecutive losses  = 0
Maximum consecutive profit        = 19294
Maximum consecutive profit/unit   = 8318
Maximum consecutive loss          = 0
Maximum consecutive loss/unit     = 0
PL distribution
0 (0, 1000] 9
1 (1000, 2000] 4
2 (2000, 3000] 2
3 (3000, 4000] 0
4 (4000, 5000] 1
PL/unit distribution
0 (0, 500] 8
1 (500, 1000] 6
2 (1000, 1500] 1
3 (1500, 2000] 1
Maximum account value             = 21194
Minimum account value             = 1887
Largest drawdown                  = -13
Average drawdown                  = -0.684210526
```

CLH06

#	CL	Cost	PPS	PPS1	PPS2	Pos2	Cash2	Equity2	Total2
0	58.9	13	1	1	1	1	5487	0	5487
1	59.55	13	-2	-2	-2	-1	6111	0	6111
2	57.75	13	2	2	2	1	7885	0	7885
3	58.05	13	0	0	0	1	7885	300	8185
4	58.1	13	0	0	0	1	7885	350	8235
5	58.7	13	-2	-2	-2	-1	8809	0	8809
6	57.9	13	2	2	2	1	9583	0	9583
7	58.09	13	0	0	0	1	9583	190	9773
8	58.11	13	0	0	0	1	9583	210	9793
9	58.7	13	-2	-2	-2	-1	10357	0	10357
10	57.55	13	2	3	3	2	11468	0	11468
11	58.56	13	0	0	0	2	11468	2020	13488
12	58.75	13	0	0	0	2	11468	2400	13868
13	59.82	13	-2	-4	-4	-2	15956	0	15956
14	58.1	13	2	5	5	3	19331	0	19331
15	58.86	13	-2	-6	-6	-3	21533	0	21533

```
  16      57.9   13    2      7      7      4   24322        0   24322
  17      58.5   13   -2     -8     -8     -4   26618        0   26618
  18     57.65   13    2      9      9      5   29901        0   29901
  19     58.43   13   -1     -5     -5      0   33736        0   33736
A0 = 5500 P&L = 13752 P&L1 = 28236 P&L2 = 28236 IM = 5500 MM = 4100
INDIVIDUAL TRADES
0 (0,1) P&L=624 SIZE=1 P&L/SIZE=624 EQ=650 COST=26
1 (1,2) P&L=1774 SIZE=-1 P&L/SIZE=1774 EQ=1800 COST=26
2 (2,5) P&L=924 SIZE=1 P&L/SIZE=924 EQ=950 COST=26
3 (5,6) P&L=774 SIZE=-1 P&L/SIZE=774 EQ=800 COST=26
4 (6,9) P&L=774 SIZE=1 P&L/SIZE=774 EQ=800 COST=26
5 (9,10) P&L=1124 SIZE=-1 P&L/SIZE=1124 EQ=1150 COST=26
6 (10,13) P&L=4488 SIZE=2 P&L/SIZE=2244 EQ=4540 COST=52
7 (13,14) P&L=3388 SIZE=-2 P&L/SIZE=1694 EQ=3440 COST=52
8 (14,15) P&L=2202 SIZE=3 P&L/SIZE=734 EQ=2280 COST=78
9 (15,16) P&L=2802 SIZE=-3 P&L/SIZE=934 EQ=2880 COST=78
10 (16,17) P&L=2296 SIZE=4 P&L/SIZE=574 EQ=2400 COST=104
11 (17,18) P&L=3296 SIZE=-4 P&L/SIZE=824 EQ=3400 COST=104
12 (18,19) P&L=3770 SIZE=5 P&L/SIZE=754 EQ=3900 COST=130
STATISTICS OF TRADES
Total P&L                         = 28236
Total P&L/unit                    = 13752
Gross profit                      = 28236
Gross profit/unit                 = 13752
Gross loss                        = 0
Gross loss/unit                   = 0
Total number of trades            = 13
Number of winning trades          = 13
Number of losing trades           = 0
Average profit                    = 2172
Average profit/unit               = 1057.84615
Average loss                      = 0
Average loss/unit                 = 0
Largest winning trade             = 4488
Largest winning trade/unit        = 2244
Largest losing trade              = 0
Largest losing trade/unit         = 0
Max number of consecutive wins    = 13
Max number of consecutive losses = 0
Maximum consecutive profit        = 28236
Maximum consecutive profit/unit   = 13752
Maximum consecutive loss          = 0
Maximum consecutive loss/unit     = 0
PL distribution
0 (0, 1000] 4
```

```
1 (1000, 2000] 2
2 (2000, 3000] 3
3 (3000, 4000] 3
4 (4000, 5000] 1
PL/unit distribution
0 (500, 1000] 9
1 (1000, 1500] 1
2 (1500, 2000] 2
3 (2000, 2500] 1
Maximum account value          = 33736
Minimum account value          = 5487
Largest drawdown               = -13
Average drawdown               = -0.684210526
```

USH06

#	US	Cost	PPS	PPS1	PPS2	Pos2	Cash2	Equity2	Total2
0	113.0625	13	1	1	1	1	1337	0	1337
1	113.40625	13	-2	-2	-2	-1	1654.75	0	1654.75
2	112.71875	13	2	2	2	1	2316.25	0	2316.25
3	113.09375	13	0	0	0	1	2316.25	375	2691.25
4	113.125	13	0	0	1	2	2303.25	406.25	2709.5
5	113.1875	13	-2	-3	-4	-2	2782.5	0	2782.5
6	112.65625	13	2	4	4	2	3793	0	3793
7	112.90625	13	0	0	1	3	3780	500	4280
8	112.90625	13	0	0	0	3	3780	500	4280
9	113.0625	13	-2	-5	-6	-3	4670.75	0	4670.75
10	112.46875	13	2	7	7	4	6361	0	6361
11	112.71875	13	-2	-9	-9	-5	7244	0	7244
12	112.65625	13	2	10	10	5	7426.5	0	7426.5
13	113.53125	13	-2	-13	-13	-8	11632.5	0	11632.5
14	112.59375	13	2	21	22	14	18846.5	0	18846.5
15	113.40625	13	-2	-34	-36	-22	29753.5	0	29753.5
16	113.34375	13	2	43	44	22	30556.5	0	30556.5
17	114.21875	13	-2	-57	-58	-36	49052.5	0	49052.5
18	113.3125	13	2	93	96	60	80429.5	0	80429.5
19	114.1875	13	-1	-58	-60	0	132149.5	0	132149.5

```
A0 = 1350 P&L = 8297.5 P&L1 = 127231.5 P&L2 = 130799.5 IM = 1350 MM = 1000
INDIVIDUAL TRADES
0 (0,1) P&L=317.75 SIZE=1 P&L/SIZE=317.75 EQ=343.75 COST=26
1 (1,2) P&L=661.5 SIZE=-1 P&L/SIZE=661.5 EQ=687.5 COST=26
2 (2,5) P&L=442.75 SIZE=1 P&L/SIZE=442.75 EQ=468.75 COST=26
3 (4,5) P&L=36.5 SIZE=1 P&L/SIZE=36.5 EQ=62.5 COST=26
4 (5,6) P&L=1010.5 SIZE=-2 P&L/SIZE=505.25 EQ=1062.5 COST=52
```

```
5 (6,9) P&L=760.5 SIZE=2 P&L/SIZE=380.25 EQ=812.5 COST=52
6 (7,9) P&L=130.25 SIZE=1 P&L/SIZE=130.25 EQ=156.25 COST=26
7 (9,10) P&L=1703.25 SIZE=-3 P&L/SIZE=567.75 EQ=1781.25 COST=78
8 (10,11) P&L=896 SIZE=4 P&L/SIZE=224 EQ=1000 COST=104
9 (11,12) P&L=182.5 SIZE=-5 P&L/SIZE=36.5 EQ=312.5 COST=130
10 (12,13) P&L=4245 SIZE=5 P&L/SIZE=849 EQ=4375 COST=130
11 (13,14) P&L=7292 SIZE=-8 P&L/SIZE=911.5 EQ=7500 COST=208
12 (14,15) P&L=11011 SIZE=14 P&L/SIZE=786.5 EQ=11375 COST=364
13 (15,16) P&L=803 SIZE=-22 P&L/SIZE=36.5 EQ=1375 COST=572
14 (16,17) P&L=18678 SIZE=22 P&L/SIZE=849 EQ=19250 COST=572
15 (17,18) P&L=31689 SIZE=-36 P&L/SIZE=880.25 EQ=32625 COST=936
16 (18,19) P&L=50940 SIZE=60 P&L/SIZE=849 EQ=52500 COST=1560
STATISTICS OF TRADES
Total P&L                          = 130799.5
Total P&L/unit                     = 8464.25
Gross profit                       = 130799.5
Gross profit/unit                  = 8464.25
Gross loss                         = 0
Gross loss/unit                    = 0
Total number of trades             = 17
Number of winning trades           = 17
Number of losing trades            = 0
Average profit                     = 7694.08824
Average profit/unit                = 497.897059
Average loss                       = 0
Average loss/unit                  = 0
Largest winning trade              = 50940
Largest winning trade/unit         = 911.5
Largest losing trade               = 0
Largest losing trade/unit          = 0
Max number of consecutive wins     = 17
Max number of consecutive losses = 0
Maximum consecutive profit         = 130799.5
Maximum consecutive profit/unit  = 8464.25
Maximum consecutive loss           = 0
Maximum consecutive loss/unit      = 0
PL distribution
0 (0, 5000] 12
1 (5000, 10000] 1
2 (10000, 15000] 1
3 (15000, 20000] 1
4 (20000, 25000] 0
5 (25000, 30000] 0
6 (30000, 35000] 1
```

```
7 (35000, 40000] 0
8 (40000, 45000] 0
9 (45000, 50000] 0
10 (50000, 55000] 1
PL/unit distribution
0 (0, 500] 8
1 (500, 1000] 9
Maximum account value          = 132149.5
Minimum account value          = 1337
Largest drawdown               = -13
Average drawdown               = -0.684210526
```

SPH06

#	SP	Cost	PPS	PPS1	PPS2	Pos2	Cash2	Equity2	Total2
0	1275.3	13	1	1	1	1	19687	0	19687
1	1279.7	13	-2	-2	-2	-1	20761	0	20761
2	1266.8	13	2	2	2	1	23960	0	23960
3	1267.5	13	0	0	0	1	23960	175	24135
4	1267.8	13	0	0	0	1	23960	250	24210
5	1271.8	13	-2	-2	-2	-1	25184	0	25184
6	1264.7	13	2	2	2	1	26933	0	26933
7	1267.9	13	0	0	0	1	26933	800	27733
8	1268.2	13	0	0	0	1	26933	875	27808
9	1276.9	13	-2	-2	-2	-1	29957	0	29957
10	1266.9	13	2	2	2	1	32431	0	32431
11	1269.9	13	-2	-2	-2	-1	33155	0	33155
12	1269.4	13	2	2	2	1	33254	0	33254
13	1276	13	-2	-2	-2	-1	34878	0	34878
14	1269	13	2	2	2	1	36602	0	36602
15	1275.5	13	0	0	0	1	36602	1625	38227
16	1277.2	13	0	0	0	1	36602	2050	38652
17	1277.6	13	-2	-2	-2	-1	38726	0	38726
18	1273.1	13	2	3	3	2	39812	0	39812
19	1276.5	13	-1	-2	-2	0	41486	0	41486

```
A0 = 19700 P&L = 20962 P&L1 = 21786 P&L2 = 21786 IM = 19700 MM = 15800
INDIVIDUAL TRADES
0 (0,1) P&L=1074 SIZE=1 P&L/SIZE=1074 EQ=1100 COST=26
1 (1,2) P&L=3199 SIZE=-1 P&L/SIZE=3199 EQ=3225 COST=26
2 (2,5) P&L=1224 SIZE=1 P&L/SIZE=1224 EQ=1250 COST=26
3 (5,6) P&L=1749 SIZE=-1 P&L/SIZE=1749 EQ=1775 COST=26
4 (6,9) P&L=3024 SIZE=1 P&L/SIZE=3024 EQ=3050 COST=26
5 (9,10) P&L=2474 SIZE=-1 P&L/SIZE=2474 EQ=2500 COST=26
6 (10,11) P&L=724 SIZE=1 P&L/SIZE=724 EQ=750 COST=26
```

```
7 (11,12) P&L=99 SIZE=-1 P&L/SIZE=99 EQ=125 COST=26
8 (12,13) P&L=1624 SIZE=1 P&L/SIZE=1624 EQ=1650 COST=26
9 (13,14) P&L=1724 SIZE=-1 P&L/SIZE=1724 EQ=1750 COST=26
10 (14,17) P&L=2124 SIZE=1 P&L/SIZE=2124 EQ=2150 COST=26
11 (17,18) P&L=1099 SIZE=-1 P&L/SIZE=1099 EQ=1125 COST=26
12 (18,19) P&L=1648 SIZE=2 P&L/SIZE=824 EQ=1700 COST=52
STATISTICS OF TRADES
Total P&L                          = 21786
Total P&L/unit                     = 20962
Gross profit                       = 21786
Gross profit/unit                  = 20962
Gross loss                         = 0
Gross loss/unit                    = 0
Total number of trades             = 13
Number of winning trades           = 13
Number of losing trades            = 0
Average profit                     = 1675.84615
Average profit/unit                = 1612.46154
Average loss                       = 0
Average loss/unit                  = 0
Largest winning trade              = 3199
Largest winning trade/unit         = 3199
Largest losing trade               = 0
Largest losing trade/unit          = 0
Max number of consecutive wins     = 13
Max number of consecutive losses = 0
Maximum consecutive profit         = 21786
Maximum consecutive profit/unit    = 20962
Maximum consecutive loss           = 0
Maximum consecutive loss/unit      = 0
PL distribution
0 (0, 1000] 2
1 (1000, 2000] 7
2 (2000, 3000] 2
3 (3000, 4000] 2
PL/unit distribution
0 (0, 500] 1
1 (500, 1000] 2
2 (1000, 1500] 3
3 (1500, 2000] 3
4 (2000, 2500] 2
5 (2500, 3000] 0
6 (3000, 3500] 2
Maximum account value              = 41486
```

```
Minimum account value          = 19687
Largest drawdown               = -13
Average drawdown               = -0.684210526
```

These statistics show what the futures market offered during one week before Christmas 2005.

The majority of corn trades, 12 of 15, could each yield an average of $200 profit per contract. This would require $340 of initial capital for the first trade. Crude oil did not have any potential profits that were < $500 per contract. Soybeans showed an optimal return on capital of 13,658 percent (not annualized, but just for five days). Cocoa had an absolute profit $322,200 and shows that one week of perfect trading would be the equivalent of a healthy income for the next year. For the S&P, this was a relatively quiet week. Indeed, it only returned $21,786 of potential profit with initial requirement at least $19,700. This explains why so many traders invest their time researching and understanding how to get a small percentage of what is offered.

In all cases, adding money management makes the crucial difference. I noticed that for some markets using just a few months of open, high, low, and settlement prices (ignoring intraday data) and applying the second P&L reserve strategy exponentially increases the number of traded contracts. The total number of contracts reaches a level so high that a standard 32-bit CPU register (which corresponds to an unsigned integer value > 4 billion) is not large enough to hold the result. These remarkable situations are quickly recognized because the output becomes very suspicious (big position numbers are followed by smaller position numbers, the result of a CPU overflow). Clearly, any trade size that begins to approach the volumes and/or open interests of a particular market would make trading impossible. Actually, trading more than 10 percent of the daily volume would increase slippage to a point where the only viable strategy is the "do nothing strategy." This is why the two reserve strategies should be applied to relatively short time intervals or with costs set up reasonably high in order to target the most important events. The program `maxprof` (see Chapter 3), which evaluates potential profit using only *r*- and *l*-algorithms, can be applied on much longer time intervals. It does not reinvest profits.

MULTIMARKET POTENTIAL PROFIT ALGORITHMS

The comparison of several markets naturally brings us to the idea of developing an algorithm of potential profit for a portfolio of markets, each reflecting individual transaction costs and margin requirements. This extension would require date and time classes in order to synchronize the events observed in different markets. The simplest approach to this algorithm would be to use individual potential profit strategies, obtained for each market, as inputs to the portfolio. An "analytical" algorithm could be rather complicated. We should not exclude that a "numerical" algorithm using *genetic algorithms* technology, operating on individual potential profit strategies simultaneous to solve the portfolio problem, could be an easier way to the final goal. In the last case, however, it is difficult to prove that the genetic algorithm solution corresponds to the absolute maximum, although the chances are very good.

EPILOGUE

It is not surprising that traders agonize over their attempt to get even a small percentage of the market's price swings, when their efforts result in losses or even financial disasters. Big money, comparable to these tremendous potential profits, is lost regularly. Alternatively, one can hope that because opportunities arise every week (the week selected was ordinary), losses can be recovered in the following week. Trading is not for everybody. After all, if all people decided that their only business was to trade, how long would society continue to exist? Maybe this is one of the reasons why 90 percent of traders lose. It maintains natural balance between the distribution of people among professions. New traders can be viewed as random people who enter the markets, lose their investments, and leave, while those who devoted lives to this hard business are able to continue.

However, if one wants to study trading, how can we ignore the style and results obtained by the absolutely best trader? This book is for them.

If one is asked to name the single most important property of markets, what should it be? Some may say *wildness*. Others would say *the inability to predict future price moves*. My answer is that *the most important market property is its offer of potential profits, which can be evaluated from the market itself*. This book is about computing this property.

CONCLUSIONS

- The three potential profit strategies are obtained for the five business dates December 19 through December 23, 2005, using the open, high, low, and settlement prices for the futures contracts CH06, SH06, WH06, LCG06, GCG06, HGH06, CCH06, KCH06, SBH06, CTH06, LBH06, CLH06, USH06, and SPH06.
- The second P&L reserve strategy is evaluated, and the statistics of corresponding trades and P&L distributions are computed for the same contracts.

Bibliography and Sources

Aho, Alfred V., Brian W. Kernigan, and Peter J. Weinberger. *The AWK Programming Language.* Reading, MA: Addison-Wesley, 1988.

Baaquie, Belal E. *Quantum Finance: Path Integrals and Hamiltonians for Options and Interest Rates.* Cambridge, UK: Cambridge University Press, 2004.

Babcock, Bruce, Jr. *The Business One Irving Guide to Trading Systems.* Homewood, IL: Business One Irwin, 1989.

Bachelier, Louis (1900). Théorie de la Spéculation. Doctoral dissertation. Reprinted in P.H. Cootner, ed. *The Random Character of Stock Market Prices.* Cambridge, MA: MIT Press, 1967, pp. 17–78.

Barndorff-Nielsen, Ole E., and Robert Stelzer. Absolute Moments of Generalized Hyperbolic Distributions and Approximate Scaling of Normal Inverse Gaussian Levy Processes. *Scandinavian Journal of Statistics*, Vol. 32, 2005, pp. 617–637.

Baillie, R.T., T. Bollerslev, and H.O. Mikkelsen. Fractionally Integrated Generalized Autoregressive Conditional Heteroskedasticity. *Journal of Econometrics*, Vol. 74, 1996, pp. 3–30.

Black, Fischer. How We Came Up with the Option Formula. *Current Contents/Social & Behavioral Sciences*, Vol. 19, No. 33. Philadelphia: Institute for Scientific Information, Inc., 1987.

Black, Fisher, and Myron Scholes. The Pricing of Options and Corporate Liabilities. *Journal of Political Economy*, Vol. 81, May–June 1973, pp. 637–659.

Booch, Grady. *Object-Oriented Analysis and Design with Applications.* Redwood City, CA: Benjamin/Cummings Publishing, 1994.

Chan, Tony F., Gene H. Golub, Randall J. LeVeque. Algorithms for Computing the Sample Variance: Analysis and Recommendations. *American Statistician*, Vol. 37, No. 3, August 1983, pp. 242–247.

Chester, Michael. *Neural Networks: A Tutorial.* Englewood Cliffs, NJ: PTR Prentice-Hall, 1993.

Connors, Laurence A., and Linda Bradford Raschke. *Street Smarts: High Probability Short-Term Trading Strategies.* Los Angeles: M. Gordon Publishing Group, 1996.

De Boor, Carl. *A Practical Guide to Splines.* New York: Springer-Verlag, 1978.

Dierckx, Paul. *Curve and Surface Fitting with Splines.* Oxford, UK: Clarendon Press, 1995.

Dugan, Ianthe J. Sharpe Point: Risk Gauge Is Misused. *Wall Street Journal*, August 31, 2005, pp. c1, c2.

Elder, Alexander. *Trading for a Living: Psychology, Trading Tactics, Money Management.* New York: John Wiley & Sons, Inc., 1993.

Gallant, Stephen I. *Neural Network Learning and Expert Systems.* Cambridge, MA: MIT Press, 1993.

Gamma, Erich, Richard Helm, Ralph Johnson, and John Vlissides. *Design Patterns. Elements of Reusable Object-Oriented Software.* Reading, MA: Addison-Wesley, 1994.

Geman, Helyette, Nicole El Karoui, and Jean-Charles Rochet. Changes of Numeraire, Changes of Probability Measure, and Option Pricing. *Journal of Applied Probability,* Vol. 32, 1995, pp. 443–458.

Harrison, Michael, and Stanley Pliska. Martingales and Stochastic Integrals in the Theory of Continuous Trading. *Stochastic Process and their Applications,* Vol. 11, 1981, pp. 215–260.

Hull, John C. *Options, Futures, and Other Derivatives,* 3rd ed. Upper Saddle River, NJ: Prentice Hall, 1997.

Hunt, P.J., and J.E. Kennedy. *Financial Derivatives in Theory and Practice.* Chichester, UK: John Wiley & Sons, LTD, 2000.

International Standard ISO/IEC 14882, 2nd ed. 2003-10-15. Programming languages: C++.

Jones, Ryan. *The Trading Game: Playing by the Numbers to Make Millions.* New York: John Wiley & Sons, 1999.

Kaufman, Perry J. *The New Commodity Trading Systems and Methods.* New York: John Wiley & Sons, 1987.

Kaufman, Perry J. *New Trading Systems and Methods.* 4th ed. New York: John Wiley & Sons, 2005.

Kelly, J.L. Jr. A New Interpretation of Information Rate. *Bell System Technical Journal,* July 1956, pp. 917–926.

Knuth, Donald E. *The Art of Computer Programming:* V.2. Seminumerical Algorithms, 3rd ed. Reading, MA: Addison-Wesley, 1998.

Koenig, Andrew, and Barbara Moo. *Ruminations on C++.* Reading, MA: Addison-Wesley Longman, 1996.

Koza, John R. *Genetic Programming: On the Programming of Computers by Natural Selection.* Cambridge, MA: MIT Press, 1992.

Lefevre, Edwin. *Reminiscences of a Stock Operator.* New York: John Wiley & Sons, Inc., 1993. Copyright 1993, 1994 by Expert Trading, Ltd. Originally published in 1923 by George H. Doran and Company.

Lippman, Stanley B. *Inside the C++ Object Model.* Reading, MA: Addison-Wesley, 1996.

Mandelbrot, Benoit, B. The Variation of Certain Speculative Prices. *Journal of Business,* Vol. 36, 1963, pp. 394–419.

Mandelbrot, Benoit B., and Richard L. Hudson, *The (Mis) Behavior of Markets.* New York: Basic Books, 2004.

Markowitz, Harry M. The Early History of Portfolio Theory: 1600–1960. *Financial Analysts Journal*, Vol. 55, No. 4, 1999, pp. 5–16.

Martin, Robert C. The Open-Closed Principle. *C++ Report*, January 1996, pp. 37–43.

Merton, Robert C. *Continuous Time Finance.* Malden, MA: Blackwell, 1990.

Meyer, Bertrand. *Object-Oriented Software Construction.* New York: Prentice Hall, 1988.

Moiseev, Nikita Nikolaevich. *Mathematical Problems of Systems Analysis.* Moscow: Nauka Publishers, 1982 (in Russian).

Musser, David R., and Atul Saini. *STL Tutorial and Reference Guide: C++ Programming with the Standard Template Library.* Reading, MA: Addison-Wesley, 1996.

Neftci, Salih N. *An Introduction to the Mathematics of Financial Derivatives.* San Diego: Academic Press, 1996.

Newborn, Monroe. *Computer Chess.* New York: Academic Press, Inc., 1975.

Pardo, Robert. *Design, Testing, and Optimization of Trading Systems.* New York: John Wiley & Sons, 1992.

Press, William H., Saul A. Teukolsky, William T. Vetterling, and Brian P. Flannery. *Numerical Recipes in C: The Art of Scientific Computing*, 2nd ed., Cambridge, UK: Cambridge University Press, 1992.

Rebonato, Ricardo. *Volatility and Correlation: The Perfect Hedger and the Fox*, 2nd ed. Chichester, UK: John Wiley & Sons, 2004.

Rogers, L.C.G., and David Williams. *Diffusions, Markov Processes, and Martingales.* Vol. 1: *Foundations;* Vol. 2: *Ito Calculus*, 2nd ed. Cambridge, UK: Cambridge University Press, 2000.

Rumbaugh, James, Ivar Jacobson, and Grady Booch. *The Unified Modeling Language Reference Manual.* Reading, MA: Addison-Wesley as imprint of Addison Wesley Longman, Inc., 1999.

Shaleen, Kenneth H. *Volume and Open Interest: Cutting Edge Trading Strategies in the Futures Markets.* Chicago: Probus Publishing, 1991.

Sharpe, William F. Capital Asset Prices: A Theory of Market Equilibrium under Conditions of Risk. *Journal of Finance*, Vol. 19, No. 4, 1964, pp. 425–442.

Shannon, Claude E. A Mathematical Theory of Communication. *Bell System Technical Journal*, Vol. 27, October 1948, pp. 379–423, 623–656.

Shannon, Claude E. Programming a Digital Computer for Playing Chess. *Philosophical Magazine*, Vol. 41, 1950, pp. 356–375.

Smith, Gary. *How I Trade for a Living* (Wiley online trading for a living). New York: John Wiley & Sons, 2000

Stevens, Richard W. *Advanced Programming in the UNIX Environment*, 18th printing. Reading, MA: Addison-Wesley as imprint of Addison Wesley Longman, Inc., 1999.

Stroustrup, Bjarne. *The C++ Programming Language, special edition.* Reading, MA: Addison-Wesley, 2000.

Vince, Ralph. *The Mathematics of Money Management: Risk Analysis Techniques for Traders.* New York: John Wiley & Sons, 1992.

Vince, Ralph. *The New Money Management: A Framework for Asset Allocation.* New York: John Wiley & Sons, 1995.

Vlissides, John. Pluggable Factory, Part 1. *C++ Report*, Vol. 10, No. 10, November/December 1998, pp. 52–56.

Vlissides, John. Pluggable Factory, Part 2. *C++ Report*, Vol. 11, No. 2, February 1999, pp. 51–57.

Williams, Larry R. *How I Made One Million Dollars... Last Year... Trading Commodities*, 3rd ed. Brightwaters, NY: Windsor Books, 1979.

Williams, Larry R. *Long-Term Secrets to Short-Term Trading.* New York: John Wiley & Sons, 1999.

Williams, Larry R. *Day Trade Futures Online.* New York: John Wiley & Sons, 2000.

Williams, Larry R. *Trade Stocks & Commodities with the Insiders: Secrets of the COT Report.* Hoboken, NJ: John Wiley & Sons, 2005.

Youngs, E.A., and E.M. Cramer. Some Results Relevant to Choice of Sum and Sum-of-Product Algorithms. *Technometrics*, Vol. 13, 1971, pp. 657–665.

About the CD-ROM

INTRODUCTION

This appendix provides you with information on the contents of the CD that accompanies this book. For the latest and greatest information, please refer to the ReadMe file located at the root of the CD.

SYSTEM REQUIREMENTS

- A PC running Windows or Linux, or Macintosh running Mac OSX
- A CD-ROM drive

USING THE CD

To install the items from the CD to your hard drive, follow these steps:

1. Insert the CD into your computer's CD-ROM drive. The license agreement appears.

   (Note to Windows users: The interface won't launch if you have autorun disabled. In that case, click Start@@>Run. In the dialog box that appears, type D:\start.exe. (Replace D with the proper letter if your CD-ROM drive uses a different letter. If you don't know the letter, see how your CD-ROM drive is listed under My Computer.) Click OK.)

(Note for Mac Users: The CD icon will appear on your desktop; double-click the icon to open the CD and double-click the "Start" icon.)

(Note for Linux/Unix Users: If your system doesn't support automount, you will have to use the disc mounting utilities on your particular system to browse the content of the CD-ROM.)

2. Read through the license agreement, and then click the Accept button if you want to use the CD. After you click Accept, the License Agreement window won't appear again.

The CD interface appears. The interface allows you to install the programs and run the demos with just a click of a button (or two).

WHAT'S ON THE CD

The following sections provide a summary of the software and other materials you'll find on the CD.

Content

All header *.h and source *.cpp files containing C++ declarations and definitions of classes, operations, and functions are described in the book and placed on the CD in a folder called "Code." These files also include C++ comments. The data input and output *.txt files represent plain text files and can be ordinarily viewed with text editors and other text processing tools. References to corresponding chapters describing the meaning of the files are listed below.

A simple makefile containing portable commands and understood by make and nmake utilities is provided for convenience and illustrates the project's organization and building the code. Building means compilation and linking of the programs. The makefile contains comments explaining where it can be customized and tuned for a compiler of your choice. It shows relationships between files required to form complete programs.

In order to compile and link the files and create an executable program, it is needed to have a C++ compiler and linker installed. The C++ code is written using portable syntax and is suitable for many modern C++ compilers of different versions. Among those are products of GNU GCC and systems such as Microsoft Visual C++. The shell scripting program multimarket.sh is for convenience and reproduces some of the results discussed in the book. It runs on UNIX or requires an UNIX shell emulator such as CYGWIN for Microsoft Windows, where the standard text processing program is installed. It is assumed that the programs `maxprof3` and evaluate executed by the script are built before running the script. Only the C++ header and source files are really needed in order to create the most important programs described in the book.

File	Where is it described and/or used?
`makefile`	See comments in makefile
`account.cpp`	Chapter 4
`distrib.cpp`	Chapter 8

evaluate.cpp	Chapter 9
maxprof.cpp	Chapter 3
maxprof3.cpp	Chapter 6
pardo.cpp	Chapter 1
Prices.cpp	Chapter 1
test1.cpp	Chapter 1
test2.cpp	Chapter 2
test3.cpp	Chapter 3
test4.cpp	Chapter 4
test5.cpp	Chapter 5
test6.cpp	Chapter 6
test7.cpp	Chapter 6
test8.cpp	Chapter 8
AccountAlg.h	Chapter 4
Cost.h	Chapter 2
CPrices.h	Chapter 1
Distribution.h	Chapter 8
EvaluateStrategyAlg.h	Chapter 8
FirstPLReserveAlg.h	Chapter 6
IPrices.h	Chapter 1
PardoPotentialProfitAlg.h	Chapter 1
Position.h	Chapter 5
PotentialProfitAlg.h	Chapter 3
PotentialProfitMinAccountAlg.h	Chapter 5
Price.h	Chapter 1
Prices.h	Chapter 1
ProfitAndLossAlg.h	Chapter 2
SecondPLReserveAlg.h	Chapter 6
Spec.h	Chapter 1
SpecCost.h	Chapter 2
Strategy.h	Chapter 2
Trade.h	Chapter 5
TradeStatisticsAlg.h	Chapter 9
multimarket.sh	See comments in multimarket.sh
CBOT_20051021_SF06_DATA.txt	Chapter 7, 9
CBOT_20051021_SF06_RESULT.txt	Chapter 7
CBOT_2005JFM_SK05_C_DATA.txt	Chapter 7
CBOT_2005JFM_SK05_C_RESULT.txt	Chapter 7
CCH06_20051219_20051223.txt	Chapter 10
CH06_20051219_20051223.txt	Chapter 10
CLH06_20051219_20051223.txt	Chapter 10
CTH06_20051219_20051223.txt	Chapter 10
GCG06_20051219_20051223.txt	Chapter 10
HGH06_20051219_20051223.txt	Chapter 10
KCH06_20051219_20051223.txt	Chapter 10

LBH06_20051219_20051223.txt	Chapter 10
LCG06_20051219_20051223.txt	Chapter 10
MULTICONTRACTS_RESULT.txt	Chapter 10
readme.txt	This file
SBH06_20051219_20051223.txt	Chapter 10
SH06_20051219_20051223.txt	Chapter 10
SPH06_20051219_20051223.txt	Chapter 10
USH06_20051219_20051223.txt	Chapter 10
WH06_20051219_20051223.txt	Chapter 10

Customer Care

If you have trouble with the CD ROM, please call the Wiley Product Technical Support phone number at (800) 762-2974. Outside the United States, call 1(317) 572-3994. You can also contact Wiley Product Technical Support at **http://support.wiley.com.** John Wiley & Sons will provide technical support only for installation and other general quality control items. For technical support on the applications themselves, consult the program's vendor or author.

To place additional orders or to request information about other Wiley products, please call (877) 762-2974.

Index

B

T

U

For more information about the CD-ROM, see the About the CD-ROM section on page 229.

CUSTOMER NOTE: IF THIS BOOK IS ACCOMPANIED BY SOFTWARE, PLEASE READ THE FOLLOWING BEFORE OPENING THE PACKAGE.